Coming Out in Christianity

Melissa M. Wilcox

Coming Out in Christianity

Religion,
Identity, and
Community

INDIANA
University Press
Bloomington & Indianapolis

Portions of Chapter 2 appeared previously in "When Sheila's a Lesbian," *Sociology of Religion* 63, no. 4 (2002): 497–513, © 2002 by The Association for the Sociology of Religion, Inc.

An earlier version of Chapter 3 was published as "Of Markets and Missions: The Early History of the Universal Fellowship of Metropolitan Community Churches," in *Religion and American Culture* 11, no. 1 (2001): 83–108, © 2001 The University of California Press.

Publication of this book is made possible in part with the assistance of a Challenge Grant from the National Endowment for the Humanities, a federal agency that supports research, education, and public programming in the humanities.

This book is a publication of

Indiana University Press
601 North Morton Street
Bloomington, IN 47404-3797 USA

http://iupress.indiana.edu

Telephone orders   800-842-6796
Fax orders   812-855-7931
Orders by e-mail   iuporder@indiana.edu

Library of Congress Cataloging-in-Publication Data

Wilcox, Melissa M., date
  Coming out in Christianity : religion, identity, and community / Melissa M. Wilcox.
    p.   cm.
Includes bibliographical references and index.
  ISBN 0-253-34278-3 (alk. paper) — ISBN 0-253-21619-2 (pbk. : alk. paper)
  1. Homosexuality—Religious aspects—Christianity. 2. Gays—Religious life. I. Title.
  BR115.H6W54 2003
  261.8'35766—dc21

                                                                      2003001815

1 2 3 4 5   08 07 06 05 04 03

For my parents:

Margaret R. Wilcox
and
W. Wayne Wilcox

THE ROAD NOT TAKEN

Two roads diverged in a yellow wood,
And sorry I could not travel both
And be one traveler, long I stood
And looked down one as far as I could
To where it bent in the undergrowth;

Then took the other, as just as fair,
And having perhaps the better claim,
Because it was grassy and wanted wear;
Though as for that the passing there
Had worn them really about the same,

And both that morning equally lay
In leaves no step had trodden black.
Oh, I kept the first for another day!
Yet knowing how way leads on to way,
I doubted if I should ever come back.

I shall be telling this with a sigh
Somewhere ages and ages hence:
Two roads diverged in a wood, and I—
I took the one less traveled by,
And that has made all the difference.

—Robert Frost

Contents

Preface

This is not a book about homosexuality. It is not a book about religion or spirituality or churches. It is a book about people. Written in the shadow of California's Knight initiative, which bans already illegal same-sex marriages, such a project only seems all the more necessary. I have long sympathized with political activists, but I find my activism in my writing and in the classroom; although I did not realize it at the time I began this project, *Coming Out in Christianity* is part of that effort. Like many of the people whose stories and opinions are contained within these pages, I believe that much—though certainly not all—of the inequity, mistreatment, and violence suffered by lesbian, gay, bisexual, and transgender people stems from misunderstanding, ignorance, and the all-too-human fear of the unknown. Education and exposure are two possible solutions to these problems, and for those reasons this is a book about people.

Today in the United States, the topic of "homosexuality" is pervasive in both religious and secular settings. The military's "don't ask, don't tell" policy has been a hot political issue for years, and many states are embroiled in debates over whether same-sex couples should have any of the rights accorded to opposite-sex partners. Same-sex marriage, though it may be the newest source of panic for moral conservatives, is barely even on the legal map. Already, however, it has become the topic of conversation in religious organizations, on talk shows, and in homes across the country. And most important for the people in this study, the issue of "homosexuality" threatens to create a yawning chasm within several mainline Protestant denominations.

But there is a problem with these debates: each takes place primarily over the heads of the actual people whose lives are affected. Lesbians, gay men, bisexuals, and transgender people struggle to make their voices heard in debates that affect their status as church members, their parenting rights, their ability to keep vigil at a dying partner's bedside, and even their safety on the streets. Yet no matter how vocal groups such as the Human Rights Coalition or the National Gay and Lesbian Task Force become, no matter how visible the LGBT activists are within mainstream religious organizations, ultimately these are still debates conducted by an "us" about a "them." In many religious groups, the situation is worse: the debate is not even about a "them" but about a behavior, such as drug abuse or swearing, that "we" consider not to be intrinsic to anyone's identity and therefore are determined to battle. Lesbian, gay, bisexual, and transgender people gather outside these gates, angrily challenging such assumptions, but their protests fall on deaf ears. For that reason also, this is a book about people.

Although it addresses current topics and debates within religious studies and the sociology and psychology of religion, and although it is written for an academic audience, this book is also intended to be useful to a more general readership. It is my hope that in time the work presented here will reach not only students of religion, sociologists, and psychologists; not only LGBT church members and pastors; but also heterosexual laypeople, religious leaders, friends, parents, teachers, and other potential allies of lesbian, gay, bisexual, and transgender Christians. If it manages to deepen even one more person's understanding of LGBT Christians, this book will have been worth writing.

Many people whose names are not on the title page were all the same indispensable to this work's production. First and foremost in any fieldwork-based study, of course, are the participants. The pastors and congregants at the pseudonymous congregations of MCC Valle Rico and Oceanfront MCC generously welcomed my presence among them and answered my many questions with patience and insight. Oceanfront's Reverend Sharon and her partner June also designed the altar featured in the cover photo. Never having been on the opposite side of things, I can only imagine how much a researcher's presence might cramp one's style at church—especially in a charismatic congregation such as Oceanfront. But people went out of their way to include me, and someone was always kind enough to offer explanations of anything I did not fully understand. I also owe a special debt of gratitude to those who took the forty-five minutes to an hour required to fill out the survey I mailed to them. Even more credit is due to those who consented to sit down with me for anywhere from half an hour to three hours, answering my questions about deeply held beliefs and sometimes painful experiences. I fervently hope I have done their stories justice in the pages that follow.

I owe the development of my thoughts on this matter, as well as whatever quality is present in my analysis and my writing, primarily to five people. Alice Bach, my mentor during my college years, sparked my interest in religious studies and feminist studies when I still thought that my career would be devoted to researching equine lameness. Her support and her faith in me over the years have kept me going when I was reticent to ask anyone else about the worth of my work. Wade Clark Roof was enthusiastic about this project from the beginning and offered helpful advice throughout. I have benefited in untold ways from my years of association with him, and those familiar with his work will spot its influence in both the underlying theory and the presentation of this book. To Catherine Albanese I owe my appreciation of the importance of historical context in even the most recent developments on the U.S. religious scene. Richard Hecht generously gave hours of his time to discuss theory with me and continuously challenged me to understand the ways in which those theories applied to the context of my research. Finally, Beth Schneider offered a reading of the manuscript from outside the study of religion—always an important corrective—and has kept me on my toes regarding my use of gender theory and queer theory. Any errors I have managed to make despite all of these positive influences are completely my own doing.

The University of California at Santa Barbara provided a significant amount of financial support for this research, first through a Regents' Special Fellowship and then through two Humanities and Social Sciences Research Grants. Among other things, the latter allowed me to hire assistants for the painstaking and time-consuming process of transcription; I am immensely grateful to Nancy McLoughlin and Kerry Mitchell for their careful efforts to transform hours of unclear audiotape into legible documents. Anna Bigelow, Suzanne Crawford, and Suzanne Stillman added their efforts to those of Nancy and Kerry just in time to bail me out as a deadline approached.

I undertook the process of revising the manuscript during my two years as a Faculty Fellow at the University of California, Santa Barbara—another opportunity for which I am deeply grateful—and I wish to thank as well all of the students, friends, and colleagues at that university whose ideas have strengthened and sometimes redirected my own. Many thanks also go to Mark Kowalewski for a careful reading of one draft of the manuscript and for offering many helpful recommendations. And most important, thanks to Robert J. Sloan, Kendra Boileau Stokes, Jane Lyle, and Kate Babbitt at Indiana University Press for their interest in the project and for helping me through the publication process.

Frank Zerilli, at the denominational headquarters of the Universal Fellowship of Metropolitan Community Churches, has been of great assistance in clarifying details about the denomination. I also owe him thanks for allowing me access to the archived collection of denominational publications that formed the backbone of Chapter 3. The librarians and interlibrary loan staff at UC Santa Barbara's Davidson Library, as well as those at Shields Library at University of California, Davis, have been immensely helpful in tracking down the sometimes obscure background sources I needed for this study.

Many thanks go to Carolyn Hartsough at the University of California at Berkeley for assistance with statistical analysis; any inaccuracies or errors that remain I have managed to make with no assistance whatsoever. I also wish to acknowledge a much older debt to Trudy Fator, who patiently taught a recalcitrant high school sophomore the writing skills she had failed to learn in school. Without those abilities, I never could have survived the rigors of advanced academic study, much less the writing of a book.

It is my parents, Margaret and Wayne Wilcox, who are ultimately responsible for this undertaking, and it is to them that this work is dedicated. From the start, they encouraged my creativity and curiosity, a fierce independence they no doubt have regretted from time to time, and the dogged determination I needed to see any project through. They have also been the source of extensive financial and emotional support.

From my father, a professor of forestry, I inherited an insatiable curiosity about how things work. Probably he is also at least partially responsible for my sneaking suspicion that nothing is fully proven without at least a few tables and statistics. From my mother, whose field is educational psychology, I gained a passion for people-watching that quashed any ideas I once had about studying ancient texts—the people are simply too hard to spot in aging manuscripts and weathered stone. Both parents are responsible for the confidence that has led me to risk a first book in a nascent field, and both gifted me with the love of teaching that initially brought me to academia.

Wynn Wilcox, my brother, has been and continues to be a fount of knowledge on such topics as cultural and critical theory, about which he understands far more than I can ever hope to comprehend. It has been an enjoyable honor to share with him the ideas, experiences, excitement, and frustration of academic work, and I look forward to having him as my most valued colleague for many long years.

I owe thanks as well to Andrea Fazel and Lynnette Hawkins, who first introduced me to MCC and who have remained my good friends despite the deleterious effects that writing a book can have on one's personality and weekly schedule. Val Williams has given generously of her time, her energy, and frequently her home over the past several years, and I am immensely grateful for her support. Dr. Jekyll and Mr. Hyde, two cats who manage to abide me even when I behave like their namesakes, faithfully provided welcome distractions and excuses for breaks throughout my research and writing. And many thanks go to my partner, Janet Mallen—not only for being both supporter and sounding board throughout the revision process but also for her careful indexing and for the beautiful photography that graces the cover of this book.

Finally, a caveat. Like any book, this one is certain to have its share of drawbacks that have escaped my attention or my ability to remedy them. Rather than detracting from the contributions this volume does make, I hope that these shortcomings will inspire future projects that improve upon the work presented herein.

Coming Out in Christianity

Prologue

A Tale of Two Communions

On a tree-lined side street near the downtown area of Valle Rico, California, stands a small building of gray stucco that looks as though it was once a house. In fact, it was not: it was built for a Seventh-day Adventist congregation and then housed a spiritualist church. But for the past several years it has been the home of the Metropolitan Community Church of Valle Rico, or MCCVR. A newcomer entering the church on this hot September morning would mount the stairs to the side of the portable wheelchair-access ramp and encounter greeters at the doorway, welcoming all who enter as well as handing out the bulletin for the day's service. Passing through the small hallway next to the church's offices, she would enter the sanctuary, a room approximately forty feet square with wood floors and walls of white and dusty rose. The two side walls hold stained-glass windows, their borders done in greens and browns but their centers light in color to add the sun's encouragement to the four small ceiling lamps that illuminate the room.

Wall hangings between these stained-glass windows, worked in an intricate design that suggests at once a tree, human figures, rainbow-colored flames, and a dove, proclaim "We Are Standing on Holy Ground," and "The Spirit of God Has Set Us Free!" On the back wall hangs a large rainbow flag with a sign next to it explaining that the flag is "intended to represent the whole human family."[1] The altar, draped today in varying shades of green, stands on a small stage that occupies most of the front of the room. Behind the large gold cross that holds pride of place on the altar are the plates and cups for communion, covered by a dark green cloth. A crystal flask containing oil for anointing sits in front of an elaborate gold bookstand that holds a black folder, and a pale green taper on either side of the cross completes the picture. To the left is an ornate gold candle stand, roughly four feet in height, which holds a large dark-green candle. The altar is flanked by green-draped lecterns, and four microphones are set at strategic points across the stage.

Six rows of dark-brown wooden chairs—nine chairs on either side of the central aisle—set the church's capacity at a little over a hundred; chairs along the back wall raise that number to nearly 120. But today, as the summer winds to a close, attendance is fairly low: roughly fifty people are seated or are milling about the room. The congregation is mostly white, as are all of the pastors, although there are a few African Americans, Latinos, Asian Americans, and Pacific Islanders present. Congregants range in age from late 20s to 70s, with the vast majority in their late 30s and 40s. About twenty of the adults present are women, three of whom are transgender; two children are also in the congregation today.

Reverend Patrick, the church's senior pastor, plays softly on the electric keyboard that sits in the right corner at the front of the sanctuary as people continue to drift in. When 10:30 arrives, Reverend Keith, the pastor in charge of music, moves to stand behind the left-hand lectern, and Reverend Patrick modulates into the key of the opening song. Right away, our newcomer knows she is not in a typical mainline Protestant church, as the standing congregation sings the following words:

> My God hears my prayer.
> My God hears my prayer.
> What I affirm, I attract to me.
> My God hears my prayer.
> My God hears my prayer.
> What I believe I will see.

This impression is confirmed when the church's third pastor, Reverend Dean, comes to the lectern as the greeters quietly close the sanctuary doors and request latecomers to wait in the hallway. Rather than welcoming the congregation or making community announcements, he asks those present to sit comfortably their chairs with both feet on the ground and to breathe deeply and regularly. He then leads a guided meditation based on a quotation in this week's church bulletin. These quotations, which change on a monthly basis, are sometimes biblical, but they may also come from the religious writings of contemporary individuals or the sacred texts of other world religions. This month's quotation, taken from the work of noted metaphysical writer C. Alan Anderson, reads: "I am an opportunity for God to accomplish something marvelous through me."

Following the meditation, Reverend Keith leads an opening hymn; members of the congregation read the lyrics either from the slim binders set on each chair or from the screen at the left front corner of the room. Suzanne, a transgender pastoral candidate who is nearing her own ordination, offers the opening prayer, welcomes the congregation, and makes announcements. One of the biweekly Reiki healing services will be held this Monday evening, she tells the congregation, and she reminds them not to forget the upcoming study session on the book *A Course in Miracles,* led by Reverend Patrick. Also forthcoming are a deacons' meeting, a movie night, the local district conference, and the annual church retreat. Suzanne reminds everyone that audiotapes of Sunday services are available free to newcomers and for five dollars to regular attenders, and she notes that prayer partners will be available in the sanctuary after the service for those in need of one-on-one support.

Those in the congregation then stand and greet each other with hugs, and the room echoes with enthusiastic greetings and the sounds of people hurriedly catching up with the events of each others' lives. Several people greet newcomers, asking whether they are attending for the first time and expressing hope that they will enjoy the service. A few notes from the keyboard send the congregation back to their seats like schoolchildren after recess, and a member of the congregation comes up on stage to give the day's Bible reading.

After the congregation sings a response to the Bible passage, Reverend Patrick takes the floor for the sermon. He is a widely read man with a strong interest in metaphysics, and his sermons are usually organized around a monthly theme. Last month's topic was M. Scott Peck's four stages of spiritual development, and Reverend Patrick identified this church's goal of developing a "stage four" spirituality—independent but community-oriented. This month's theme is "Turning the World Inside Out: A Crash Course in Metaphysics." Having spent the first Sunday of the month telling the story of Unity founders Myrtle and Charles Fillmore, today Reverend Patrick reminds the congregation that the Fillmores experienced "spiritual healing."[2] He brings this discussion together with a somewhat esoteric quotation from the apocryphal Gospel of Thomas in order to arrive at his message for the day: that God is expressed in the world through humans and that people must align their eyes with God's eyes, their minds with God's mind, in order to allow that expression to take place.

The sermon is followed by a period of community prayer, during which two members of the congregation read aloud from prayer cards that people have filled out before the service began. These cards, all anonymous, ask for blessings for ill family members and help with difficult times; they also express gratitude for new jobs, regained health, and other positive developments. While one person reads these prayer requests, the other lights the large candle that stands near the lectern. A common sight in MCC services, this "candle of hope and healing" is used in some congregations as an AIDS and breast cancer memorial. At MCCVR it serves the broader purpose of emphasizing all of the prayers offered during this period of the service.

Following the offering is the most remarkable, and for many the central, part of any MCC service: communion. Unlike some Protestant churches, MCC offers communion at every service and emphasizes that one does not need to be "a member of this church, or of any church" to take part. Christian belief is sufficient in any MCC, and at MCCVR even that belief is loosely defined, since communion is viewed as a meal shared in remembrance of a great teacher.

As happens frequently at MCCVR, a member of the congregation serves as celebrant today. Leading the congregation in a communal confession and a Sanctus sung in both Spanish and English, the celebrant then turns to the black folder on the altar to conduct the consecration. Holding up the pita bread that serves as the host in this church, he breaks it in half and then leads the congregation in a responsive reading before inviting everyone to the "table."

Ten people come forward first, including Reverend Dean, Reverend Keith, Suzanne, several deacons, and other members of the congregation. Reverend Patrick seats himself behind the keyboard and begins to play quiet instrumental versions of favorite hymns; some people in the congregation sing along softly, and during a particularly moving song, two or three from more charismatic backgrounds raise a hand, palm forward, toward the altar as they hum or listen. Splitting into five pairs, the servers spread out across the front of the room, each pair supplied with a cup of grape juice and a plate of communion wafers. Ushers indicate which rows may approach the altar, and a line forms down the center aisle as people wait their turn to receive communion from one of the pairs in front of the stage. Some go up alone, while others stand in line with partners, hand in hand. Two men who are regular attenders are the fathers of a toddler, and today all three are taking communion together, their son sitting on one father's shoulders.

Taking communion at an MCC church involves more than simply accepting the bread dipped in juice (or wine, which is optional at some churches) and receiving a quick blessing. Instead, after serving the individual, couple, or family that has come forward, the pastor or congregation member embraces them loosely and prays over them quietly for anywhere from thirty seconds to a few minutes. During communion, the entire front of the church is occupied by these small huddles of people, and beneath the keyboard music and the soft singing from those still seated runs the quiet murmur of several voices offering prayers.

Communion rounds out the MCCVR service, and after those serving communion have served each other and Reverend Patrick, they return the dishes to the altar and cover them. Reverend Keith leads the congregation in a closing hymn, but the service has not yet ended. The congregation stands to recite together the benediction, a prayer also used by the metaphysical Unity churches:

> The light of God surrounds us.
> The love of God enfolds us.
> The power of God protects us.
> The presence of God watches over us.
> Wherever we are, God is. And all is well.

Regular attenders make a slight alteration to the final line, grinning as they proclaim: "And all is swell!" Congregants then join hands to sing a final song whose words are projected on the screen at the front of the room:

> Love can build a bridge
> between your heart and mine,
> Love can build a bridge,
> Don't you think it's time,
> Don't you think it's time?

One of the pastors reminds those present to gather in the social hall that stands behind the church, and the service closes as people look around to greet old friends, introduce themselves to newcomers, scan the flyers and pamphlets available on a table in the back of the sanctuary, or drift out the door.

A 40-minute drive away, and several hours later, the members of Oceanfront Metropolitan Community Church (OMCC) are preparing for the evening service in the coastal city of La Playa. Oceanfront draws its congregation from a wide geographical area, and for several years it has held its morning and evening services in two separate cities, La Playa and Seaview. OMCC is too small a church to have its own building; its evening service takes place instead inside a local United Methodist church.

Hanging outside the church is a faded canvas banner reading "Oceanfront Metropolitan Community Church." In the doorway a rainbow flag patterned after the U.S. flag, with pink triangles in the blue field where stars would be, swings gently in the breeze. Inside, one side of the sanctuary is set up for an MCC service. Because the pews are arranged in a U-shape, and because its attendance is only a fraction of that at the Methodist church, OMCC uses one side branch of the U and sets its altar in front of these pews. On the left side of the altar, from the congregation's point of view, stands a large gold cross identical to the one at MCCVR. Flanking it are two lavender candles in gold candlesticks, and at the center of the table are the communion vessels: a cream-colored ceramic goblet decorated with a gold UFMCC logo and a matching shallow bowl, both covered with a rainbow-colored cloth. On the right side of the altar is a small box, decorated with rainbow crepe paper, that is used to collect private prayer requests and a small wicker basket for the offering. Next to the altar on the same side is a wooden lectern. To the altar's left, an overhead projector and a makeshift screen—constructed from a white sheet stretched over a PVC-pipe frame—complete the simple setup, which must be erected and then removed for each OMCC service at this church. Slim, orange-covered booklets are spread across the front four pews: these contain the lyrics to OMCC songs and hymns.

Entering the church a few minutes before the beginning of service, our newcomer finds Reverend Sharon, the church's only pastor, and her partner June preparing for the service. The church's music director and her partner, who like Reverend Sharon and June travel from La Playa to Seaview and back every Sunday, are setting up the musical parts of the service—tuning a guitar, testing the small sound system, reviewing chords, and checking to make sure the correct transparencies are readily accessible for those songs not included in the songbook. Today there are two other women present when the service begins; three more drift in during the next ten minutes.

About five minutes after the official starting time of 5:30, the music director moves to stand next to the altar. She announces the title of the first song, and as people flip through their songbooks or

peer at the overhead, she strums the opening chords. A few know
these songs by heart; others follow the words and the music leader's
voice. Although there are some fairly typical Protestant hymns in
Oceanfront's repertoire, many of these introductory praise songs are
taken from contemporary Christian artists and are most familiar to
those who listen to Christian radio stations or follow Christian rock
and pop groups.

The congregation sings a second song before the music leader
introduces the opening hymn, a more solemn introspective song
that marks the formal beginning of the worship service. With so
few people in attendance, the singing at OMCC is quite different
from that heard at MCCVR. Some people sing only softly or do not
sing at all; at times only June and the music director can be heard,
despite June's tireless efforts to raise the energy level and involvement of the congregants. For the opening hymn, the music director
asks everyone to stand, and as Reverend Sharon walks into the
room and up to the altar, a member of the congregation lights the
altar candles.

Reverend Sharon welcomes everyone to the church and asks
whether there are any announcements. When no one responds,
she mentions the upcoming district conference and a workshop
on diversity that is to be held in La Playa next week. She offers an
opening prayer, then sits down in the front pew as the music director comes forward to lead the congregation in four more songs.
During an especially moving song, one woman sings with her arms
slightly outstretched, palms up and eyes closed. Others simply sing
along, preferring not to express themselves in charismatic form.

Following the singing, the music director sits down and another
member of the congregation comes up to the altar to lead the community prayer. Unlike MCCVR, where requests for prayer are
anonymous, at Oceanfront MCC those in need of prayer announce
their requests to the congregation. The woman leading it today
explains the process briefly, saying that it is a time to share needs
or thanks for blessings bestowed; she then asks whether anyone has
something to share. After a long period of silence, June asks blessings for a family member and Reverend Sharon offers thanks for a
recent experience. The woman leading community prayer asks for
God's presence and guidance in her life, and June adds a prayer
for the people of a country embroiled in civil war. Another period
of silence ensues, and the lay leader then closes the prayer session.

Reverend Sharon returns to the altar at this point to pass around the offering basket and the box for private prayer requests. Most people drop in a small offering; no one fills out a prayer card. When the box and basket have been returned to the altar, June comes to the front with her Bible to read this Sunday's scriptural passages. Having finished, she returns to her place in the front pew, and Reverend Sharon moves to the lectern to begin her sermon. Her theme today is taken from Psalm 1, which speaks of the blessed person's trees bearing good fruit (in traditional versions it is the blessed man, but both MCC Valle Rico and Oceanfront MCC use gender-inclusive language in their services). What fruit, Reverend Sharon asks the congregation, does your tree bear? What fruits do you expect the trees of others to bear? Using a casual conversational style, she encourages responses from those present and goes on to say that people often bear the fruits of anger and ill temper while expecting others to bear those of kindness. Upon concluding, she closes the sermon with a prayer.

As at MCCVR, communion is the final part of Oceanfront's service. Although communion at the two churches is essentially the same, there are a few noteworthy differences. One concerns the "host" at Oceanfront. Reverend Sharon originally used communion wafers, but for several reasons these became impractical for the church. Begun by accident but continued in an effort to sanctify the everyday, the current tradition at Oceanfront is to make use of anything that can be dipped in juice and placed in someone's mouth. Most common at the La Playa services are cheddar cheese goldfish crackers, but during my fieldwork I saw everything from a peanut butter cookie to a scone appear on the communion plate. In addition, the juice is not always grape juice. Because Reverend Sharon does not prepare the altar, she is occasionally surprised by what appears when she removes the cloth covering the communion elements, and sometimes a short discussion ensues to determine exactly what the "host of the day" actually is.

Today there are goldfish crackers on the plate. After taking a moment for silent confession, Reverend Sharon offers a prayer and leads the congregation in a brief statement of faith, then consecrates the communion elements. When she invites people to come forward to receive communion, she adds that anyone who wishes can also be prayed over without taking communion. The music director returns to the front and begins playing her guitar softly, and her partner puts song lyrics on the overhead projector as a few people begin humming quietly. No one else comes forward for a few seconds, but

goldfish crackers?

eventually June stands and approaches the altar. Reverend Sharon serves her and then embraces her while praying softly. When June returns to her seat, another woman goes up to the altar. She says something quietly to Reverend Sharon, who nods, serves her communion, and then begins to pray over her. After about a minute, Reverend Sharon catches the eye of another member of the congregation without breaking stride in her prayer. This member touches another on the arm, and both move to stand behind the woman over whom Reverend Sharon is praying, hands held out at chest level with their palms facing pastor and congregant.

Keeping one hand on the woman's shoulder, Reverend Sharon holds the other, palm down, just over the woman's forehead. She begins to pray more fervently as the woman lifts her palms toward the sky. After a few minutes the woman collapses backward into the waiting hands of her fellow congregants, who lower her gently to the ground. She lies there, eyes closed, experiencing the overwhelming and intimate divine contact that charismatic Christians call being "slain in the spirit." Reverend Sharon squats by her head, one palm stretched over her, and continues to pray. Another minute goes by, and the woman opens her eyes and smiles. Reverend Sharon smiles back and returns to the altar as the woman slowly rises and walks to her pew. Three others come up to take communion, but today no one else is "slain."

When communion is finished, the music director returns to the front pew. Reverend Sharon places the cloth back over the goblet and dish and then offers a closing prayer. People slowly stand and greet each other as others begin to put the altar materials back in a closet to be stored until next Sunday. June and Reverend Sharon make a point of speaking to the rare newcomer, welcoming her and expressing their hope that she has enjoyed the service and will return again. Although Oceanfront does not have an official social hour as does MCCVR, it is common for people to adjourn to a nearby restaurant for a late dinner; today is no exception.

I first learned about the Universal Fellowship of Metropolitan Community Churches (UFMCC)[3] years ago during a long-distance telephone call from a close friend while I was spending a year in England. As I strained to hear her over the chattering of Yorkshire accents in the dining hall, my friend told me with some reticence that she and her partner had begun attending church and that while she found some parts of the service discomfiting, overall she was enjoying the experience.

Like most non-Christian lesbian, gay, bisexual, and transgender (LGBT)[4] people, my reaction to the idea of an LGBT Christian church was one of incredulity. While I respected my friend's judgment and that of her partner, and while I was willing to support heartily anything that they found enriching, I could not fathom why any self-respecting feminist lesbian would want to be involved with a religion so heavily implicated in the battles against women's and LGBT rights. Needless to say, I have learned a great deal since then.

Part of my astonishment also stemmed from the fact that my friend, with whom I had embarked on the spiritual explorations of my early college years, had almost no religious exposure at all as a child and during our college years had shown far greater interest in things New Age than in anything remotely Christian. I began to wonder what drew people to MCC and whether it was common for non-Christians to convert to Christianity through this church. As it turns out, neither of the churches in this study has a significant number of converts, and my friend herself did not become a Christian—in fact, she and her partner no longer attend MCC. But my curiosity was piqued.

As I continued to foster a growing interest in the roles religion can play in creating and resisting oppression, MCC remained in the back of my mind. I found Christianity to be particularly interesting in this regard because although it is frequently typecast as either oppressor or liberator, in reality its roles have spanned a wide range, from fierce oppression to oblivious neutrality to outright radicalism. After discovering how little the area of LGBT studies in religion had been explored to date, I decided to undertake a research project on the Metropolitan Community Church.

LGBT People in Religion

Robert Frost wrote metaphorically of two roads diverging in a wood and of his difficulties in making the irrevocable decision between the two, not knowing what lay ahead on either one. For LGBT people who were raised within Christianity, this is often a familiar dilemma. In many churches and among many Christian families, the two identities are mutually exclusive: one cannot be openly and proudly lesbian, gay, bisexual, or transgender and also be Christian. For Christians, then, and for numerous others from traditional religious backgrounds, awareness of same-sex attraction or transgender identity leads to this crossroad, presenting one with the difficult choice between religious commitment and one's sexual or gender identity. Some choose their religion and struggle to become heterosexual or to identify with their socially assigned gender. Others choose LGBT identity, forcefully rejecting the religion that denigrates who they are.

There are some, however—and their number may be larger than anyone suspects at this point—who refuse to make that choice and instead reconfigure the map. Out of two diverging roads they create two converging ones, reinterpreting their belief systems in such a way that LGBT identity and religious commitment are not just compatible but are also intertwined. Some undertake these reinterpretations independently; others rely on assistance from books, Web sites, friends, and even religious leaders. And for a few the whole process is unnecessary, because these two facets of their identities were never divergent.

These people sometimes practice their religion alone or with their partners and/or children; others attend a wide variety of congregations. Some of the latter remain closeted in order to continue attending the church of their choice; some attend liberal churches or LGBT-supportive congregations; some become activists for LGBT rights within their denominations; while others, like most of those in this study, take part in congregations that are led, run, and frequented primarily by LGBT people.

Despite the relevance of these processes of identity negotiation and community support to current research in psychology, sociology, and religious studies, little work has been done to date in this field. Although primary sources—collections of reflective essays on religion written by LGBT people—and resources for LGBT theology have increased steadily over the past fifteen years, secondary studies of contemporary LGBT people in religion include only a few scattered books, a handful of articles, and some unpublished dissertations and master's theses. Only two attempts have been made so far to bring these works into conversation with each other.[5]

Another fascinating development of the past few decades is the appearance and growth of LGBT congregations: religious groups that serve primarily or exclusively lesbian, gay, bisexual, and transgender people. Some of these are fully self-contained congregations, holding regular services and offering all of the assistance and amenities of any other congregation. Others are better characterized as support groups; they offer resources for those struggling to integrate religious and LGBT identities, but for religious services one must go elsewhere. At the time of this writing, roughly fifteen in-depth studies of such congregations or their participants in the United States are publicly available, and several studies from Britain have been published recently. Only five of these works are book length, and to date no attempt has been made to consolidate this body of research into a cohesive set of findings.[6]

1st Study!

Existing Studies

The first ethnographic study of a gay and lesbian (and perhaps bisexual and transgender) congregation was published in 1974 by Ronald M. Enroth and Gerald E. Jamison. Appearing both as a book (*The Gay Church*) and an article ("The Homosexual Church: An Ecclesiastical Extension of a Subculture"), the study focused on the importance of a gay-specific congregation for those attending MCC San Francisco.[7] Following closely on the heels of Enroth and Jamison was Paul F. Bauer, whose "The Homosexual Subculture at Worship" was based on research at MCC Denver.[8]

In some ways, these very important inaugural studies reveal more about the culture of the time than they do about LGBT religiosities in general. All three publications reflect an underlying assumption that "homosexuals" (mostly gay men, to judge from the evidence cited) are in some way psychologically abnormal. The nature and source of this abnormality vary: none of these authors necessarily wishes to claim that homosexuality itself is disordered. However, their discussions betray dated stereotypes of the sex-crazed gay socialite and the tragically delicate fairy—figures they suggest have been damaged not so much by their homosexuality itself as by societal rejection. Aside from this stereotyping and an inaccurate summary of MCC's theology as "fundamentalist," Bauer offers a cogent reading of MCC as a community that supports the resolution of cognitive dissonance. Enroth and Jamison, in contrast, leave the reader with the impression that "the homosexual church" is little more than a dressed-up version of the bathhouses, a new place to cruise where the atmosphere is quieter and the men perhaps more respectable. Viewing "homosexual" congregations more as coping mechanisms than as legitimate religious groups, Enroth and Jamison leave us with a useful (though skewed) outsider's view of early MCC churches but cannot offer a helpful theoretical perspective.

Taking up that task from where Bauer left off was E. Michael Gorman, whose 1980 dissertation in anthropology at the University of Chicago was sorely needed yet also far ahead of its time.[9] In "A New Light on Zion," Gorman presents the results of his fieldwork at three gay congregations in what he calls "Lake City": an MCC, a chapter of the Catholic organization known as Dignity, and an LGBT synagogue.[10] Providing a ground-level view of pre-AIDS (again, mostly male) gay culture that is occasionally chilling when read nearly twenty years after the appearance of the disease, Gorman's work is the first to give serious in-depth consideration to the importance and function of LGBT religious congregations.[11]

Comparing Protestant, Catholic, and Jewish congregations, Gorman concludes that the overall benefits of gay congregations are similar regardless of religious context. He understands such congregations as communities in which to develop a sense of pride—for him, to move from being "homosexual" to being "gay"—and as mediators between conflicting gay and religious identities. He also sees them as critical sources of support for same-sex relationships, which often suffered (and still suffer) from the pressures of societal disapproval. Finally, Gorman was the first to note the defiantly individualistic claim among religious lesbians and gay men: "This is my religion too!"

Eleven years passed after Gorman's dissertation was filed before another notable study appeared in 1991. Scott Thumma's article "Negotiating a Religious Identity" is one of the few available studies of the identity crisis faced by gay men and lesbians in conservative religious traditions.[12] It focuses on a small local organization that Thumma dubs "Good News," which ministers to gay and lesbian evangelical Christians. Although the group met regularly during the course of Thumma's research, only a small number of core members were involved in person. Much of their work was accomplished through a newsletter and through answering individual letters from Christians struggling to reconcile gay or lesbian identity with fundamentalist or evangelical beliefs. Members of the organization responded to these letters with explanations of the theological and biblical perspectives that supported the validity of a gay or lesbian Christian identity—providing tools, Thumma suggests, for the negotiation of a newly integrated religious identity.

Similar themes are evident in much of the other research published on LGBT religiosity in the 1990s. Foremost among these works are Leonard Norman Primiano's dissertation on Dignity-Philadelphia and Moshe Shokeid's book on New York's Congregation Beth Simchat Torah (CBST).[13] Both authors discuss a number of different facets of congregational life, but both also pay significant attention to the question of identity. Primiano echoes and amplifies Gorman's work in his valuable discussion of vernacular religion in the lives of lesbian and gay Catholics. In the claim that "this is our religion too," he sees an individualistic form of religiosity whose self-definition is affected by but not dependent upon official religion. While he suggests that Dignity-Philadelphia provides communal support for such religious identities, the initial steps toward integration seem to take place outside the church. This suggestion correlates well with the findings of Glenn Wagner and his colleagues.[14] Studying the self-acceptance of gay Catholics who were members of Dignity and those who were not, these researchers posited a significant difference due to the positive influence of Dignity but in fact found little divergence between the two populations.

Despite working in a different city and a different religion—and despite not having read Primiano's work, to judge from his bibliography—Shokeid reaches many of the same conclusions. Finding, as Primiano did, that people attending CBST have at least begun to integrate their Jewish and gay or lesbian identities, he also suggests that the synagogue is a central source of support and affirmation—a resource, as he puts it, for "restoring [a] cracked self-image and identity."[15] As at Dignity-Philadelphia, this support comes from many sources: ritual (services), theological resources such as the rabbi and the congregational library, the presence of a community, study groups, and so on.

In a 1995 article, R. Stephen Warner, on the other hand, focuses on intellectual resources. Relying mostly on UFMCC publications and interviews with denominational leaders, he points to a combination of essentialism and Pentecostal theology as the key to MCC's success in supporting the integration of Christian and gay or lesbian identities.[16]

Ritual is also important in a very different religious setting studied by Edward Gray and Scott Thumma in the mid-1990s.[17] The Gospel Hour was a drag show performed in an Atlanta gay bar that carried explicit religious overtones and was patronized largely by gay men who were former conservative Christians. Some of these people attended the local MCC; some found it too liberal or too socially oriented for their tastes and attended nowhere; some went back to their home churches occasionally, keeping their gayness deeply hidden; and a fourth group was alienated enough from Christianity that they no longer attended at all. But all came to the Gospel Hour to hear and sing the songs of their childhood, reaffirming a Christian background or identity in an overtly gay context.

Several other works appeared after 1995 that broadened the study of LGBT people in religion. Gary David Comstock's groundbreaking book *Unrepentant, Self-Affirming, Practicing* addressed in depth for the first time the experiences of lesbians, bisexuals, and gay men in non-LGB religious organizations.[18] It brought together numerous previous studies of LGB religiosity (often included as a small portion of a broader study), along with his own work on LGB members of the United Methodist Church and United Church of Christ. Though Comstock's analysis focuses more on experiences (congregational involvement, experiences in ministry, and so on) than on belief (which occupies only one chapter of the book), there is evidence throughout his book that LGB people in mainstream religious organizations rely on the same individuality, the same vernacular religion, identified in studies of gay and lesbian congregations.

That same year, Kimberly Mahaffy published an article that addressed identity crises among lesbian Christians through the lens of cognitive dissonance.[19] Using quantified interview data, she found (as was suggested by Thumma's study of Good News) that evangelical Christian identity predicted dissonance both internally (dissonance within oneself) and externally (dissonance between one's own beliefs and the beliefs of those around one). Participants in her study reacted to this dissonance in three different ways: by altering their beliefs (mostly in the case of internal dissonance), leaving their church (in the case of external dissonance), or choosing to live with the dissonance. These patterns, too, are suggested by previous studies and are supported by the work presented here.

In 1996, the first study of gay male religiosity in Britain reached publication in the form of two articles authored by Andrew K. T. Yip, a sociologist whose first book on the subject was published the following year and who has continued to be extremely productive in this area.[20] Focusing his discussion of religion on strategies for creating and maintaining an integrated gay/Christian identity, Yip seconds Warner's suggestion that a religiously rooted essentialism—the belief that "God made me this way"—is an important part of such identity integration. Furthermore, like the participants in Mahaffy's study who changed their beliefs in order to reduce internal dissonance, most of Yip's respondents have developed strategies that allow them to discount church teachings while continuing to attend services. In a 2002 article based on a large quantitative and qualitative study, Yip echoes several previous authors in stressing the importance of individual beliefs and practices over institutional influences in the identity negotiations of what he calls "non-heterosexual" Christians.[21]

Finally, Eric M. Rodriguez and Suzanne C. Ouellette have recently written a handful of articles on MCC New York (MCCNY), the most relevant of which focuses again on the processes of identity integration among gay and lesbian Christians.[22] Rodriguez and Ouellette found that the majority of participants in their study (all of whom were involved in MCCNY) had integrated their religious and sexual identities and that MCCNY had played an important part in that integration process. They note, however, that their study does not examine the actual process or stages involved in such integration; it also does not discuss in depth the specific roles played by the church, although it does stress the importance of MCCNY for many respondents.[23]

Despite the recent growth in this field of study, therefore, many gaps remain—as one might expect, given that most of the influential literature is less than ten years old and can be summarized in a few pages. One of these gaps is analytical literature about MCC. Because of the denomination's status as the first LGBT religious group to spread beyond a single city, its prominence in LGBT histories in the United States, and the number of existing publications on the UFMCC, this is somewhat surprising. However, the only book-length study of the denomination is Enroth and Jamison's early and by now far outdated work. Furthermore, of the studies that appear to be relatively free of homophobic stereotypes, only Gorman's and Rodriguez and

Ouellette's are based upon extensive fieldwork and interviews with individual members.[24]

More remains to be done as well on the question of identity. Though a number of authors have discussed the importance of this topic, only a few have explored it in depth. Moreover, the interaction of individual and community also deserves further in-depth study—along the lines, especially, of the work of Gorman, Shokeid, Gray and Thumma, and Rodriguez and Ouellette. Insufficient attention has been paid thus far to the role of ritual and symbol in LGBT congregations and the ways in which they might be just as important as pastoral care in the support of LGBT religiosity.

Why This Study?

This study is designed to address the aforementioned gaps as much as possible given the limitations of a single researcher, the UFMCC itself, and the two congregations on which the study focuses. Its central aim with regard to LGBT studies in religion is to elucidate further the interactions between religious beliefs and practices and LGBT identities. As only the third book-length congregational study in this area to reach publication, it adds to scholarly understanding of the complexities of LGBT religiosity and I hope it will inspire future studies in the areas I have been forced to leave inadequately addressed.[25] However, the book also makes a number of contributions to religious studies and LGBT studies in general.

For example, much attention has been paid in recent years to the increase in religious individualism in the United States. However, LGBT Christians—and LGBT people of many other faiths as well—are unusual in that they do not always choose such individualism so much as they have it thrust upon them. Many are rejected by their religious organizations or are aware that they would be rejected were they to reveal their sexual or transgender identity. Therefore, forging their own religious and spiritual paths is more a necessity than a new route to fulfillment for many LGBT people. Because of this fact, LGBT communities present a particularly interesting opportunity for studying contemporary religious individualism.

The study of LGBT Christians also offers new perspectives on other theoretical issues. For instance, the affirmation of LGBT identity that takes place on both symbolic and verbal levels during MCC services suggests a new angle on the study of religious symbolism and ritual. On a more sociological level, the importance of community for many of the participants in this study recalls the work of Peter Berger and Thomas Luckmann on plausibility structures and the social construction—or in this case, reconstruction—of reality. The role of religion in power dynamics and social control is also highly relevant here, as religious beliefs help to shape the self-image of many participants. And as Bauer, Mahaffy, Rodriguez and Ouellette, and others have already observed, the acute crisis of identity suffered by some LGBT Christians suggests interesting new directions within the field of psychology as well.

Finally, within LGBT studies as a whole, a great deal of attention has been paid to the "queering" of various social institutions: the challenges made by same-sex couples to traditional models of marriage and the family, for instance, or the politics of gender. Yet like feminist theory and women's studies, queer theory and LGBT studies have been reluctant to address the topic of religion. Perhaps this is due to the strong influence of Marxism in both feminist and queer theory; yet as early as the work of Antonio Gramsci (and, some would argue, in Marx's writing itself), Marxism has recognized at least a faint counterhegemonic potential in the religion of the people—that which we might today call "lived religion." Thinkers from Gustavo Gutierrez to Otto Maduro have seen the potential for combining Marxism with theology in Latin America, and it is the liberation theology of Gutierrez and others in which much LGBT theology is rooted.

Perhaps the neglect of religion within LGBT and queer studies also stems from a perception that few LGBT people are religious. As the growing body of work discussed above demonstrates, however, this is not the case. Furthermore, as scholars delve more deeply into non-organized religiosities in these communities, it is likely that we will discover greater religious depth and diversity among LGBT people than is even suspected by most contemporary observers. As with marriage, family, gender, and many other social institutions, there have been many "queerings" of religion in its institutionalized, individual, and communal modes. Understanding these alterations and the variety of roles religion plays in the lives of LGBT people will refine our analyses of such diverse phenomena as coming out, identity formation, and general mental health.[26]

Studying MCC

As Comstock has pointed out in his work on LGB people in religion, and as R. Stephen Warner has noted in the context of immigrant congregations, studying what others do and say *about* a group of people is interesting but is entirely insufficient if one wishes to understand that group. A "focus on congregations," Warner says, "means that we look at what the various communities do religiously for themselves, not what others do or do not do on their behalf."[27] And Comstock asserts that "religious bodies most often choose to engage in abstract discussions about homosexuality and to prohibit homosexual behavior rather than to examine the actual lives of lesbians, bisexuals, and gay men and to take seriously the many dimensions of their lives."[28]

Comstock's observation could be applied as well to the sociology of religion, which has found its attention captured by debates over homosexuality in the mainline churches but has seen far less concerted development in studies of the actual people whose "behavior" is the subject of these debates. In large part, this study represents an effort to correct that imbalance by presenting the cares and concerns, trials and triumphs, of people who have removed themselves from such discussions by joining a church in which both their Christianity and their LGBT identity are welcomed without question—even if they themselves have not yet reached that level of self-acceptance.

Introducing the Churches

The UFMCC

Troy Perry founded the first Metropolitan Community Church in Los Angeles during October of 1968; the Universal Fellowship of Metropolitan Community Churches held its inaugural general conference in 1970 with five member churches represented. Perry, who had been defrocked by the Church of God in Prophecy when he revealed his homosexuality to his bishop, felt a divine calling to create a church that would minister to gay and lesbian Christians; the denomination's mission statement still defines it as "a Christian Church founded in and reaching beyond the Gay and Lesbian communities." It adds: "We serve among those seeking and celebrating the integration of their spirituality and sexuality."[29]

Unfortunately, the UFMCC does not keep demographic or other statistics on its membership. It is generally assumed, however, that the over 40,000 members of its roughly 300 churches continue to be predominantly LGBT. Its congregations are small, averaging in my experience between fifty and one hundred regular attenders. But while some MCC services take place with as few as four or five people present in the pews, Dallas's Cathedral of Hope MCC has the distinction of being an LGBT megachurch with approximately 3,000 members.

The denomination's early years were marked by the struggles of lesbian members and pastors for equal representation, inclusive language, and other issues of gender equality. In March 2000, a denominational official estimated that the number of female clergy has now slightly surpassed the number of male clergy; however, no figures are yet available on the gender breakdown of MCC's membership.[30]

The UFMCC currently recognizes several underserved populations within its ranks; whether these are also underrepresented among clergy (with the exception of women) or relative to the general population is often unclear. These populations include laity in general, people of color, non–English-speaking church members (presumably within the United States as well as internationally—the UFMCC has churches in eighteen countries), youth and young adults, and women pastors. Only a few of the larger MCC congregations in the United States offer special worship services or outreach programs for people of color; MCC Los Angeles and MCC New York are both notable for holding a Spanish-language service, and the latter church offers special ministries for its congregants of African descent. Although recent years have seen the beginnings of organization among the Asian and Pacific Islander members of the denomination, these developments are still in their infancy. There is no movement that I am aware of within the denomination to address the concerns of its American Indian members or those of Middle Eastern descent.

In 1998, the UFMCC's doctrine, as outlined in its by-laws, proclaimed adherence to Christian beliefs and asserted that the denomination "moves in the mainstream of Christianity." This general statement was followed by only seven points. These include belief in the trinity; the divine inspiration of the Bible; the dual human and divine nature of Jesus; the presence of the Holy Spirit as God's love in the world; justification by grace through Christian faith; the special power of grace to save humans from "loneliness, despair and degradation"; and an evangelistic mission that mandates regular worship services as well as "edification through the teaching and preaching of the Word."[31]

Clearly, although these statements explicitly define MCC churches as Christian organizations, they leave a great deal of theological leeway for individual congregations. The by-laws on sacraments, rites, and church services are equally permissive. In fact, although many MCC congregations do follow a certain pattern in their services, the only official requirement is that churches hold at least one worship service, offering communion, every Sunday.[32] As a result, services at individual congregations within the denomination reflect the wide range of Christian backgrounds among both congregants and pastors.

Thus, despite Perry's Pentecostal heritage, one can easily find within MCC not only services based on conservative Christian practices and theology but also "high church" services that attract members from Catholic or Anglican backgrounds, gospel services, services that closely resemble those of mainstream Protestant churches, and even services incorporating New Age, metaphysical, or Goddess-based beliefs and practices. In the larger churches, members often can choose between an early morning "high-church" service, a late morning "mainline" service, and an evening "low-church" service. While this diversity has led to no small amount of tension within the denomination, it makes the UFMCC a fascinating organization to study as well as an excellent resource through which to contact LGBT Christians from a wide variety of religious backgrounds.

Because I was interested in obtaining as diverse a sample as possible given the limitations of a single researcher, I chose to work with two MCC churches rather than a single one. I intentionally selected widely different congregations, hoping to determine whether there were any notable variations between the two in demographics, reasons for attending, or effects on congregants' lives.

Metropolitan Community Church of Valle Rico

MCC Valle Rico[33] is located near the heart of a city with just under a million inhabitants. The church was founded in the early 1970s, shortly after the UFMCC's inaugural conference. By the summer of 1998, it had a mailing list of more than 300 and a weekly budget of just over $1,800. Attendance at its single Sunday service during that summer averaged around fifty-five, although special services with guest choirs or speakers drew larger numbers. Women typically constituted between 25 and 40 percent of the congregation during the course of my study, and several transgender women were present at most services. Transgender men were less common, although one attends occasionally and a second, a former MCCVR pastor, visits from time to time.

According to the 2000 census, Valle Rico's population is roughly 36 percent white, 30 percent Latino, 27 percent Asian, and 3 percent black or African American; just over 50 percent of its inhabitants speak only English in the home. Despite being located in a highly diverse section of the city—one passes storefront signs in both Spanish and Vietnamese while walking down the block—MCCVR does not reflect this ethnic diversity. At any given service, one can expect to find seven or eight congregants who are African American, Latino, Asian American, or Pacific Islander; the rest are white. The church offers no advertised services for attenders who do not speak English.

MCCVR had three pastors on staff, all gay men, during the summer of 1998. It also sponsored a transgender lesbian pastoral candidate who was nearing her ordination; she now serves as pastor at another MCC church in the area. When she left in the fall of 1998, the church added a fourth gay man to its clergy. All but the senior pastor, Reverend Patrick, work only part-time for the church.

Because of Reverend Patrick's strong interest in metaphysics, services at MCCVR have a decidedly different flavor from that of many MCCs—at least at points. Although the presence of several formerly charismatic or Pentecostal Christians in the congregation has led some in jest to call MCCVR a "meta-costal, Pente-physical" church, the pastors also have been known to advise inquirers from conservative Christian backgrounds that MCCVR may not suit their needs. In fact, one couple that I interviewed first attended MCCVR during one of its more experimental services and denounced it as simply "not Christian." When a subsequent discussion with a pastor convinced them that not all services were that radical, however, they returned and enjoyed attending for several years.

Oceanfront Metropolitan Community Church

Although La Playa had a male-pastored MCC congregation at one time, Oceanfront MCC dates from the arrival of Reverend Sharon in June of 1988. Always a small and somewhat experimental church, it attracted more women than men from the start. With a budget of just under $2,000 per month (in contrast to MCCVR's comparable weekly budget), OMCC employs only a single half-time pastor and struggles to meet its financial obligations. Human obligations, too, frequently outstrip the church's budget. Reverend Sharon generally works more than forty hours per week on church-related matters and considers the extra twenty or more hours she puts in each week to be a donation to Oceanfront.

In the early years, the church's morning and evening services met in two separate locations in La Playa. Concerns over accessibility for congregants with disabilities as well as recognition of the growing number of congregants who drove in from outlying areas to attend services led the church to move one service to Seaview; and services were held in both locations throughout the time of my fieldwork with the church. In 1999, however, Oceanfront MCC lost its Seaview lease, and the morning service moved to the small La Playa LGBT community center.

La Playa, Seaview, and Valle Rico differ widely in ethnic composition; La Playa and Seaview are far less diverse than the larger city nearby. La Playa, which had a population of 55,700 in 1999, was 72 percent white, according to the 2000 census. Latinos were the largest minority then, comprising over 17 percent of the population; Asians represented nearly 5 percent and blacks and African Americans less than 2 percent. The smaller city of Seaview, which had a population of 33,100 in 1999, was 75 percent white in 2000, with Latinos, Asians, and blacks/African Americans comprising 10.9 percent, 7.3 percent, and 2.4 percent of the population, respectively.[34]

During the summer of 1998, attendance was almost entirely female and overwhelmingly white at both OMCC locations; the church has no notable transgender population. Overall, attendance during that summer was quite low. The La Playa services typically had four or five people in the congregation, in addition to Reverend Sharon and the music director; Seaview services usually attracted around ten people. A special service celebrating the church's tenth anniversary was held in mid-June and attracted sixteen people; this was the largest attendance I saw at any Oceanfront service.

Although Reverend Sharon told me that the attendance in 1998 was at an all-time low in the ten-year history of the church, Oceanfront has always been small. Because of this, it is also especially vulnerable to personal tensions and the upheavals caused by change. One of the most disruptive events in its brief history was the move toward charismatic practice initiated by Reverend Sharon and June.

This development began at a denominational general conference in 1993, when Sharon and June went to hear a friend preach. It was a healing service, which for charismatic Christians refers to healing through prayer, and the pastor eventually called for people to come to the altar for healing. June, who only recently had become Christian, was horrified when many of those over whom the pastor prayed were "slain in the spirit," collapsing as they experienced an overwhelmingly intimate contact with the divine. But later that evening, after she had recovered from her shock, June began to believe that this was the proof of God's existence for which she had been praying. She and Reverend Sharon discussed the issue repeatedly over the next several months.

Among California MCC churches, several are well known for being charismatic or offering charismatic services. One of the most prominent of these is MCC Long Beach, which holds an annual charismatic conference. After the experience at the general conference, Reverend Sharon decided to attend this charismatic conference, and June accompanied her. June received the gift of tongues, or glossolalia, a form of sacred but unintelligible speech which she now calls her "personal prayer language." After this point, Reverend Sharon began to attend healing services outside OMCC and to hold such services within the church—and charismatic expression began to take place at OMCC.[35]

This development precipitated a crisis in membership from which the church is still recovering. While some people from charismatic Christian backgrounds were newly attracted to Oceanfront because of these developments, others became distinctly uncomfortable and left the church. Although OMCC held healing services at both of its locations, when it left Seaview and returned both services to La Playa, it also changed its approach, advertising the evening service as Oceanfront's "charismatic service," and the morning one as its brief "contemporary service." The church attracted a few new members after making these changes, but the gains were offset by a schism:

several members, including the music director, left during the summer of 1999 to form their own church. Hence, Oceanfront MCC continues to struggle.

Healing services, which have played such an important role in OMCC's recent history, also take place at MCCVR—and the contrast in these services provides a humorous but accurate summary of the differences between the two churches. The special service held at OMCC to commemorate its tenth anniversary was a charismatic healing service, and a pastor and musicians were brought in from a large MCC in another part of the state. When I mentioned to someone at MCCVR that I had attended a healing service at Oceanfront, the person expressed great surprise, commenting that perhaps the congregations had more in common than most people knew. Likewise, when I commented to someone at OMCC that I was attending biweekly healing services at MCCVR, I was met with incredulity.

The cause of these reactions? Unlike at Oceanfront, the healing services in Valle Rico involve not charismatic experiences but Reiki, a form of energy-based healing favored by those interested in things metaphysical. People at each church, however, assumed that the other church's healing service was the same as theirs. So those at MCCVR were shocked to hear that people at charismatic OMCC were practicing Reiki (which they were not), and those at Oceanfront were equally dumbfounded at the news that charismatic services were taking place at metaphysical Valle Rico (which they were not). Healing work comes in many forms.

Introducing the Project: Fieldwork and the Researcher

From 1997 to 1999, and most intensely during the summer months of 1998, I attended weekly services, special services, and meetings at MCCVR and at both the La Playa and Seaview locations of OMCC. In addition, in July of 1998 I mailed a 61-item anonymous questionnaire to all individuals on each church's mailing list. Included with the questionnaire was a form that respondents could mail back separately if they wished to volunteer for interviews.

Although both churches were careful to check personal and professional references before allowing me to proceed with my fieldwork, being accepted by these congregations was a fairly simple process. Many LGBT people today feel that education is the best route to ending the hatred and bigotry directed at them, and to this end they are often more than happy to share their stories, especially if there is a chance those stories will be widely disseminated.

This is not to say that there was not some suspicion of me and of my project; surveys at MCC Valle Rico were sent out without a pastoral cover letter, and despite reassurances in my own cover letter about the anonymity of the questionnaire, I received several irate phone calls from people who demanded to know how I had obtained their addresses. Although I explained to them that the mailing lists had remained confidential and I did not have a copy of them, these few persisted in believing (incorrectly) that I had used a code that would allow me to connect the information on each survey with a person's name and address. Clearly, the legacy of decades of police entrapment and bar raids has not yet died.

While those whose contact with me was restricted to the survey packet sometimes remained suspicious of my intentions, those who attended services might have discovered several factors that argued for my acceptability in the community. For one thing, I knew former members of both churches, whom some people remembered and trusted. Second, the pastors in each church had spoken to me about the project and had approved it. And third, aware that I was working among a community still suspicious of the motives of heterosexual researchers, I brought my partner to services at each church at least once. Being an insider in terms of sexual orientation was a greater advantage in these communities than being an insider in terms of religion would have been—especially as some of these people have received their most serious mistreatment at the hands of heterosexual Christians. I also shared white ethnicity with the majority of each congregation—which is one possible explanation among many for the small number of people of color who volunteered for interviews.

Providing me with more of an outsider perspective, however, was the fact that I am not Christian and for many years had been an advocate of the feminist critiques of that religion as sexist, heterosexist, implicated in racism and genocide, and anti-environmentalist. Three semesters at a school affiliated with a United Methodist seminary began to change my mind about such absolutist statements, but when I began research in MCC I was still distinctly uncomfortable with Christian ritual. Though this perspective made the research a personal challenge for me, it also made it necessary for me to ask more questions than a committed Christian might have asked about the ways in which Christianity affirmed LGBT, feminist, and other identities for the people in this survey. The answers to these questions have contributed significantly to the depth of this project.

In recent years, questions of voice have come increasingly to the fore, especially in fieldwork-based research. Although I make an effort throughout this book to provide sections in which participants' voices are relatively free of my interpretive and editorial interventions, the analyses and organization in the remainder of the text are heavily affected by my own perspectives. In writing, I have chosen to remain in the outsider and insider positions of my fieldwork: that is, I write as a non-Christian but also as a member of the LGBT community. Thus, while I bracket questions regarding the actual truth of the Christian message and focus instead on the ramifications of such beliefs in participants' lives, I am less reticent when it comes to asserting the reality of oppression in the lives of LGBT people.

In addition, my main concern in this study is to explore and understand the experiences of LGBT Christians during the late twentieth century. For this reason, I do not make use of analytical techniques that challenge or undermine the verity of participants' self-perceptions. I have become increasingly wary of concepts such as "false consciousness" because I suspect that they mask an analytical elitism, a claim that "we know you are oppressed even if you do not." Such claims typically oversimplify the situation and invalidate the experience and subjectivity of those involved. However, my wariness certainly does not amount to a rejection of the idea that cultural beliefs and values can support social inequality. But rather than present those experiences with suspicion, I approach them sympathetically, providing what anthropologists often call an "emic," or insider, perspective. This both supports the goals of my own work and allows readers to draw their own conclusions regarding my findings.

Results: A Brief Overview

Surveys

Returns on the questionnaire were disappointingly low despite a reminder letter mailed a month later. Of a total of 384 surveys mailed (292 at MCCVR and ninety-two at OMCC), 117 usable ones were returned (ninety from Valle Rico and twenty-seven from Oceanfront). Percentage returns for each church were nearly identical: 30.8 percent for MCCVR and 29.3 percent for OMCC. The overall return rate was 30.5 percent. However, more than 65 percent of those who returned surveys also volunteered for interviews.

In-depth demographic data from the survey are provided in the appendices, but a few points are worth noting here. Despite the overwhelming presence of women at Oceanfront's services, 44 percent of the surveys returned from that church were completed by male church members or church affiliates. At MCCVR, 59 percent of the respondents were men. Five transgender people completed the survey, all from MCCVR. Just under 7 percent of respondents (7.8 percent at MCCVR; 3.7 percent at OMCC) identified as heterosexual; the others were lesbians (33 percent overall), gay men (50 percent), bisexuals (8 percent), and questioning (4.3 percent).

Ethnically, the responses to the survey reflected and at times even exaggerated the lack of diversity at the churches. Overall, 82 percent of respondents were white (86 percent at MCCVR and 69 percent at OMCC), a total of forty-one women and fifty-four men. Chicanos and Latinos made up 4.3 percent of respondents (three women and two men), Asians and Pacific Islanders 3.4 percent (one woman and three men). One respondent, a transgender woman, was Native American. Nearly 10 percent of respondents—six women and five men—reported being biracial (white and Asian/Pacific Islander or white and Native American) or multiracial. No African Americans returned the survey. The mean age of respondents, which was nearly identical for both churches, was 48. Female respondents were slightly younger, on average, than male respondents; the mean age for women was 46 while for men it was 50.

Education levels at both churches were relatively high; 61 percent of MCCVR respondents and 52 percent of OMCC respondents held at least a bachelor's degree. Reported individual incomes spanned a wide range, from below $15,000 to over $90,000, but the average was approximately $30,000. Incomes at Oceanfront were somewhat lower than those at MCCVR. Occupations, too, were extremely varied. Although nursing, teaching, accounting, and technology jobs were among the most common, participants also were auto-repair workers, peace officers, quality inspectors, human resources and management personnel, artists, and consultants—among others. Several were disabled or retired, but only one reported being unemployed.

Only 44 percent of respondents were currently members of an MCC church; of those, 87 percent belonged to MCCVR or OMCC. Forty-three percent attended at least once a month, but 25 percent attended less than once a year and just under 10 percent never attended. Among respondents who did attend MCC, 82 percent attended MCCVR or OMCC more frequently than any other MCC church. Another 11 percent spent more of their time attending a larger MCC church in the area, while seven respondents attended other MCC churches in California or the West Coast because they traveled or had moved.

Correlating with the UFMCC's self-understanding as an ecumenical organization was the range of denominational backgrounds among survey respondents: nearly equal numbers of survey respondents came from mainline Protestant and Catholic backgrounds. Among MCCVR respondents, conservative Protestant churches were the next most common background, followed by no religious background and liberal Protestantism. It is interesting that among respondents at the charismatic OMCC, these final three categories were reversed: liberal Protestants and those with no religious background tied for third place, while conservative Protestantism was the fourth most common background.

Because of my interest in obtaining as much in-depth information as possible, especially in light of the low returns on the questionnaire, I interviewed all volunteers who returned their interview cards before a cutoff date, roughly a month and a half after the surveys had been mailed. Including those with pastors, I conducted a total of seventy-two semistructured interviews, lasting between thirty minutes and three hours each, with an average length of just under an hour. All but a few interviews were audiotaped, with participants' permission, and I took copious notes as well during the interviews in case of tape malfunction. The tapes were later transcribed by myself or one of several research assistants.

Overall, I interviewed thirty-four women and thirty-eight men; the interviews nearly leveled the gender imbalance in the survey responses. Interview participants from the MCCVR mailing list included twenty-one women, two of whom were transgender, and thirty-one men, including the three pastors. Among those contacted through the OMCC list were thirteen women, including the pastor, and seven men. Ethnic minorities were represented far more poorly in the interviews than were women, with no African American participants and only one Latino, one Native American (a transgender woman), and one Filipina participating. Five of those I interviewed were biracial (three women and two men), and three (one woman and two men) identified as multiracial.

The ages of interview participants ranged from early 30s to mid-70s, and slightly over half—a larger percentage than among survey respondents—were current members of MCC. Seventy-four percent had attended MCC for at least three years, and 31 percent for more than ten years. Some were currently highly involved in the church and others attended on occasion; several had been involved in the past but had developed religious interests or needs that MCC could not fulfill and had moved on to other churches. A few had attended an MCC church in a former area of residence but had discovered that MCCVR and OMCC were different from their previous churches and thus had stopped attending MCC altogether. Tables containing complete descriptive statistics for the interview participants can be found in the appendices.

Although many of the interview respondents would have been happy to have their real names used in this study, some members of these churches are still highly vulnerable to discrimination because of their jobs, families, church affiliation outside MCC, and so on. For that reason, I have chosen to follow the sociological convention of using pseudonyms for everyone involved in this study as well as for the churches. Those who are sufficiently familiar with California MCCs will recognize these two congregations, and close friends of individuals in the study may recognize familiar stories. I have made every effort, however, to exclude personally identifying information when discussing the interview material, especially in the case of particularly sensitive issues. For the convenience of those who wish to trace personal stories across the chapters, I have included in the appendices an index of the people who appear in this book, cross-referenced to the pages that contain a quotation or narrative from each person.

Qualifications, Caveats, and Controversies

Statistical Data

The low returns on the survey make it a resource for indicative rather than conclusive results. Moreover, it is unfortunately quite difficult to obtain statistically meaningful comparisons between the two churches with such a small sample. The interviews suffer from a similar problem: although the large number of interviews conducted makes it possible to trace highly suggestive patterns, I make no claim that these are representative of the experiences of all LGBT Christians, all MCC members, or even all current and former members of these two congregations. I have retained the descriptive data and some of the correlations, however, because I find them suggestive in combination with the interview data. I hope that future studies will expand upon the tentative conclusions suggested here.

Such difficulties, in fact, arise in any study of LGBT people in religion: no research can be considered to be truly representative or to be a truly random sample because it is quite likely that some groups will self-select out of the study. The group most likely to be underrepresented is comprised of people who are still struggling with LGBT identity. Some of these people are deep "in the closet," concealing their same-sex attraction or transgender identity from everyone, and they feel immensely threatened by any stranger's attempt to discuss this identity with them. Others may feel too much internal conflict to be willing to discuss such a difficult issue with an outsider. As a result, although some people in this study are indeed still in the throes of a struggle over identity, they are probably underrepresented.

Ethnic minorities, transgender people, and women are also underrepresented in this study—the former two groups more severely than the latter. In large part this is due to the disproportionate number of whites, men, and people of orthodox gender identity in the congregations themselves—a problem that reflects in turn divisions within LGBT communities at large. While I take this lack of representation into account, I have attempted in response to make especially audible those transgender people and ethnic minorities who did participate in this study. Perhaps their stories will spark the interest of others and lead to a more representative body of research in the field.

Inclusivity and Terminology

This discussion leads to a related and equally important issue: the advisability of including bisexuals and transgender people at all in such a study, especially when they make up such a small percentage of the sample population. Since the use of "LGBT" became popular several years ago, some have rightly expressed concern that this might be simply a new and empty form of political correctness: that researchers and others would offer this linguistic nod to bisexuals and transgender people without actually including them on an equal footing with lesbians and gay men. Indeed, the same problem has arisen repeatedly around the equal inclusion of lesbians under the term "homosexuals." Others have worried that by lumping these groups together into one unpronounceable acronym, we will encourage the assumption that all of these very different people share identical experiences.

In part, these worries reflect very real problems: studies of religion in the lives of transgender or bisexual people are extremely rare, and little primary literature exists on this topic.[36] Other gaps that are even less frequently addressed glare just as strongly: there is also, for instance, appallingly little work to date on religiosity among LGBT people who are members of ethnic minorities, and although several notable studies focus exclusively or primarily on men, only one (Mahaffy's) focuses on women. The (usually male) authors of male-focused studies sometimes cite a dearth of women in the group under consideration;[37] others explain their unilateral focus as a reluctance to speak for women or to assume that men's and women's experiences might be comparable. To my mind, these reasonable reservations should provide the impetus to include the voices of women—however few they might be in the data at hand—and not to efface their presence. For the same reason, despite the small number of bisexuals and transgender people taking part in this study, I have chosen to include their voices rather than erase them by focusing solely on lesbians and gay men.

Let me underscore that this is not to suggest that the experiences of bisexuals, transgender people, lesbians, and gay men can be melded into one another. But they cannot be completely separated, either—if for no other reason than because some transgender men are gay, some transgender women lesbian, and others bisexual. The challenges faced by members of LGBT communities differ not only because of gender identity or sexual orientation, but also because of biological sex, race, ethnicity, class, physical ability, and a host of other factors. While it is critical to be sensitive to these differences, I do not believe that they should preclude all attempts at generalization, especially because carefully drawn, limited generalizations can be useful on a practical level. The conclusions reached in this book *do* include bisexuals and transgender people, not because those populations were represented in statistically reliable numbers—no group was, and that is a goal that has been met by few studies of LGBT religiosity to date—but because bisexuals and transgender people were involved in the study, and their experiences actually did resonate noticeably with those of lesbians and gay men. This similarity is not entirely surprising given that much religiously based oppression of LGBT people comes from heterosexual orthodox-gendered populations that persist in conflating gender identity with sexual orientation.

Narrative and Memory

Despite their widespread use in historical, sociological, and psychological research, life stories are among the more controversial sources of data in all of these fields. Human memory is notoriously unreliable, and the urge to create a cohesive narrative often leads people to alter their stories over time. The presence of a researcher also inevitably impacts narrative: people may screen out particularly uncomfortable or unflattering episodes in their lives or may discuss only those experiences they believe are relevant to the researcher's interests. In fact, as Guy Widdershoven has argued, events and stories have an almost cyclical interaction. Socially available narratives affect how an experience is initially perceived, the experience alters the story, and the altered story in turn reshapes the next experience or is altered further by other or newly available narratives.[38]

These complications are particularly relevant to the life histories of LGBT people—gays and lesbians especially—for whom the coming-out narrative has a standard and stylized format that people often expand or alter but from which they rarely depart entirely. As Kenneth L. Cuthbertson has pointed out, this story bears strong similarities to the conversion narratives that have prevailed in mainstream U.S. culture since the colonial period.[39] Despite its apparent novelty, therefore, the coming-out narrative resonates with a trope familiar in the dominant culture, and the general outline of individual coming-out stories might be influenced by that trope as well as by the standard narratives found within LGBT communities. These common themes shape the ways in which many LGBT people speak about coming out; they affect which events people remember and which they emphasize. They also are responsible in part for a reinterpretation of the past: for instance, LGBT people frequently recall events from their childhood that seem to prefigure a non-normative gender or sexual identity. The truth underlying these interpretations is difficult, if not impossible, to ascertain.

It is also quite likely that the process of completing the survey and being interviewed for this study triggered further identity construction or reconstruction in some cases. A number of participants remarked that the survey, the interview, or both had led them to think in a new way about the connections between religion and their sexual or gender identity. This could be an advantage: without a previously existing story into which to fit their experiences, these participants might have been less likely to reinterpret or selectively remember the events I asked them to recall. Yet, my questions about the relationship (or lack thereof) between religion and LGBT identity may have led participants to see connections where previously there had been none. Thus, I make no claim to be studying the unadulterated "facts" of respondents' lives—if, indeed, such a feat is ever possible.

Most likely to be affected by such retellings and reinterpretations, however, are not recollections of specific events or emotions but evaluations of the importance and meaning of such experiences. Although this interpretive work is sometimes not noticeable, many people mark it with phrases such as: "Now that I look back on it, I realize that . . . ," or "I think I was really feeling. . . . " In such cases, I have made the reinterpretations visible by including the "marker" phrases in quotations or by explicitly stating that these are the speaker's current understandings of a past event.

That these rereadings of one's life will affect studies such as this is inevitable. First and foremost, life histories demonstrate how people understand their past through the lenses of the present. Yet I do not believe that scholars should entirely discount such histories, either. While someone may remember an emotion as being stronger or weaker, or more or less important, than it actually was, her recollection of having experienced that emotion is likely to be fairly reliable. Furthermore, the concern here is with overall patterns— and although it is remotely feasible that such patterns could be a secondary effect of culturally shaped narratives, I am reluctant to assign culture such an extreme influence.[40]

Members, Attenders, and Seekers

The wide distribution of the questionnaires among members, former members, and affiliates of MCCVR and OMCC led to an unexpected advantage: in addition to receiving responses and interview offers from current MCC attendees, I also had the opportunity to learn from those who once had been involved with the church but eventually left as well as those who were on the mailing list because they had visited once or twice but had found MCC not to their liking. This enabled me to explore the reasons that MCC did *not* attract people as well as the reasons it did do so; it also gave me the chance to consider people's reasons for leaving in addition to their reasons for staying.

The purpose of the following chapters, then, is to trace patterns of religious and sexual or gender identity as they have been told to me in the life histories of current, former, and tangential associates of two Metropolitan Community Churches. The chapters examine people's initial experiences with the tensions between LGBT identity and Christian belief, their struggles (or sometimes lack thereof) to integrate those two aspects of their lives, the reasons for their attendance at MCC, and the roles that MCC churches have played in their lives. In the process, each chapter brings in current theories—predominantly from the fields of sociology and religious studies, but also from psychology, anthropology, cultural studies, and other areas—that help to elucidate the various individual, collective, social, and symbolic processes involved in this complex set of data. It is my contention that a single field cannot completely understand the wide variety of issues at stake here. While this approach may make me vulnerable to charges of theoretical dilettantism, I prefer José Cabezón's term: "theoretical promiscuity."[41]

Overview

The chapters in this book are organized into three parts—Identity, Community, and Identity in Community—which roughly follow the typical course of the identity-integration process from individual struggles to community support to an integration of individual and communal strategies. Most chapters contain narratives or summaries from the interviews and from my fieldnotes in addition to presenting and analyzing data. Although my voice intrudes in the narratives from time to time in order to give details or to summarize, one of the primary purposes of these sections is to allow the voices of those I worked with to come across as much as possible. The stories told and analyzed throughout this book are theirs, first and foremost, and ought to be heard as I heard them; several of the narrative sections give the reader an opportunity to see portions of these stories as they were told to me. The second purpose for including the narratives is to offer examples of the patterns or stories discussed in the chapter, again allowing the reader to see the entire story in context rather than relying solely on the brief quotations or survey data presented in the rest of the chapter.

Chapter 1, "Converging and Diverging Roads," explores the hypothesis that for Christians, an emerging LGBT identity typically conflicts with the existing religious identity. Beginning with a discussion of changing attitudes toward homosexuality in the twentieth-century United States and Europe, the chapter examines the growth of debates in U.S. religious organizations over the nature of homosexuality and homosexual people. It then examines survey and interview data in order to determine exactly how much exposure the participants in this study might have had to anti-LGBT religious teachings and what effect those teachings had on participants' self-understanding.

The following chapter, "Christians Coming Out," discusses the process of coming out as lesbian, gay, bisexual, or transgender and of reconciling that sexual or gender identity with religious beliefs in light of sociological approaches to religious experience and religious individualism. Exploring the religious, spiritual, and theological resources utilized by the study participants, the chapter identifies five main patterns in the process of identity reconciliation. Tellingly, four of the five, which represent the vast majority of study participants, depend on individual initiative rather than on church support. The chapter concludes by exploring specific strategies of identity, exegesis, and theology that were utilized by participants during the coming-out process.

"Individualism," Wade Clark Roof wrote recently, "is more than a one-way influence shaping styles of institutional commitment; it also opens up new possibilities for religious institutions and changing modes of personal commitment."[42] This may indeed be one of the driving factors behind the success of the UFMCC, but there are others as well; the book moves here from focusing on individuals to looking at some of their sources of community. Chapter 3, "Creating a Space," is the pivotal chapter of the book, shifting the analytical focus from individual to community as Part II begins. In order to locate OMCC and MCCVR within a broader subcultural and social context, this chapter turns from ethnographic to historical data in order to explore the denomination's early growth in relation to factors both internal and external to the organization itself—such as social changes, new approaches to Christian theology, and strong leadership.

Chapter 4 returns to the fieldwork data to examine the process of "Creating New Worlds." This chapter argues that many of the religious options currently available to LGBT Christians represent an old world wherein LGBT identity and Christian belief are still divergent. Within MCC and other LGBT congregations, however—just as in the lives of most study participants—those two roads converge. Why is MCC more attractive than other options to those who do attend? For those who do not, why is MCC *not* as attractive an option? This chapter explores the pathways that brought participants to MCC, the events that led some out again, the point in the process of identity integration at which they began attending, and the reasons for which they came.

The resources offered by MCC, however, are not limited to the sympathetic ear of a deacon or the exegetical prowess of a pastor; affirmation of LGBT Christian identity takes place through a variety of symbolic media both within and outside of the Sunday church services. Chapter 5, "Re-Creating the World," explores these resources, relying on the theoretical insights of scholars such as Peter Berger, Thomas Luckmann, and Bruce Lincoln. It concludes that the symbols and sources of community available at MCC literally construct a new world in which the combination of Christian belief with LGBT identity is not only normative but also highly valued.

Chapter 6, "We Took the One Less Traveled," moves into Part III, "Identity in Community," and brings together the topics discussed in Chapters 1 through 5. Revisiting each aspect of the identity-integration process—initial divergence, growing suspicion of the divergence, individual strategies for identity reconciliation, and the roles played by community—this chapter considers the ways in which theoretical approaches to religion, culture, and the self might be applied to this process, above and beyond the theoretical contributions already explored within each chapter. In addition, it moves beyond the previous chapters to explore two final topics: an affirmative theme that links individual and community and the role of MCC as a public institution.

Finally, the epilogue turns to considerations of the future of LGBT people in Christianity. Troy Perry was a key speaker at the April 2000 Millennium March on Washington and an officiant at a massive public wedding for same-sex couples the day before the march, and LGBT Christians in general and the UFMCC in particular are demanding increasing recognition and respect. The epilogue ponders the roles LGBT Christians may come to play in academic research on religion and in the "real world" of U.S. churches.

Part One
Identity

1   Converging and Diverging Roads

Suzanne is a transgender lesbian who was raised as a Catholic in Texas, was born again during her college years, and attended both Episcopalian and Presbyterian churches while in college and graduate school. When I met her she had been involved in MCC for nearly a decade and was finishing ministerial training; she is now an ordained pastor within the UFMCC. Over lunch at an Indian restaurant near her home, she shared with me her experiences of discovering both a sexual and a gender identity that clashed with expected norms. "When I transitioned," she explained, referring to her shift from living as a man to living as a woman, "[I was] in law school, my last semester in law school. And I got a letter from the president of the Christian Legal Society, who was a friend of ours— he was the president of the student government— . . . basically saying that he loved me and didn't want me to go to hell, and . . . there was this whole time [when] . . . I would tell people at the church about who I was. And encountered a lot of resistance. . . . The priest at the Episcopalian church performed an exorcism on me." As she discussed reactions to her transgender identity among Christian friends and acquaintances, she added, "I was tired of being told . . . that I was saying God had made a mistake [by putting a woman in a man's body]."[1]

Comments from an anonymous survey respondent, whom I did not interview, represent this study's most chilling example of the deleterious effects of religious homophobia. A Filipino in his 40s, this man was raised attending Catholic services at least once a week. He now identifies as gay. He still considers himself Catholic and attends a Catholic group on a weekly basis; he also is interested in MCC but has not yet attended. Asked to reflect on the ways in which his process of coming out as a gay man had been affected by religion or spirituality, he wrote the following: "Coming out and spiritual activities are two different worlds. It's like heaven and earth. I stop praying to God to change me. I have to suffer till my last end. I cannot stand being made fun of and object to jokes and snide remarks. I just have to pray that I'll die very soon because I cannot kill myself. It's against God's law." In response to a question at the end of the survey about the interaction of sexual orientation and religion in his life, he continued: "My life is a big disappointment. God knows I do not like to be a homosexual. I thought I can change myself: I keep asking God, why me? Sometimes I'm happy but most of the time I am depressed. Sometimes I think crazy. I wish somebody will kill me. I like to evaporate from this world. I like to love but I'm disgusted. My upbringing has something to do with it. . . . I have to hide, pretend, so shameful about my innermost being. I have no other recourse but to ask God for mercy and forgiveness for all this mess and confusion."[2]

Anthony was raised in a Presbyterian church in California and converted to Catholicism in 1958, at the age of 18. Shortly before his eighteenth birthday, he came out to someone at his school. Here is what Anthony told me about this experience: "The first person I ever remember telling about this was at the military academy. And this was in nineteen . . . fifty-eight. And at that time, homosexuality was regarded as being one of the five mental illnesses that could actually wind you up in a state institution in the state of California for the rest of your life. And that was not stopped until 1965. So when I told, uh, the headmaster . . . actually, it was the commandant, . . . former retired colonel, World War I. . . . But when I told him about this thing, you know, I was in an extremely vulnerable position. And he informed me at that point in time that I was totally, hopelessly . . . mentally ill." Anthony paused. "So I spent a lot of time trying to figure out—well, why, you know. I couldn't understand it as being mentally ill. I mean, you know, I wasn't having hallucinations, I wasn't having delusions. . . . I mean, I didn't have any of the symptoms other than the fact that I happened to be a homosexual who is now categorically mentally ill. And certifiable now to go to a state mental institution for the rest of my life. In fact, they were going to . . . in fact, they did put me in a—in a psychiatric hospital, because they were going to do a lobotomy on me. Just to get—and then, as they said, to bring me back slowly to heterosexuality." Anthony managed to avoid the lobotomy, but several years later the medical establishment returned to haunt him. When he underwent a physical exam as a final prerequisite for entry into the Dominican order, the doctor asked whether he was homosexual. Anthony answered in the affirmative, and the doctor wrote in his report: "This person is a homosexual." The Dominicans immediately terminated his application.[3]

Each of these stories shows a different aspect of the challenges faced by LGBT Christians during the latter half of the twentieth century. Anthony's brush with brain surgery came at a time when the definition, diagnosis, and treatment of homosexuality were still predominantly the domain of science. His later experience with the Dominicans, along with Suzanne's encounters with Christian friends and the anguish of the anonymous respondent, came about as a result of a shift in the social domain that defined LGBT identities. The focus of scientific scrutiny throughout most of the century, homosexuality became subject instead to religious moralizing in the 1960s. As sickness or as sin, LGBT identities and their expression have been off-limits to many who strive to fulfill their churches' and families' definitions of a "good Christian." As a result, Christianity and LGBT identity have become diverging roads in the life paths of many.

Psychology, Morality, Religion

Although same-sex erotic activity has been recognized across time periods and cultures,[4] within Western cultures the practice of defining a central aspect of one's identity by such acts arose only in the nineteenth century. In fact, Foucault argues that it was a specific shift in the sociopolitical dynamics of power that brought sexuality to the forefront as a topic of concern. As the focus of power relations moved from power to control a person's death to power to control her or his life, both biological regulation and control over the body gained in importance. Consequently, sexual function came under increased scrutiny, and "deviance" from social norms of sexuality became an increasingly serious offense.[5]

This emphasis on controlling the body, however, also meant that sexuality and sexual "deviance" were studied and treated under the same rubric and by the same professionals as other bodily ills: they were considered medical (or later, psychoanalytic) concerns and were addressed by doctors. This medicalization of homosexuality, bisexuality, and transgender identity—not to mention the confusion between the three in early literature on "gender inversion"[6] —had two crucial effects on society at large, at least within the United States. First, with medical attitudes toward homosexual activity culturally pervasive by the early twentieth century, there was a sense of illness surrounding same-sex eroticism. Acts that would have been viewed a century before as "perversions" or at least as strange and perhaps indulgent sexual tastes now held the added stigma of being symptoms of stunted psychological development, a kind of psychic retardation.[7] This did not prevent the existence of a homosexual subculture that waxed and waned in population and visibility as the social climate shifted; on the other hand, medicalization also did not prevent homosexuality from being included on the roster of criminal activities in the United States.

The second important result of medicalization lay in its clear designation of medicine and psychoanalysis as the proper fields to study and treat homosexuality. As a result, and quite in contrast to the situation today, homosexuality was not a central issue for religious leaders.[8] As an illness or perhaps a temporary developmental disability, it was considered to lead to outrageous behavior, but it was not primarily a moral issue and thus was not a topic of religious exhortation.

Anthony, whose story appeared at the beginning of this chapter, noted that his experiences with medical definitions of homosexuality came near the end of this phase in Western attitudes. Up to this point, those fighting for recognition and acceptance of homosexuals also had been working primarily within the medical arena, attempting to undermine the association of homosexuality with mental illness.[9] However, as social protest and especially the civil rights movement grew through the 1960s, a new group of homosexual activists came on the scene, bringing with them a radically different approach to the issue. Although their New Left strategies and rhetoric had roots in the early Communist-influenced years of an older homosexual rights group, in the late 1960s the time was ripe for new tactics. Claiming as its official birthdate the June 1969 riots at New York's Stonewall Inn, the gay liberation movement burst onto the scene with an innovative message for mainstream United States society: homosexuality was not an illness or an aberration but a valid and innate identity.[10]

This claim sparked a debate that still rages today over the rights of lesbians and gay men—and now bisexuals and transgender people as well—to have equal access (opponents call it special privileges) to employment, housing, parenting rights, and so on. Central to this debate is a deeper question: Are sexual orientation and transgender identity unchangeable ontological realities, freely chosen behaviors, or something in between? The medical definition of homosexuality lingers still, but it has shifted focus considerably due to one important event: the official demedicalization of homosexuality.

In 1974, the American Psychological Association published the third edition of its *Diagnostic and Statistical Manual*. For the first time, it did not define homosexuality as a mental disorder.[11] At the same time, the more conservative elements of United States society were reacting to the ongoing sexual revolution. Sexual activities previously considered undeniably wrong and even socially destructive were now being reconsidered and accepted. Certainly teenagers in the West had been engaging in sexual activities before marriage for centuries, but now it appeared that such activity would come to be viewed as acceptable. Abortion had been decriminalized. From a Foucauldian point of view, the technologies of power were shifting; from a conservative point of view, time-honored values were being thrown to the winds.

No longer able to rely on the medical or legal establishments to keep society in line, those who held to such values turned to that other bastion of social control: religion. Morality became an important rubric for defining sexual norms and sexual deviance, and religion became the forum in which to discuss such issues. On the subject of homosexuality, as with other topics such as gender roles and the family, conservatives appealed to an image of "traditional" moral values and the "traditional American family" as standards for behavior.[12] Religion, and especially Christianity, was a central buttress for these arguments.

As a result, it quickly became necessary for religious organizations to clarify their positions on the issues raised by the visibility and vocal nature of the gay liberation movement. First to be addressed was the question of how homosexuals (bisexuals and transgender people generally were not recognized during these years) should be treated by society: Did they deserve basic human rights? Non-discrimination policies? Full equality? The second question was more difficult: How were homosexuals to be understood on an ontological level? Was one born irreversibly homosexual? Was it an innate proclivity that could be resisted? Or was it a perversion of one's natural heterosexuality, perhaps as a result of a less-than-ideal upbringing or exposure to the baser elements of society? Third, religious leaders and organizations had to address the issue of sexual activity as it related to ontology and soteriology: Were homosexuals to be cured and encouraged back into heterosexuality? Was it best simply to recommend celibacy? Could homosexual relationships perhaps be condoned, and if so, under what circumstances? All of these questions, however, led to the two that were critical now that homosexuality lay within the domain of religion: What did the sacred texts teach about it, and how could homosexuals be honorable members of their religions?[13]

Although religious groups had been discussing these issues prior to the late 1960s, the early 1970s saw a virtual explosion of official religious statements that paralleled the explosion of the gay rights movement onto the streets of the metropolitan United States.[14] Responses varied widely, even in these early years. In 1973, for example, the National Conference of Catholic Bishops produced a set of guidelines for confessors who counseled homosexual parishioners. After reviewing at length both biblical and scientific perspectives on homosexuality, the document offers a distinction between "temporary homosexuals" and "apparent permanent homosexuality." Confessors are advised to encourage the former to avoid contact of any sort with homosexuals in order to prevent such a temporary state from becoming permanent. In the latter case, they are to counsel celibacy. Furthermore, seminarians are considered as a special case: those judged to be permanently homosexual, the document claims, usually have more far-reaching psychological problems that will lead to poor performance as priests.[15]

Conservative Protestant organizations made the issue of sexual morality not only explicit but also relevant on a national level. In 1979, for example, the Assemblies of God proclaimed:

> One reason why Christians are deeply concerned about this problem is that a nation's tolerance or intolerance of homosexuality is one indication of the nation's spiritual condition. When Israel drifted away from God, it tolerated various evils, including sodomy (1 Kings 14:24). When Israel returned to God, homosexuality was not tolerated (1 Kings 15:12).[16]

The document goes on to assert that homosexuality is a sinful behavior that can be removed by the power of God.

On the other end of the Protestant spectrum, however, in 1972, the United Church of Christ (UCC) became the first non-LGBT denomination to ordain an openly gay minister. The question of whether to adopt a policy supporting the ordination of homosexuals was debated by the denomination's Executive Council in 1973, but no official statement was made at that time. In 1975, however, the Tenth General Synod of the UCC issued a document containing the following statement:

> Without considering in this document the rightness or wrongness of same-gender relationships, but recognizing that a person's affectional or sexual preference is not legitimate grounds on which to deny her or his civil liberties, the Tenth General Synod of the United Church of Christ proclaims the Christian conviction that all persons are entitled to full civil liberties and equal protection under the law.[17]

Although it takes no explicit position regarding the ontological or soteriological status of "affectional or sexual preference," the Synod's language and its reference earlier in the document to the Kinsey reports suggest an understanding of sexual orientation as an intrinsic identity.

The religious situation with regard to homosexuality has not changed substantially over the past three decades. A few Protestant denominations, including the United Church of Christ, now allow the ordination of lesbians and gay men, and their current issue of debate is same-sex marriage. Many other denominations, however, in an intense struggle that has been compared to the debates and divisions over slavery, are still deciding whether or not to accept and support openly lesbian and gay members.[18] Several denominations now have More Light or Open and Affirming movements, wherein individual congregations make the decision to declare themselves supportive of lesbian and gay Christians (bisexuals and transgender people continue to be relatively invisible in these situations). Such a move is often more radical than it appears, even in mainline Protestantism: in 1999, several churches were expelled from the American Baptist Conference for declaring themselves Open and Affirming.

Moreover, as liberals have made some strides in the direction of acceptance, conservative Christians have further institutionalized their own approaches to homosexuality. Most evident, in this case, is the existence of a parachurch organization known as Exodus Ministries, which is only one of several groups offering to help LGBT people find healing and heterosexuality through God. Exodus holds meetings and conferences nationwide; in 1998, it provoked significant controversy by promoting its services with flashy full-page advertisements in major metropolitan newspapers in the United States.

The theological theme uniting all of these debates, however, concerns not identity but activity. Whether they are literalists or not, most Christians do at least consider biblical teachings when deciding their stance on moral questions —and it is around biblical statements on homosexual and transgender activity that most of the other debates over LGBT identities ultimately revolve. At issue are a total of eight texts in the Hebrew Bible and the Christian New Testament: Genesis 19:4–11; Deuteronomy 20:5 and 23:17–18; Leviticus 18:22 and 20:13–14; 1 Corinthians 6:9; 1 Timothy 1:10; and Romans 1:26–27. The most well-known is the Genesis text, the story of Sodom and Gomorrah that gives us the English word "sodomy." Close runners-up are the two texts in Leviticus, which declare male homosexual activity to be toʿevah—a word usually translated in English as "an abomination." The second Levitical passage establishes the death penalty for such wrongdoers. The Deuteronomy passages are similar in declaring the woman who wears men's clothing, the man who wears women's clothing, and the qadesh (previously translated as "sodomite," now more frequently as "temple prostitute") to be "abominations" to God.[19]

Perhaps more troubling to many Christians are the New Testament passages. Because Paul taught that believers in Jesus followed a new law that invalidated the old ones, LGBT Christians can argue that texts such as those found in Leviticus and Deuteronomy do not apply to them. The topic of homosexual activity, however, also appears in the letters of Paul, and it receives the same condemnation. There is no reference in the Gospels themselves to anything that could be construed as homosexual or transgender behavior. However, even this fact can be used either for or against LGBT people. Those in support of the inclusion of LGBT people in Christianity argue that Jesus spoke up about the crucial issues and neither homosexuality nor transgenderism was one of them; opponents typically respond brusquely that Jesus also did not discuss child molesters.

The fiery debate over these eight brief texts has taken many forms. At the extreme end of conservatism, some have pointed to Leviticus 20:13 as a justification for violence against LGBT people.[20] More frequently, conservatives rely on both Hebrew Bible and New Testament texts to argue that although homosexual activity is sinful, God offers salvation to all and therefore homosexuals and transgender people, like other sinners, can be saved if they agree to give up their sinful ways.[21]

Those arguing that LGBT people express valid and God-given identities employ several tactics with respect to biblical texts. One common approach is linguistic: returning to the original languages of the texts, some point to variant uses of the same word that suggest a retranslation or reinterpretation. Thus, toᶜevah may be retranslated as "ritually unclean," and qadesh may be changed from "sodomite" to "cult prostitute" or "temple prostitute." As the latter example suggests, historical approaches also frequently prove useful. In arguing against the typical anti-gay interpretation of Genesis 19, for example, a pro-LGBT theologian may discuss the importance of hospitality in ancient Mediterranean cultures and thereby reinterpret the "sin of Sodom" as an extreme display of inhospitality. A similar approach can be used with the three New Testament passages, arguing that Paul's condemnation was directed at man-boy relationships rather than committed long-term relationships between adults. Although there are other approaches to the texts themselves, a final common response to these issues rejects such complex arguments entirely, pointing out that Jesus's first and foremost teaching was not to condemn others for their sins but to love unconditionally.[22]

Initially, the medical view reduced homosexuals to maladjusted neurotics, then it defined homosexuality as a severe illness requiring institutionalization or even corrective brain surgery; now scriptural debates, theological arguments, and fierce battles take place on both denominational and congregational levels—how does all of this affect the people who are the objects of these policies? It is fairly easy to form hypotheses. First, and beyond any content-based issues, it is crucial to note that despite the presence of a small number of very vocal LGBT activists, the vast majority of this lengthy debate has been conducted over the heads of LGBT people themselves. This exclusion itself carries a strong message of inferiority, a sense of being second-class humans, in the same way that Western discourse often has marginalized and devalued ethnic minorities and women. Second, as with medical views of homosexuality, religious views do not remain within church or temple walls; especially when they are shared by culturally influential groups, religious values diffuse throughout society at large.

Third, and equally if not more important for the people involved in this study, children raised within religious groups that are embroiled in the homosexuality debates may be exposed to negative attitudes and animosity before they begin to come out as homosexual, bisexual, or transgender. LGBT people who attend religious services as adults may continue to be exposed, perhaps at even greater levels than children, to hostility, uncertainty, and biblical debates. It is not unreasonable to surmise that the prognosis for a positive self-image in such situations would be poor.

Indeed, many have made exactly that assumption. It is part of the story that Troy Perry tells about founding MCC: an encounter with a young man who has been rejected by his church is the event that sparks Perry's sense of God's call to found a congregation for those people whom the other churches refuse to serve.[23] It also continues today as a central theme in the UFMCC. Nancy Wilson, denominational elder and formerly senior pastor of the UFMCC's mother church, asks: "What are the wounds of our people—the gay, lesbian, bisexual, transgender communities and tribes?" She answers:

> Clearly, rejection and abandonment are at the top of the list. Rejection and abandonment by our families, churches, synagogues, governments. But also high on the list for me is the damage caused by *slander*. There is no explicit condemnation of homosexuality among the Ten Commandments in the *Bible*, but there *is* a commandment against *bearing false witness against your neighbor.*[24]

Wilson adds that one major source of this damaging false witness is the anti-LGBT rhetoric of the religious right.

Even within the two MCC congregations I studied, the idea that LGBT people are frequently psychologically injured by their religious upbringing was commonplace. During an interview, for example, Reverend Sharon commented: "I just think we're just really battered and bruised . . . if we're gay and lesbian in particular, transgender. And bi, for a different reason there. . . . You know, because we've felt shut out of mainline churches in particular, Christian ones."[25] Other people told me stories, both during formal interviews and at church services, about friends or acquaintances who had experienced such suffering.

It is not solely within MCC, however, or even within religious settings in general, that attention has been paid to the connections between LGBT self-acceptance and religious teachings. J. Michael Clark, Joanne Carlson Brown, and Lorna M. Hochstein, for instance, used case studies of Catholicism and the United Methodist Church to explore the deleterious effects of Christian teachings about homosexuality on lesbian and gay people as well as on the parents of lesbian or gay children. They conclude that

> far from providing religious support and/or spiritual nurture, even for gay/lesbian believers, institutionalized Judaeo-Christianity has actually been the arbiter of homophobic judgment, fostering rejection and alienation not only within gay/lesbian individuals and gay/lesbian relationships, but also between gays/lesbians and both their families of origin and their native cultural ethos.[26]

Despite the prevalence and logic of these assumptions about the effects of religious upbringing and religious environment, there have been few opportunities to test them. It is worth asking, therefore, how these factors affected the participants in the present study. There are two steps to answering this question. The first involves exploring whether participants were in fact exposed to such teachings as children, teenagers, or adults. If they were exposed, it is also important to know how this took place, to what they were exposed, and how often.

Exposure to Religious Teachings

Upbringing

The distribution of religious upbringing in this study clearly indicates that most survey respondents were raised within religions that might have exposed them to negative teachings about homosexuality, or at least to the often venomous debates on the topic. The vast majority, not surprisingly, were raised as Christians; 12 percent of these were raised in conservative Protestant denominations, 33.3 percent in mainline Protestant denominations, and 6 percent in liberal denominations. Just under 30 percent of the survey respondents were raised Catholic.[27]

However, such exposure would be most intense if people actually attended services as children; here again, the survey results are unsurprising for a sample drawn from church mailing lists. During both childhood and teenage years, roughly three-quarters of the respondents reported attending at least once a month, and over 60 percent had attended other religious organizations such as parochial schools or youth groups as well. Among the latter group, 42 percent had attended more than one type of organization. Thus, most participants in this study were in a position to be exposed to negative religious attitudes toward LGBT identity: they were raised within religious groups that have been ambivalent or openly hostile toward LGBT people, and they were regularly and often heavily involved with these groups.

The possibility of continuing exposure is also important, however. After all, with a mean age for the respondents of 48 years (in 1998), it is likely that many people's childhood and teen years took place before the issue of homosexuality became a central topic of religious concern. Anyone of this generation who left the church in her late teens and did not return would have avoided exposure to most of the homosexuality debates within her religious tradition. However, as the mean age listed for coming out was in the 20s, the majority of respondents would have come out either as the debates were beginning or after they were underway. Moreover, there was a strong correlation in this sample between age in 1998 and age at coming out.[28] Those born earlier came out, in general, at a later age than those of a younger generation, making it even more likely that most respondents came out after religious groups began actively to discuss homosexuality.

Coming Out

During the time when they were coming out as lesbian, gay, bisexual, or transgender, over 42 percent of the respondents attended religious services at least once a week; nearly 60 percent went to services at least once a month.[29] Although attendance levels dropped relative to the childhood and teen years, they remained quite high considering that respondents were dealing with nascent LGBT identities during this period. Many LGBT people leave religious organizations by choice or by force upon coming out, but if they did in fact leave their congregations, it seems that the majority of the participants in this study switched to a different congregation rather than leaving organized religion altogether.

In fact, over 25 percent of respondents had at least some contact with MCC during this period. This figure is interesting in itself, however, because it actually represents a combination of two separate attendance patterns: roughly 15 percent of respondents reported MCC as their sole religious affiliation during this period, while 10 percent attended both MCC and another religious organization—mostly mainline Protestant or Catholic. Those who did not attend MCC at all while coming out included just over 20 percent who attended mainline Protestant services, roughly 15 percent who attended Catholic services, 11 percent who attended conservative Protestant churches, nearly 8 percent who went to metaphysical or New Age groups, and just under 7 percent who attended liberal Protestant services.

With relatively high religious attendance in childhood and teenage years, as well as during the year before coming out (these time periods overlap, of course, for some), and with the vast majority attending either Protestant or Catholic services throughout, participants in this study seem highly likely to have been exposed to debates about the nature of homosexuality and its compatibility with Christianity. A more definitive answer on this question, however, comes from the narrative responses in interviews and open-ended survey questions.

Most of the people I interviewed mentioned being currently aware of the negative attitudes toward homosexuality that are held by many Christians and Christian organizations. Indeed, such awareness is difficult for anyone to avoid, given that the issue has gained an increasingly high profile over the years. Only about 60 percent of those interviewed brought up the topic in relation to their own experiences, but almost without exception, the stories they told involved encountering negative images of homosexuality. The three stories that opened this chapter are typical examples of such images.

Some respondents observed that the apparent animosity between religion and LGBT identity was reinforced within the LGBT community. Peter, for instance, is a gay man who was actively involved in the Methodist church as a child and a teenager. He was one of the few participants who had received a fully supportive response from his pastor when he came out, and he reported that he has never felt any personal conflict between being gay and being Christian. But when I asked him how non-Christian LGBT people respond to the fact that he is both gay and Christian, he told me that some people say that is impossible—the church, they say, doesn't want him. Some have even told him "God doesn't love gay people."[30]

Although only one other person reported such explicit rejection of religion on the part of LGBT people themselves, many heard this message from other sources before or during their process of coming out. Even here, however, the picture is complex. Despite the strikingly powerful degradation of LGBT people evident in the opening narratives to this chapter, not everyone learned of negative attitudes toward homosexuality from religious sources—in fact, only about two-thirds of those exposed to such images before or during the coming-out process learned of them solely through religion. Around a quarter of the same group encountered the negative attitudes socially rather than in religion, and four people found them in both places. Matt, for example, did not attend religious services while growing up and marked "none" in the survey when asked about his religious upbringing. Nevertheless, he was aware of a disapproval of homosexuality in both Christianity and society at large. In high school, he told me,

> I kind of, like, knew that [same-sex attraction] wasn't acceptable, but I didn't know why. And then you hear things—comments made. . . . I knew that it's not something you really want to talk about and you certainly don't want to act upon. You see, that's the part I was saying: it's just kind of part of the society. And I really—I can't even tell you, other than that one program [a radio program in which the topic was debated from a Christian standpoint] where I've heard that. I just knew that was true.[31]

Others told me that God and religion had no relation whatsoever to negative attitudes toward homosexuality in their lives.

Both before and during the coming-out process, then, many participants in this study were exposed to negative beliefs about homosexuality—and this exposure took place in several different ways. Even more interesting, however, are their responses to such beliefs. Although about 70 percent report that they subscribed to or at least considered these negative perspectives for a period of time, the other 30 percent found them ludicrous, even at a young age. Lacey, a Filipina lesbian in her 30s, told me that because she came out at the early age of 8, her lesbian identity was accepted by her family. As a result, although both the nuns and the other students at her Catholic school made it quite clear that lesbianism was unacceptable, "I did not pay attention to that." She laughed: "I said, 'Oh, Lord, I love you, but what am I gonna do? This is the way I am.' You know. If people got upset, people's upset."[32]

Abigail, in contrast, went through a long period of ambivalence. A white lesbian in her 40s, Abigail was raised in Methodist and Episcopalian churches. She told me that when she started to come out around the age of 14,

> it seemed like a lot of people who were real sure that they understood the will of God were also very sure that being gay was, at the very least, sinful. And innately bad. Rotten, kind of. And I had a conflict with that, because that really was not how it seemed to me. On the other hand, some of these people . . . sure had a lot more experience with God than I did. So I thought maybe I was supposed to listen to that.[33]

Although Abigail continued to stand by her belief that being a lesbian was not sinful, it took several long conversations with Reverend Sharon for her to resolve the issue on a biblical level.

Effects of Religious Teachings

These last two stories lead directly into the second aspect of the question posed at the beginning of this chapter: How were LGBT people affected by exposure to the homosexuality debates? As Lacey's and Abigail's experiences make clear, answers to this question vary widely. Before examining individual responses, however, it is also informative to consider the overall picture suggested by the survey.

Participants were asked to recall their attitudes toward homosexuality during the year before coming out and to rate those attitudes on a scale from 1 to 5, with 1 representing "very negative," 5 "very positive," and 3 "neutral/didn't think about it." The average response among the entire sample was 3.1: almost exactly in the center. However, only 21 percent of the respondents actually reported holding a neutral position during this time period. Most cast their votes in the "somewhat" category, and with a total of 38 percent reporting negative feelings toward homosexuality and 40 percent weighing in on the positive side, opinions were clearly mixed.

To gain a better understanding of the complex stories underlying these measurements, it is necessary to follow the process of reconciliation in the lives of individual people. Some of these journeys are brief and painless, others are lifelong and arduous, and some bring the traveler close to death once or many times. However, despite the image of MCC as companion and community during this journey, for many the church was instead the final destination of their travels. Reflecting a current trend in religiosity in the United States, the central theme of these journeys is not the community but the individual. From a sociological standpoint, each of these travelers journeyed alone. From their own Christian perspectives, each journeyed with God.

2 Christians Coming Out

Despite widespread exposure to the homosexuality debates in the mainstream denominations and to negative messages about homosexuality, many of the participants in this study never took such messages to heart. A Latina woman in her early 50s clarified this process of self-affirmation in a written response to the survey. "Religious teachings," she wrote, "taught me 'we are all God's children.' I never doubted God's love, Jesus' love or non-acceptance from either. My parents taught me if I followed the Catholic training as a child to my adulthood, I was 'good' in God's eyes. But Catholicism also denounced homosexuality. This confused me. If I was 'good,' why not accepted for this reason alone? I chose to feel accepted rather than rejected by God even though my teachings did not [accept me]. I was convinced otherwise; I found too much in Jesus' teachings to feel I should not be accepted by my Savior. I chose to shun the 'religious community' until I joined MCC."[1]

For others, the process was not so simple. In fact, for some, the issue of whether or not God is anti-LGBT can be resolved only through a kind of empirical testing. One example of this approach comes from Bill, a white man in his early 40s who had accepted his gay identity only about two years before we met. Although he had been aware of his same-sex attraction for most of his life, he had firmly believed in the sinfulness of homosexual activity and had spent two decades struggling to become heterosexual.

After navigating the complex security systems of the technology industry, I met with Bill in his office over cups of specialty coffee, and he told me about his journey. "I spent twenty years trying to overcome it [homosexuality]," he recalled, "and wanting to overcome it, and choosing to overcome it, and not doing anything that would, you know, complicate the matter in terms of sexual behavior, and it just didn't happen. So if there's anybody who should have succeeded in changing their orientation, I would have been a classic example of that, and yet I failed miserably. So when I realized that, it was much easier for me to accept myself."

I asked Bill to explain the tactics he used in his attempts to "overcome" his homosexuality. "I tried to . . . put as much distance as possible between me and the gay community. . . . I tried to immerse myself in a gay-hostile environment, which was fundamentalist churches . . . Baptist and Mormon. . . . And I just assumed that if God had—did not want me to be gay, that he would provide a way for me to escape that through a relationship with a woman that would take away all these problems. And after twenty years, and nothing happening, I began to realize that maybe I'm going down a dead end."

Bill kept his struggles to himself. Although one of his churches offered "homosexual recovery workshops," the classes met at the front of the building near a large sign that declared their purpose, and so despite being tempted to join, he never did. Moreover, unlike others in this study, he did not confide in his pastor or ask church members to pray for him. In fact, he only told one friend from his conservative churches about his homosexuality—and that was after having come out. "It wasn't while I was in the struggling process. All that was internal. I mean, when I came out it was basically 'here I am, I've done it on my own.'" He decided eventually to test his growing suspicions that God did not want him to be straight, and to do so he selected what he thought would be the least potentially harmful LGBT institution: a church. Meeting other LGBT Christians at MCC, he says, "burst the chain."[2]

While these two stories show different journeys, each journey resulted in the conclusion that God does not condemn homosexuality. Some people, however, take such conclusions to an entirely different level: for them, sexuality and spirituality are closely linked. Andrew, for instance, believes it was God who helped him to discover his gay identity. Such beliefs, moreover, are not only evident among those with liberal religious backgrounds. Andrew's parents were missionaries with the Independent Fundamentalist Churches of America, and when he came out he was attending a Southern Baptist church.

Once we finished discussing our shared interest in rock-climbing, I asked Andrew whether he had ever questioned his relationship with God while he was coming out. He answered: "No, I don't think so, because . . . I feel it was . . . my relationship with God that actually kind of brought me out. . . . I had been praying for about a year to really know myself better, because, you know, I was twenty-seven, I was kind of at a—at one of those places where—you know, you get close to thirty, you feel like you're grown up and still don't know what you are. . . . And so I was asking to know myself better, and so . . . my sexuality, although I'd hardly ever thought about it, was definitely one of the things that kept coming up." Laughing, he explained further: "You know, when you look at a couple and realize you're not looking at the woman—you know, you would really rather be with a guy. . . . And . . . I was living alone at the time . . . I spent enough time alone that . . . I had to face those things."

Andrew read a few books on homosexuality and decided that his feelings definitely fit their descriptions. And although no one at his churches had made pronouncements about homosexuality, he knew that some people claimed that it was wrong. "So I got out my *Cruden's Complete Concordance,* and I wrote on a sheet of paper every possible reference to Sodom . . . and having relationships with men, who slept with who, knew who, all of that stuff that I could think of. And I just went through the Bible looking it up. And I said, 'Oh, that's no big deal.' That's basically what I said."[3]

Individualism, Essentialism, Religion, Identity

Chapter 1 explored the homosexuality debates in the mainline denominations of the United States and asked how those debates had affected the participants in this study. Continuing that line of inquiry, this chapter examines the roles played by religion and by the more individual "spirituality" of the contemporary United States in the coming-out process. As is clear from the stories related above, many LGBT Christians face a serious dilemma when they acknowledge their sexual or gender identity. While they may feel that LGBT identity is an intrinsic and perhaps even positive part of their being, many religious groups teach otherwise. This conflict of opinions is something that LGBT Christians must solve internally if they are to continue to claim both the religious and the sexual or gender aspects of their identities.

Religion and Individualism

When Robert Bellah and his colleagues wrote *Habits of the Heart* in the mid-1980s, they were concerned with the ways in which their country's historic legacy of individualism had developed in the past few decades. Sheila Larson, one of the participants in their study, exemplified this "expressive individualism" in her religious beliefs: not affiliated with any official religion, she called her faith "Sheilaism."[4] To Bellah and his co-authors, this form of religiosity smacked of self-absorption, of a disaffiliation from community that they also saw in many other areas of respondents' lives. And indeed, for decades sociologists have viewed such individualized religiosity as evidence of a severe decline in the importance of religion in general in the United States.[5] Yet psychologists have rarely been as concerned as sociologists over the deleterious effects of individualized religion, even if some have argued for the deleterious effects of religion in general.[6] And of late, sociologists and historians, too, are conceding that the increase in individuality within the religious sphere may in fact herald not a decline but simply a shift in the "spiritual landscape," as Martin Marty has called it.[7] Recent works have focused on the wide-ranging beliefs encompassed under the currently popular term "spirituality," seeking to understand not only their attractiveness but also their importance in the lives of people in the United States today. Two important examples are the work of Robert Wuthnow and Wade Clark Roof.

In *After Heaven*, Wuthnow argues that during the latter half of the twentieth century, religiosity and religious identity in the United States underwent a shift from a "spirituality of dwelling" to a "spirituality of seeking."[8] The former, he explains, is exemplified by the concept of a spiritual home, usually a congregation and sometimes also a building in which people experience spirituality and a sense of permanent sacred space. Those who take part in a spirituality of dwelling define their religiosity through this home: they are Catholic, for example, because they were raised within Catholicism. In a spirituality of seeking, though, "status is attained through negotiation. A person does not have an ascribed identity or attain an achieved identity but creates an identity by negotiating among a wide range of materials. Each person's identity is only understandable through biography." Self-definition is no longer reliant "on the statuses that institutions confer."[9] In this case, someone is Catholic less (or not at all) through having been raised that way and more because her personal beliefs resonate most closely with those of Catholicism as she understands it.

In exploring the potential assets of a spirituality of seeking, Wuthnow discusses two participants in his study whose life experiences have differed somewhat from the norm: one is a survivor of childhood sexual abuse while the other had a father who was manic-depressive and alcoholic. These two, and those like them, he argues, "have been jarred out of socially acceptable ways of living and thus cannot create a self by playing the roles prescribed by social institutions. If their lives are to have coherence, it must be of their own making."[10] For LGBT people in the United States today, the experience of coming out is not always one that jars them "out of socially acceptable ways of living." However, it generally does at least raise questions regarding their social acceptability, and it certainly suggests to the heterosexual world a drastic change in *something*—judging, at least, from the frequent appearance of the puzzling term "the gay lifestyle." Certainly within the confines of Christianity, coming out still tends to call into question the validity of one's faith and even of one's existence. Reverend Sharon, for example, told me that when she came out to her parents, her mother's first words were: "I thought you believed in God!"[11] In such cases of uncertainty about or direct challenge to one's place in the social order, the shift toward religious individualism may make it easier for LGBT Christians to create coherence between their religious and sexual or gender identities.

Wade Clark Roof provides further insight into this shift toward the spiritual. In *Spiritual Marketplace*, he suggests that the relatively new term "lived religion" is helpful in understanding the current conglomeration of institutional and personal beliefs and practices in the United States.[12] Roof suggests that there are three central aspects of lived religion: scripts, practices, and human agency. Scripts, which for LGBT people can be either negating, affirming, or neutral, come from the religious group in which a person was raised, the teachings of his parents, his partner's current beliefs, ideas embodied in the culture, and so on. Thus, Roof argues, spirituality is never entirely an individual issue because it is inevitably shaped by surrounding institutions and influences.

Practices, too, Roof suggests, are rooted in community, even if they are performed by the individual. They may link that individual, however tenuously, to her community, but they also reinforce scripts, influencing belief through action, mind through body. Lest we find ourselves in a Gramscian world where hegemonic discourse determines individual belief and identity, however, the third aspect of agency enters to complicate the other two. Roof explains: "People make choices, selectively engage scripts and practices, reflect upon themselves as meaning-making creatures. In this process biography and faith traditions interact to produce discursive strategies toward religion."[13] Invoking a language of "human dilemmas and existential concerns," Roof argues that in such situations, "it becomes necessary to carry on a creative dialogue with tradition." Echoing Wuthnow, he continues: "And in so doing, individuals configure new spaces for making meaning and engage in a process of interiorizing and authenticating their own affirmations."[14]

For those involved in this study, the conflict between LGBT identity and traditional Christian views of gender and sexuality clearly poses a human dilemma or even an existential concern (Why me? What does my life mean? How am I to live? Or, more to the point here: How can I continue to be an upstanding Christian?). Roof's and Wuthnow's works explain why such a process may be unnecessary for some: rather than being a rule book, religion has become a resource to be utilized when it is expedient and ignored or re-written when it is not. As one bisexual man explained to me, "I take from the Bible what I can use, and I disregard a lot of what I can't use."[15]

This "biblical buffet" strategy has been noted in other groups as well. Coin-ing the term "sifting" to describe the process of selective religious identificat-ion, Lynn Resnick Dufour explores the processes of identity construction among Jewish feminists. She identifies three major types of resultant iden-tity—inclusionist, transformationist, and reinterpretationist—that resonate with the various reinterpretations of Christianity produced by participants in this study. Most important here, however, is the process by which those in Dufour's study integrated their Jewish and feminist identities. Dufour ex-plains:

> Sifting is a process by which many people construct cohesive, non-conflicted identities out of potentially conflicted ones. This process in-volves trying-on various practices and attitudes of a given reference group, evaluating them based on one's personal values, needs, or feelings, and then either identifying with them or "screening them out" of one's identity.[16]

Like the feminists in Dufour's study, the LGBT people discussed here sifted through the practices and attitudes of Christianity in order to assemble a Christian identity that could be integrated with their LGBT identities.

Identity and Essentialism

In recent years, essentialism has become the sordid past that femi-nist and queer theory valiantly attempt to reject. Much early feminist dis-course tended toward biological essentialism, lauding "women's" way of doing things and suggesting that female-run enterprises would be more nurtur-ing and egalitarian than those run by men because (these theories claimed) women are "naturally" gentler and less competitive than men. In contrast, contemporary theories of both gender and sexual identity are best repre-sented by the radically constructivist work of authors such as Judith Butler. Moving beyond those constructivists who argue that biological sex deter-mines the type of gender conditioning a child receives, Butler contends that our interpretation of biological sex—indeed, even the concept itself—is also socially determined. In a kind of infinite regress, she undermines any cer-tainty except this determinative power of society and culture, and argues that subversive performances such as cross-dressing are the formula that can re-veal the invisible ink of culture.[17]

While the current fashion in constructivism allows scholars the opportu-nity to explore the intricate despotism of what Adrienne Rich once called "compulsory heterosexuality,"[18] it often proves unhelpful to oppressed communities. Certainly this is the case with some LGBT people: it is easy to see how disadvantageous a constructivist interpretation would be, for instance, in arguing against conservative Christianity's interpretation of homosexuality or transgender identity as "sinful." Somehow, "God made me this way" seems to hold more water than "homosexuality is a concept coined by medical professionals in the nineteenth century in an attempt to bring human sexuality more fully under medical control. My own identity is the social descendant of that process."

Diana Fuss has argued for the political utility of certain forms of essentialism. Prompted by a student's wholesale rejection of essentialist theories, in *Essentially Speaking,* Fuss explores both essentialism and constructivism in depth, showing that each perspective, when pushed to its limits, reveals the other at its base.[19] More important for this study, she examines the uses of essentialism in African American literary theory and lesbian/gay politics and concludes that in certain situations and with certain types of essentialism, an essentialist view of identity can be both empowering and politically expedient. The specific circumstances in which this can happen, Fuss argues, must involve a group that has suffered oppression—one whose identity has been challenged, degraded, or denied by the dominant culture. Additionally, the types of essentialism she finds useful explicitly exclude the universalizing and deterministic essentialism of white second-wave feminism. For Fuss, effective forms of essentialism are those recognizing that physicality, body, and appearance affect the experiences of individuals because they are the signifiers upon which a constructed identity is built.

Though he does not cite Fuss, R. Stephen Warner makes a similar case for the uses of essentialism within MCC. Pointing to Troy Perry's claim to have been gay since ovum and sperm first met to form him, Warner suggests that an essentialist understanding of lesbian and gay identity, when combined with what he calls a Pentecostal theology, provides a strong affirmation of identity. "The power of gay Christian essentialism," he argues,

> is that it (1) invokes a powerful and benevolent God to proclaim the issue of homosexuality to be beyond human control, thereby concentrating the energy of gays themselves on changing their circumstances; (2) frees parents from doubt; (3) denies that homosexuality is in any way contagious; (4) expresses solidarity with grass roots gay culture; and (5) demands, as a matter of simple justice, inclusion of gays as simply another tile in the American mosaic.[20]

While I disagree with Warner's assessment of MCC as espousing a Pentecostal theology—the denomination is too theologically permissive to be categorized easily as espousing *any* specific image of God—this study supports his assertions about the power of combining theological themes with identity.

To claim an essentialist identity, as Fuss has shown, can be a powerful self-affirmation; for a Christian to claim not only that her sexual or gender identity is innate but that it is God-given provides an unshakable counter-argument against those who would have her believe she is sinning or demon-possessed. In fact, some participants in this study go beyond even the position that their identity is God-given; they claim a mystical understanding of themselves as a part of God and of God as a part of them. The implications of such an understanding can be quite radical.

Religion, Spirituality, and Identity

Several of the survey items were designed to address issues surrounding the role of religion in affirmation or acceptance of LGBT identity. Because of the centrality of the coming-out experience as a turning point in the self-understanding of many LGBT people, this section focuses explicitly on that period of time. Respondents were asked several questions about religious attendance and about attitudes toward homosexuality, organized religion, and spirituality during the year before they came out. The same questions were then repeated for the year after coming out. This tight time structure obscures the length of the self-acceptance process for some people, but such difficulties often were resolved through the interviews. Even taking this limitation into account, the survey results offer some extremely suggestive insights into the relationships among religion, spirituality, and identity.

Religion as Resource

Participants in this study attended a wide variety of religious groups while they were coming out, ranging from Catholic and fundamentalist Protestant to MCC; some did not attend services at all. Judging from the stereotypical coming-out story and the equally stereotypical anti-LGBT image of all but liberal Christian denominations, one might expect to see not only a large positive shift in attitudes toward homosexuality from before to after coming out but also a link between greater shifts, or perhaps more negative attitudes overall, and attendance at the more conservative denominations. In fact, the former assumption proves to be only somewhat true, while the latter fails entirely to be upheld by the data in this study.

On a scale from 1 to 5, with 1 indicating very negative and 5 very positive attitudes, the average attitude toward homosexuality after coming out was

3.88: just slightly on the positive side of the survey choice of neutral. While only 9 percent actually reported a neutral attitude, a full 20 percent reported still having negative feelings about homosexuality during the year after coming out. However, the remaining large majority—over 70 percent—reported feeling either "somewhat positive" or "very positive" toward homosexuality. It is interesting that on average these figures represent only a small change from the year before coming out: nearly 50 percent reported no change at all. And although just over 50 percent reported a positive change in attitude, the vast majority shifted only one or two points on the five-point scale. These numbers suggest that for this group, at least, the experience of coming out involves not a sudden shift in attitudes or identity but rather a gradual development—a conclusion consistent with current theories on the stages of gay and lesbian identity development.[21]

Likewise, there was little overall change in religious attendance during this time. Again contradicting stereotypes about the deleterious effects of organized religion on LGBT identity, 36 percent of respondents reported attending religious services at least once a week during the year after coming out. Those attending at least once a month made up 56 percent of the sample, and a full 78 percent reported attending at least once a year. These high attendance figures are largely due to studying a sample drawn from church mailing lists; such a population would be expected to have a history of more regular religious attendance than the general public. Despite this fact, however, it is significant that members of a notoriously homophobic religion, many of whom were attending denominations not known for their unconditional acceptance of LGBT people, still attended services so frequently during the year after they came out.

For over half of the respondents, moreover, these figures represented no change whatsoever in religious attendance. In fact, 14 percent even reported increased attendance, while 33 percent reported a decrease. But there is a noticeable difference here between certain denominations. On average, those attending services at Catholic, conservative Protestant, or mainline Protestant churches cut their attendance in half during the coming-out period. Conservative Protestants showed the most severe drop in attendance, while mainline Protestants showed the smallest of the three; liberal Protestants did not change at all. Those attending only MCC, though, quadrupled their attendance. The other groups represented among those reporting increased attendance were unspecified Protestant, New Age, and metaphysical.

The drop in religious attendance for those groups known to teach more negative attitudes toward homosexuality is fairly logical. It becomes much more interesting, however, when combined with the predominant lack of change in attitude regarding homosexuality and the prevalent positive attitude toward homosexuality after coming out. Two key possibilities suggest themselves as explanations for this phenomenon. First, those who left their churches may have accepted the idea that one cannot be both LGBT and Christian and may have chosen LGBT identity over Christian identity. However, they also might have reinterpreted that belief as a choice between LGBT identity and Christian *belonging,* carrying on, as Roof puts it, "a creative dialogue with tradition." The interview data support both of these possible paths.

Religion as Useful Resource?

If religion is a potential resource, the next question to ask is: How useful is it? In this section and the following one, I break with standard academic usage of the word "religion" and confine the term to organized religion, because that is the way in which respondents consistently used it in surveys and interviews.

In an attempt to measure participants' assessments of the relationship between organized religion and the coming-out process, I asked them to rate their level of agreement with the following statement: "My attendance at religious services and/or my religious community helped me through the coming-out period." As with several of the survey items discussed earlier, responses to this statement were strongly bimodal and showed large differences between religious groups. Only 9 percent gave a neutral response to this statement; 53 percent of respondents disagreed with it, and 37 percent of respondents disagreed with it strongly. On the other side, 38 percent of respondents agreed with this statement, and 27 percent of respondents agreed with it strongly. While conservative Protestants averaged a response of 1.1 on this five-point scale and Catholics averaged 1.4 (close to "strongly disagree"), those attending MCC averaged 4.2 and those attending MCC along with another church averaged 4.5 (between "agree somewhat" and "strongly agree"). Only two other groups showed a positive response, and neither score was as strongly positive as those for MCC: those attending Protestant services of unspecified denomination averaged 3.2, and those attending metaphysical or New Age groups averaged 3.6 on this question.

As MCC is the source of most of these positive responses, it seems that religion may be a useful resource during the coming-out period only if it is explicitly affirming of LGBT Christian identity. In light of these answers, in fact, it may well be the case that even open and affirming heterosexual congregations were of insufficient assistance for those in this study. Recall that the turning point for Bill was attending a service at MCC and being in the company of other LGBT Christians.

Also relevant here is another intriguing aspect of the role of religion. Those who attended MCC while they were coming out, with or without attendance at the services of another religious group, came out as lesbian, gay, bisexual, or transgender at almost the highest average age of all the religious groups.[22] Why does the most affirming religious group have one of the highest average ages for coming out? I suspect the answer goes back once again to the fact that coming out, especially for those affected by negative social and religious opinions on LGBT identities, is a long and often arduous process. It is quite possible that the mean age for MCC is pushed up by "switchers" such as Bill: those people who move from condemning to supportive denominations in order to gain support from a religious community while they are coming out.[23] Many of those who came out within MCC might have struggled with LGBT identity and religion for years before making the decision to switch, thus coming out at a later than average age.

What about Spirituality?

The term "spirituality" reflects the essence of the turn toward individualism in U.S. religious cultures; it is used by people today to describe beliefs, individual practices, heartfelt connections, religious experiences, and more. Roof has indicated that among the baby-boomer generation, this term currently enjoys a far better reputation than does "religion."[24] Since religious individualism seems to be an important resource for LGBT Christians, and since over half of the survey respondents are part of the boomer generation as Roof defines it, it is logical to suspect that they might look more kindly on "spirituality" than they do on organized religion.[25]

The contrast, in fact, is stunning. While opinions of organized religion were 48 percent negative, 17 percent neutral, and 35 percent positive, opinions on spirituality were only 14 percent negative and 20 percent neutral. A full 66 percent of survey respondents reported having a positive attitude toward spirituality during the year after coming out. Moreover, respondents' views on spirituality changed even less than did their views on religion across the coming-out period: 71 percent reported no change. Those whose opinions did change were fairly evenly split: 14 percent reported having a lower opinion of spirituality after coming out, while 15 percent reported a more positive opinion.

Respondents also were asked to respond to a statement about spirituality that paralleled the one about religious organizations that was described above: "My religious belief, faith, or spirituality helped me through the coming-out period." While 38 percent of respondents agreed with the statement on religion, 57 percent of respondents agreed with the one on belief and spirituality and 38 percent of respondents agreed strongly.

Although these results are suggestive rather than conclusive because of the size of the survey, they point toward a role for both religious organizations and individual religiosity in the coming-out process. Individual belief, faith, or spirituality appears to have the upper hand, however. If this is in fact the case, it means that LGBT people are among those groups who benefit from the religious phenomena identified by Wuthnow, Roof, Dufour, and others. Lacking easily accessible ascribed identities, instead they may be sifting through their religious resources to create those identities on their own.

Christians Coming Out

Matt spoke in the previous chapter about social influences on his understanding of homosexuality. Although my interview with him lasted for nearly an hour, the most eloquent retelling of his spiritual journey appeared in response to a question on the survey; it highlights the clear contrast between the roles of external and internal forces in the self-understanding of LGBT people:

> I've never identified myself by focusing on my sexual nature. Somewhere
> along the line of my experiences I was told what I enjoyed sexually was
> bad & because of that I was bad. I went into hiding behind closed doors
> like Adam's fig leaf. I lost my Father in the process. Luckily for me He
> knew where I was, followed me never letting go until the day He brought
> me meditation and helped me to release all of the troubling self inflicted
> thoughts. Slowly, sometimes painfully slow, He gave me a new understand-
> ing of my true identity and His incredible, inexhaustible love for me. I will
> never forget the meditation in which I had the courage to say "Hello" to
> the Supreme Being and He said ever so quietly, but oh so powerfully, "I love
> you. Come home." Every day I walk another step toward the Mother of all
> Creation and I am content. In the process I am learning that love not sex is
> what I must come to terms with.[26]

The surveys and the interviews contained other stories like Matt's and also stories very different from his. Most notable, in fact, is the wide variety in the roles played by religious communities and religious belief, in the interactions of religion and nascent LGBT identity, and in the time periods spanned by these events. In general, however, the stories I heard and read constituted five major patterns. These confirm the picture suggested by the surveys: in four of the five patterns, the main events take place outside of religious communities, sometimes but not always culminating in a return to congregational attendance. Only the fifth pattern—followed by the fewest respondents—relies significantly on community *during* the coming-out process as well as after the fact. As with any sociological model, these patterns are types rather than strict categories into which every possible religious coming-out story can be fitted, and it is quite conceivable that some stories might bridge two or more of these types.

1. Separating Religion and LGBT Identity

For some people, sexuality and gender identity are unrelated to either religion or spirituality. Among these respondents, religious teachings about homosexuality never made an impact or, if they did, that impact or even the religion itself was permanently gone from the individual's life by the time she or he came out. Just as there was no negative impact, however, there also is no positive connection for these respondents between religion and LGBT identity. Following the traditional Christian understanding that God and religion are concerned with spiritual rather than bodily matters and that the spiritual and the earthly are not closely linked, these people simply do not find religion and LGBT identity to be related.

While this may be the case permanently for some of the people in this category, it is instructive to look in more depth at the story of Anthony, who spoke in the last chapter about his adventures in evading a lobotomy. Anthony eventually did make it into the priesthood, but he had learned well from his earlier experiences of telling others about his homosexuality. By the time he was ordained, he told me, he was keeping sexuality strictly separate from the rest of his life. I asked if he had remained closeted during his time as a priest, and he responded:

> Oh, totally. Oh, yeah. Every now and then I'd be asked about it, casually, by a priest friend. And I would always . . . deny it, because of the fact that I just didn't see what would be the point in telling him I was gay. What's the point? You know, nothing I'm doing [professionally] has anything to do with my private life. . . . I kept the two . . . totally separate.

Yet despite its importance at the time, the separation took its toll on him; it "eventually became . . . a part of the problem without my realizing. You have to be integrated, I think, in your life." Anthony told me that he came to see the split between his religious identity and his sexuality as "a sham . . . sort of hiding behind the collar in a way." "I felt like it was . . . phony," he explained. "You know, keeping your life . . . separate like that."

Anthony eventually left the priesthood in disgust. "I just left with a lot of anger," he recalled. "A lot of disappointment, but I think primarily anger. . . . Not at anything in particular, just angry. Denying anything having to do with the church. I threw absolutely everything I had . . . away in the garbage can. . . . I didn't want to see it; I didn't want to be reminded of it." Anthony avoided churches for a year and a half, but he recently began attending MCC in an attempt to put his shattered beliefs back together and perhaps to reenter the ministry—this time, one would assume, with an integrated identity.[27]

Anthony's story suggests that there may be two subgroups within this pattern. One is the group described above: the people for whom religion and spirituality are permanently unrelated to sexual or gender identity. However, there may be others—perhaps among those who left conservative churches when they came out—for whom this apparently simple separation is forced. In fact, temporary separation of the two identities plays a central role in the second pattern.

2. Grappling with Each Identity in Succession

This pattern also involves a separation of religion or spirituality from LGBT identity in order to deal with the two issues separately. The previous pattern involved viewing LGBT identity as unconnected to religion or spirituality while still retaining both in one's life; those who follow this second pattern reject religion initially (usually because it has rejected them), and along with religious attendance they also reject most belief or spirituality. Others leave religion for different reasons entirely—disaffection with policies on gender, for instance. Freed from these potentially fettering influences, the people in this group explore their sexual or gender identity and generally become wholeheartedly accepting of it. Eventually, however, they feel an urge to return to some sort of spiritual or religious practice. Secure in their LGBT identity, they seek a group—in this study, often MCC, but there are many other possible resources—that will affirm them as LGBT people while allowing them to develop or practice a spirituality integrated with that identity.

Walter, who spoke earlier in the chapter about his understanding of God, is one example of this pattern. When he began in college to acknowledge his gay identity, he was aware that the conservative churches he had attended while growing up taught that homosexuality was wrong in the eyes of God. He spent several years attempting to overcome this aspect of his identity, but "finally realized it was . . . ingrained in me." Meeting a group of gay people in the mountains one summer, he "realized that they were real people and that maybe this wasn't so bad after all." As a result, he pushed religion aside, saying, "'Okay, that doesn't fit.' And 'leave it behind.' I really did leave it behind." Curious about how deep the rejection had gone, I asked Walter if he had left God behind as well. "Yes," he answered, "definitely so. I just kind of compartmentalized it off and set it off over here." He laughed. "Where I didn't have to deal with it. I'm sure I thought about God in those times and I probably even prayed to some degree. It's just that it didn't have a logical . . . frame of mind to put it into. So I tended to ignore it." He paused, then added, "I mean, denial is a very handy thing."

About ten years later, Walter returned to religion through MCC. During his sixteen years with the church, he feels, the spiritual side of his life has developed and become more prominent. This has been a positive change for him in general, and it also has been a source of strength during the years since he developed AIDS.[28]

3. Relying on Spirituality

The third pattern is the direct opposite of the one just discussed. In this case, rather than rejecting religion or spirituality because of its negative influence, people embrace an individualistic spirituality as a source of support during the coming-out process. Often in these stories, spirituality is strictly opposed to the teachings and communities of organized religion, which play the same oppressive role here as they did in the pattern of dealing with each identity in succession.

There are several different variations on this particular coming-out pattern. For some, there is a long period of struggle, often encompassing years and even decades. During this time, the person takes to heart religious teachings that LGBT identity is a sin or a temptation from the devil and makes an active effort to overcome that identity. For people such as Bill, the turning point is empirical: having spent years doing everything they could to eradicate same-sex desire or transgender identification and attaining no results, they conclude that perhaps the church is wrong and God does not want them to change. This is the other possible explanation for the high number of conservative Christians who left their churches during the coming-out process.

Others come to the same conclusion in a more experiential way. Carrie is part of this latter group. For her, the journey from her conservative church to self-acceptance was a three-step process. Although she initially believed that her attraction to women was caused by demons, eventually the growing visibility of gays and lesbians in the media convinced her that homosexuality might not be as terrible as she thought. The years of self-recrimination had taken their toll, however, and she soon found herself heavily involved in drinking and drugs in an effort to "fit in."[29] Throughout these developments, though, she told me:

> I always prayed, and even if I didn't go to church, I always read the Bible, I always had talks with God. I always felt a bond with God, though. No matter what may be with people, but I could always talk to God, and I always did, and I knew what was wrong. And I thought, 'I don't need to fit in that much. Because this [drug and alcohol abuse] is hurting me.' And I knew it was wrong because we're not supposed to damage our bodies.

This realization, obtained at least in part through her personal connection with God, led her into a residential treatment program and then out of her home state to California, where she discovered MCC.[30]

A third pathway within this pattern is no less agonizing than the others, but the agony lasts only weeks or months instead of decades. In this case, the person coming out immediately challenges the church's teachings about LGBT identity rather than initially accepting them and working to change herself. She grapples with the conflict between her sense that this is an intrinsic and harmless—perhaps even good—part of her identity and the apparently clear biblical teachings against it. The person who follows this pathway refuses to capitulate entirely yet wishes to remain true to her religious beliefs. In keeping with the pattern, it is spirituality—religion on a personal level—that pulls her through. One example of this variant is Terry Rose.

Terry, who chose to use her pen name for this study, came out at a women's college in Texas. Having fallen in love with a close female friend, she tried to avoid religious questions about their relationship. She was deeply involved in a Southern Baptist church, however, so God was rarely far from her mind, and the questions about what she was doing refused to go away. "I was quite suicidal for a while," she recalled when we talked at her home.

> I'd go through my whole day, and do real well, and fake it, fake it, fake it, and then I'd go into my room and sit on my bed . . . and this friend had given me a poster that was kind of psychedelic looking, and it said "Jesus, lover of my soul." . . . And I would look at that poster, and I would cry. Wailing crying—wailing, screaming crying—and I would sing the song to myself, "For Those Tears I Died." . . . And . . . it was what held me there. I thought, "If I can stay on this bed, I won't go kill myself." And that somehow Jesus understood this, because the song says that Jesus cries too.[31]

Earlier in our conversation, Terry had told me of a time during her coming-out period when she was in church praying "and saying, 'I just can't understand why I can't love her, why it's against the rules.'" In response, "the word 'lust' came into my head." She looked up Romans 1, wherein the word appears in reference to homosexuality, and read the passage. "And it was like a huge light bulb. . . . This was not me."

She did not *lust* after her friend, Terry realized; she *loved* her, and the biblical injunction was against lust. Perhaps the clearest turning point for Terry, however, was another conversation with God:

> I was walking across campus, and it was a beautiful, sunny day . . . and it hit me that I was a lesbian. And I got really, really pissed at God. And I literally shook my fist at this patriarchal God that I knew, and said, "How dare you do this to me! All I've ever wanted was to be normal, to fit in, and then you pull this kind of garbage on me?" Oh! I was—I was furious. And it was one of those times when you—when—I literally heard a voice that was inside me and everywhere else, and it was . . . a voice from, I believe it's in Isaiah, that said . . . "Can the pot tell the potter what to make?" And then . . . this real calm feeling, this real beautiful peace that said, "Trust me, it'll be more beautiful than you ever imagined." . . . So I kind of gained strength from there.[32]

Terry, and others like her, have a distinct advantage over those who follow the other two paths possible within this pattern. This advantage, gained from a refusal to accept church teachings on homosexuality, does not spare them the pain of struggling to integrate spirituality with sexuality, but it does save them years of time and agony. Most fortunate, however, are those for whom spirituality or religion and LGBT identity were always integrated.

4. Connecting Religion and LGBT Identity

People in this fourth group are parallel in some ways to those in the first, in that the struggle experienced by others in this study is never an issue in their lives. Contrary to those in the first group, however, these individuals experience a strong connection between spirituality and sexuality; contrary to those in the second and third groups, for these people the two have never been separate.

One subset of this group encompasses those such as Andrew, whose story opened this chapter—people who believe that it was God who encouraged them to come out. Another subset includes those whose relationship with God allowed them to ride out the condemnation and rejection from their churches, and a third group sees LGBT identity itself as sacred.

Margaret and Cynthia are peripherally associated with MCC and currently claim a pluralist spirituality rather than a Christian identity, though both were formerly Christian; they discussed this issue when I interviewed them.

In the conversation quoted below, Margaret was trying to explain her understanding of the connection between spirituality and sexuality, which both women had emphasized in their surveys. Her partner helped her along:

Cynthia: Do you mean that . . . you are who you are . . . as an expression of
    Spirit?
Margaret: Yeah, that's what I mean. . . .
Cynthia: Part of that is being a lesbian, and so it's a holy and sacred thing.
Margaret: It's a holy thing. It *is* sacred.
Cynthia: Is that what you mean?
Margaret: That's what I mean. That—that I am sacred, because what God—
    because I'm an expression of God. . . . I always laugh to myself when I
    see a sign that says, "We are an open and affirming congregation," be-
    cause I feel like I don't need anyone else to tell me that I am a child of
    God.[33]

The number of people following this pattern, however, is small. Behind most stories of integration and wholeness, it seems, there lies at least a short period of uncertainty and self-doubt.

5. Coming Out in a Religious Community

This fifth pattern is the only one in which the individual relies on religion-based community support (or has such support available) *during* the coming-out process. Even here, however, community resources alone are rarely sufficient; this strategy frequently is combined with previously discussed patterns. For instance, when someone such as Anthony has divorced his spirituality from his sexuality, he may turn to MCC or a similar group for help in reintegrating the two. For people who have been trying to change, such as Bill, a supportive religious community can provide the final impetus for acceptance of LGBT identity. And at some point on the timeline, it seems that community becomes important for many.

Others, however, apparently avoid struggles like Anthony's and Bill's entirely, drifting into MCC through chance or choice and then coming out. One respondent, for example, related in her survey that she had had a crush on one of the nuns who taught at her Catholic high school. At the time, she said, she did not admit to herself that the attraction was physical as well as nonphysical. When we spoke after church one day, she told me a fascinating story about the process of coming out that occurred later in her life.

She first discovered MCC while she was beginning to explore the possibility that she might be lesbian. Having seen the church advertised as "a Christian group affirming gays and lesbians," she decided to attend. At her first service, she recalled, "I . . . went up afterwards . . . and they said, 'Well, how long have you been out?' And I literally looked at my watch and said, 'About forty-five minutes now.' " We both laughed at that, and she continued, "Because it's just—it was so clear to me that . . . it was okay to be a lesbian. And I—I just felt so at home and so comfortable in the surroundings that I just truly felt that God was being very clear: this is an okay place to be."[34]

Identity, Theology, and Coming Out

Essential Identities

Influenced by Warner's thoughts on essentialism in MCC, but also aware of the existence of a strongly anti-essentialist tendency among some feminist lesbians, I asked during interviews whether people believed themselves to have been born LGBT or whether that identity had developed over the course of their lives. Most people did not even let me finish the question—by the time I finished saying "born" they were nodding, and some even jumped in with an "absolutely" or a "definitely." Many followed this assertion with supporting statements: stories from early childhood emphasizing greater affiliation with the same sex, gender identification with the opposite sex, or simply a sense of difference.[35] A few women claimed their lesbian or bisexual identities to be chosen, and several people mentioned the possibility that sexual identity could perhaps be a choice for others.[36] Some frankly told me they did not know what the roots of their sexual or transgender identity might be, and a few who believe in reincarnation suggested that their souls might have chosen to be born LGBT in order to broaden their experiences. For the vast majority, however, essentialism reigns supreme.

If there is a choice to be made, respondents suggested, it is the choice of whether or not to express one's true sexual or gender identity. Many framed this choice as a decision between living a lie and being true to oneself. Wayne, a gay man who has been closely involved with MCC for ten years, believes that "the only choice is whether or not you live your life with dignity and integrity intact. And for many of us . . . it's a journey to the place of coming out where we can affirm who we are and what we are."[37] Handing their young son over to Wayne, his partner Robert added: "I can choose . . . emotionally and physiologically, to be attracted to women. That's not what my heart is and . . . that's not my life. . . . I guess what I'm trying to say is we can . . . change our behavior—we cannot change our orientation."[38] Robert believes that many people who change their behavior in this way do so because they are unaware that coming out is a viable option.

Beyond Warner's suggestion that essentialism removes blame and guilt from LGBT people and their parents and beyond Fuss's argument that it can be politically expedient, there is an even more powerful reason for LGBT Christians to embrace such a self-definition: the homosexuality debates are predicated on exactly this question. Most anti-LGBT Christian groups consider minority sexual or gender identities to be false, brought about through bad influences, misperceptions, poor upbringing, or even the devil. The emotional pain associated with identity crisis in many LGBT Christians is interpreted by these groups as indicating that LGBT identity is akin to an illness and that its sufferers are therefore in need of healing. Among the anti-LGBT Christian groups, only the Catholic Church has stated clearly that homosexuality is an inborn trait, and to my knowledge it has not weighed in on the subject of bisexual or transgender identities.

In response to claims that their identities are freely chosen, LGBT people frequently point to the oppression suffered by many of their group, asking what the rewards might be that would influence such a large number of people to choose to be lesbian, gay, bisexual, or transgender. When I questioned Matt about the possibility that LGBT identity might be a choice, he replied: "Why would people choose to do something that would cause them so much grief and so much pain that they would commit suicide? I mean, if it was a choice and it was so simple, just a simple thing, they would just stop."[39] Moreover, many LGBT Christians from conservative backgrounds say that their own inability to change has disproved the theory that LGBT identity is optional and can be rejected. Thus, although it is theoretically quite logical to assert that there might be an aspect of choice or social conditioning to LGBT identity, for many of the people in this study choice is not an option.

While recent genetic studies have given essentialists a strong platform on which to stand when claiming the inborn nature of LGBT identity, the people in this study have a second argument at their disposal: God. In an age and among a group in which scientific and religious beliefs hold equal sway and are often intertwined, the use of both to argue for an essentialist identity is doubly powerful: it lends credibility within both rationalist and religious circles. Furthermore, a claim to have been created lesbian, gay, bisexual, or transgender by God is much stronger in most Christian subcultures than a claim to have been born that way. The latter claim can still lead, as it does in the Catholic Church, to a position that such identities are harmful proclivities. While the former claim could still imply a testing by God rather than the granting of a valued identity, it at least obviates the need for exorcisms, "healings," and other painful results of the anti-LGBT constructivist position.

Those who believe their identities to be God-given offer two diametrically opposed interpretations of this fact; which one is relevant to a given individual probably depends on how positive his experiences have been as an LGBT person. For some, this identity is a test or a trial. Miguel, a gay Latino who was raised within the Salvation Army, says that he is "a firm believer that God made me gay," but he continues to be puzzled by passages in the Bible that he interprets as saying that homosexuals are condemned by God. "I can't believe that God would have made me this way simply to condemn me," he told me.

Miguel's ambivalence appears in another way, too. "I believe that God gave each of us a gift," he explained, "and at the same time he gave us a cross to bear. . . . I believe that God gave me the cross to bear of being gay." However, the gift that accompanies this cross is also present in his life, as he makes eloquently clear. When I asked Miguel whether he felt that being gay was good, he thought for a while, sighed, and then responded:

> I feel that if I wasn't gay I wouldn't be as sensitive to people—to the needs of people and to the hurt that people have. I feel that all of this is from my gay side. . . . I look at a tree blowing in the wind and see more than just that. I see the symmetry of the tree. I see the leaves as they shimmer. You know. And I think those are all part of my gay nature, a sensitive, more tuned-in side of me. . . . And . . . I accept being gay and I really value it— you know, as something very important to me. . . . But I just go through this dilemma of what is the purpose of my life as a gay person if I'm already condemned.[40]

For Miguel and others like him, LGBT identity is "a cross to bear," even if it comes with advantages. For others, however, the gift comes without the cross. Recall that Andrew believed that God had helped him to come out, in answer to his prayers to "know myself better." A few others, such as Margaret and Cynthia, explicitly told me that their LGBT identity was a gift from God. In cases such as this, the imagery of God becomes even more important. Not only can LGBT Christians claim their identity to be genetically determined, not only can they claim it to be God-given, but the additional claim that it is a sacred gift makes LGBT identity something not just to be endured but to be celebrated.

This raises once again the issue of theology. It is apparent that Warner was indeed correct in arguing that essentialism is an important part of identity affirmation for those involved in MCC. But if participants in this study do not hold to the Pentecostal theology that is part of his thesis, how does their theology interact with their essentialism? Several answers to this question have been given above. However, in understanding how LGBT Christians connect their sexual and religious identities, it is essential to explore in depth both their understandings of God and their answers to the supposedly anti-LGBT biblical passages.

Theology

Images of God varied widely among those I interviewed. Many from MCC Valle Rico described a mystical and often immanent God that resonated with their church's focus on the metaphysical. On the other hand, those who had found MCCVR too theologically liberal for their tastes often espoused a more traditional theology. For some, God is a father; others think of God as "parent" or "mother/father." And some speak more loosely of an energy, a flow, a life force, the Universe. Few images, however, were monolithic, and none were formulaic.

Several people included a negative component in their understanding of God: a statement of what God is not. Most common among these characteristics that explicitly did *not* describe God was "judgmental." God also was described as not damning, not angry, not petty or vindictive, not gendered, not anthropomorphic, and not "the great big daddy God of the Christian Bible that we were raised with."[41] Many of these negative descriptions reject traditional images of God; some of them reject theology that is used against LGBT people, who may feel, as Miguel does, that both the church and the Bible teach God's condemnation of them.

If God is not any of these things, then what *is* God? Though respondents rarely agreed on this topic, one aspect received overwhelming support. When I asked what the most important characteristics of God might be, the response was often both immediate and concise: "love." Some people elaborated; Jeffrey, a gay white man in his 30s, told me: "I really believe . . . that our God is a loving, accepting God, for who we are. . . . Exactly how we are. And it's that love and acceptance that draws us to Him . . . and helps us to love Him back."[42] Others were more succinct, like Lacey, who said: "For me, God is love." She paused. "That's it."[43] Metaphysical or traditional, mystical or parental, many of the images of God that respondents described to me shared this aspect.

Another important aspect of God, expressed more frequently by those involved with MCCVR, was God's immanence. Respondents described God as omnipresent, as being always nearby, being "in the world," or even being in each person. Walter, a gay man who has been involved in MCC for over fifteen years, shared the following:

> My understanding of God is spirit, and it kind of never . . . ends, and I
> consider that each and every one of us, our spiritual self is connected with

God and kind of is all intermingled. . . . We often hear the universe is one, that there really is only one spirit and we are all part of that spirit. And I do think that that's very true, because I feel so connected to so many people, especially within this church—and outside the church too.[44]

Such an understanding of God has several implications for LGBT people. First, if they hold this belief while coming out, it means that God can be present for them in a very real way during this process—as was the case with Terry Rose. Second, love and immanence can be combined to lead to the conclusion that God loves everyone and is present in all people and all relationships. Third, and most radically, if God is not only ever present but is actually present *in* each person, as Walter suggested, and if each person is made in the image of God, then God could be understood at least in part to be lesbian, gay, bisexual, and transgender.

Though no one actually made this connection, I had a fascinating conversation with another gay man, Marc, about its possibilities. Speaking in his office at a local research facility, he told me the following: "My concept of God is all that there is. . . . It's bigger than anything that I can conceive of. And that God had this image of—of wanting to materialize itself. And this is the result. . . . I am 'I AM' in my own way, the living Christ."

I responded: "Seems to me that would be an incredibly strong affirmation of being gay. To consider that you are part of the living God and that means all of you, including your gayness. . . . Do you experience it that way, or is that just an interpretation I'm putting on it?" He laughed, somewhat uncertain, and stumbled through an answer.

> Well, yeah, that was—um, it was interesting, 'cause as I was listening to you, it sounded, um, a little foreign to me. Um—but, it sounded like something that—and I don't know—you know, if I sat and thought about it that it was there—but it was like, "Well, of course." But it felt—in a way it sounded like I was hearing it for the first time. And, um, maybe that's what I needed to hear.

He paused. "I guess—so I think I—I maybe have never really heard that. I may have felt it, or lived it, or been it, but not associate—given it a definition. But it made perfect sense."[45]

It is not surprising that even a metaphysically inclined person such as Marc, someone who already envisioned himself as the image of God, would never have thought of God as encompassing homosexuality. As Howard Eilberg-Schwartz has pointed out, the sexuality of God is adamantly avoided in the Hebrew Bible.[46] Jesus' sexuality became important for some medieval women mystics, and metaphors of marriage and sexual fidelity appear in Puritan religious discourse, but each of these contexts remained explicitly heterosexual.[47] More recently, with the resurgence of paternal images of God in traditional religious contexts, sexuality has again retreated from the divine image. Yet as Margaret and Cynthia pointed out earlier, such an all-encompassing vision of divinity has the potential to sacralize sexuality, thus providing an eminently powerful affirmation of what Comstock (and the Presbyterian Church-USA) has called "unrepentant, self-affirming, practicing" LGBT identity.[48]

Exegesis

The wide range of divine imagery utilized by participants in this study is paralleled by the wide range of tactics for dealing with the "anti-homosexuality" texts in the Bible. As the arguments against such interpretations of these texts were discussed in Chapter 1, I will confine my discussion here to exploring how these arguments are mobilized by study participants.

One might assume, especially given the theological liberalism of both MCC congregations in this study, that most of the interview participants adhere to a metaphorical understanding of the Bible, seeing it as a source for spiritual reflection rather than a rule book for moral living. However, despite the liberalism of the churches they attend now, some respondents still treat the Bible as the word of God. How, then, do they reconcile their acceptance of LGBT identity with these texts?

The answer lies in a moderate approach to the Bible. Refusing to read it as metaphor, literature, or a useful but optional resource, these people instead rely on the sacred texts' historical and cultural context. Mandy, a lesbian in her late 50s, put this approach most clearly: "I believe that the Bible is God's divine word," she told me while her young grandson piled toys in her lap. "However, in order to put His word in black and white, God had to use people." She chuckled. "All of these things that make up me, I'm going to read into or see into whatever work I'm doing. So it's the same with those who wrote and then eventually translated the Bible."[49]

Others who wish to continue a modified literalist reading of the Bible point to the fact that Christians do not follow any of the other Levitical laws; therefore, they argue, it is hypocritical to apply one of those laws to LGBT Christians without also requiring that all Christians abstain from pork, wear only fabric made from a single type of fiber, and so on. Some also point to the fact that there is no record of Jesus himself saying anything about homosexuality.

More liberal readers argue that homosexuality and transgender identity as we know them today did not exist when the Bible was written. They offer the arguments mentioned in Chapter 1: that words translated as "homosexual" really mean "temple prostitute," or refer to man-boy relationships. And quite a few make things even simpler: they ignore the texts, preferring to rely on their own experience of God's love and acceptance rather than on a book that is the result of centuries of oral tradition, centuries more of transcription, and several translations. Carrie, for instance, whose story was told above, went through years of trying to change her sexual orientation before she finally came out. Now, she says, "I still have immense respect for the [Bible] because I feel all in all, you just eat the meat and spit out the bones. So I don't take every single thing—I just read it, and I let the Spirit guide me to the meaning."[50] Anti-LGBT passages, for Carrie, are simply bones to be tossed in the trash.

Permutations of a Larger Pattern?

While the pathways and strategies described in this chapter may be specific to religious LGBT people, LGBT Christians, or even the participants in this study, they also resonate in a number of ways with broader patterns in U.S. religiosity. As a result, the theories and the findings discussed herein have much to offer each other. While theories about contemporary religiosity can help to elucidate the beliefs and practices of respondents, respondents' beliefs and practices also can expand and complicate existing theories. This is true both for questions of identity and for those of religious individualism.

Identity

On the subject of essentialist identities, the ideas of both Fuss and Warner are eminently applicable to the stories described above. The vast majority of interview participants hold to some level of essentialism in their self-depictions. They go farther than Fuss suggests, however, adding to their essentialism the same divine connection that Warner noted in 1995.[51] Not only do many of them believe that they were born lesbian, gay, bisexual, or transgender; in addition, they claim to have been born that way by divine decree.

The participants in this study also go farther than Warner suggests. Though he comments on the efficacy of attributing one's sexual or gender identity to "a powerful and benevolent God,"[52] the theological beliefs of the people with whom I spoke extended far beyond this description. Certainly there were no images of God among those I interviewed that were *not* powerful or *not* benevolent, but the images that prove useful to LGBT people are much more varied than that. Some people take refuge in a parental God or a brotherly Jesus who offers them support; others find an image of omnipresence to be more powerful. Some focus on the idea that they are the image of God or the children of God, while others speak of a comforting, strengthening energy or flow. Benevolent? Absolutely, but the word is not strong enough: for most of these people God is love, and unlike many of their childhood churches, a God of love would not want them to suffer the loneliness and despair that attend efforts to eradicate minority sexual or gender identity.

Religious Individualism

By now, the importance of religious individualism for those involved in this study should be evident. Individualized spirituality constantly received much higher ratings from this group than did organized religion, and those who believe that their spirituality or religious beliefs helped them to come out far outnumber those who feel that their religious community or religious attendance helped. The survey and interview data suggest that some of those who were attending the most theologically conservative churches while coming out changed not their opinions of homosexuality, not their opinions of organized religion or spirituality, but merely their attendance. Faced with ideas that negated their newly claimed identities, they neither argued nor capitulated; they simply left.

As the interviews show, however, this process was not in fact simple. By focusing only on the year before coming out, the surveys missed much of the complexity of what can sometimes be a decades-long process. However, the interviews confirm that even the longer processes revolved around the individual rather than relying on community support. Self-definitions (essentialism) and a variety of independently defined theological positions, not to mention exegetical strategies tailored to each person's view of the Bible, lent themselves to the eventual integration process as study participants sifted through their traditions, seeking to construct a coherent identity. Moreover, four out of the five patterns of coming out for LGBT Christians and LGBT people involved with MCC had little to do with community: they were personal struggles that were sometimes undertaken in silence, in the company of God alone.

"Self-definition," Robert Wuthnow has argued, "is . . . more contingent on one's own thoughts and feelings than on the statuses that institutions confer"; this is not to say that institutions do not play a role, but that individual strategies seem, in the end, to be more influential.[53] That this was so in the late twentieth-century United States is fortunate for many of the people in this study. I noted above that Roof has described three key aspects of this individualized form of "lived religion."[54] In the context here, the scripts—Roof's first aspect—are the teachings, both positive and negative, of an influential religious organization. These teachings, however, are also seeds that sprout plants never anticipated by many religious authorities. From these seeds come images of God and Jesus and understandings of the Bible that affirm and celebrate LGBT identities. The practices are those learned in religious training: services, certainly, but more important here, prayer. People learned to talk to God, and when their lives reached a crisis point, most of them turned to a personal relationship with the divine rather than to a human being. Ultimately, they affirmed, God did not let them down but instead let them know, sometimes even in words, that they did not need to change.

Roof's third aspect explains how these religious resources were reclaimed and reinterpreted in so many different ways by so many people: agency. In a culture in which people "selectively engage scripts and practices" and "reflect upon themselves as meaning-making creatures,"[55] and where numerous Christian churches remain unwelcoming or incompletely welcoming of LGBT people, it is not surprising in the least to find individuals forging their own paths to self-acceptance and spiritual wholeness. Faced with a sometimes overwhelming crisis of identity, these people turned to their religious resources, sifting through them until they found an answer to their dilemmas. Some were prepared with the answer before the question was even posed; others thought they had found an answer but later discovered a different one. And a few are still searching, certain the answer is out there but unsure where to find it.

Robert Bellah and his colleagues never reveal (indeed, probably never asked about) Sheila Larson's sexual orientation. If she was lesbian or bisexual, she probably found little contradiction between her highly personalized love-based beliefs and her sexual orientation. However, if she was heterosexual, she was among the vast group of people in the United States for whom religious individualism is an option, a new and perhaps more fulfilling route to explore. For many LGBT Christians, individualism is a necessity, without which they would remain trapped in divinely ordained closets. In the absence of the current trend that has been so aptly characterized by Wuthnow and Roof, in the absence of the sifting strategies analyzed by Dufour, Christians coming out would be forced to choose between affirming their sexual or gender identity and embracing their religious convictions. Instead, linking an essentialist understanding of their sexuality or transgender identity to an all-embracing, non-judgmental image of the divine, they bring LGBT and religious identities together in an integrated sense of self. Many commentators have worried about the deleterious effects of religious individualism, but for the people in this study it has been a fortuitous development.

Perhaps, indeed, it has been more than fortuitous. Those who have written about religious individualism and the rise of spirituality identify the 1960s as the period that greatly augmented these developments. It is significant that MCC was founded in the late 1960s. Although LGBT religious groups had formed occasionally throughout the century, MCC was the first one to grow to any significant size—and its growth rate has been remarkable. Could it be that LGBT people are becoming more visible in religious circles not only because of the gay liberation and lesbian/gay rights movements but also because of religious trends in the United States at this point in history?

Part Two
Community

3   Creating a Space

At 75, Bobby represents an older generation of LGBT people. Having acknowledged his gay identity roughly two decades before the start of the gay liberation movement, he embodies the values of the mid-century homophile organizations. Bobby believes that political activism is not the route to social acceptance for gays and lesbians; rather, he advocates discretion and impeccable self-conduct. He is somewhat aghast at the increasing visibility and radicalism of the LGBT community over the past few decades. Nonetheless, he does see some positive developments during this time, including the founding of MCC. Bobby became a part of MCC Los Angeles in 1971, just three years after the church was founded. There he met and married his life partner, whom he lost to AIDS in 1995.

Bobby was raised in Catholicism, a faith with which he still identifies, and he remembers years of worry about the sinfulness of homosexuality. Though he is like the majority of study participants in that he resolved some of these issues on his own, it was both his partner and his contact with MCC that helped bring him to his current place of comfort and confidence in his identity.

Over cookies and demitasses of coffee, Bobby told me about discovering MCC. "I think I was going to brunch," he related. "I think this is what happened one Sunday. And I was in the car with these friends and we went by this theater on Melrose. And whoever I was with said, 'Oh, that's the gay church.' I never even heard of it. And, you know, I said, 'Well, what in hell is a gay church?'" Bobby laughed. "And they said, 'Well, it's really, really great. And to a great extent they followed the—or copied the liturgy of the Catholic Church. And you should really go.' So I went, 'Oh, what the hell, why not?' You know—so I went and I loved it."[1]

Four years after founding MCC, Troy Perry reflected: "It seems to me, now, that it must have been a matter of timing, and I think that it was fate, too!

God chose me for my mission at a time when He knew the world would respond, once the need was made clear."[2] While the question of divine ordination is beyond the scholar's jurisdiction, the question of timing is a crucial one for sociological and historical inquiry, and Perry's remarks show an insightful awareness that the success of the Universal Fellowship of Metropolitan Community Churches was due in large part to this factor. As with any successful religious group, however, the seeds of the UFMCC germinated, sprouted, and grew as a result of a multitude of interconnected factors, including both external factors in U.S. society at large and internal factors within the UFMCC itself.

Changes in U.S. Culture

In the 1980s, Frances FitzGerald undertook a study of four widely diverse communities that had taken shape during the 1960s and 1970s: San Francisco's Castro district, Jerry Falwell's Liberty Baptist Church, the Sun City retirement community, and Rajneeshpuram.[3] Rather than simply portraying the differences between these communities, FitzGerald saw in them similar results of both time-honored tendencies and recent but fundamental changes within mainstream U.S. culture.

The title of FitzGerald's book, *Cities on a Hill,* suggests the nature of the continuities she sees between these contemporary communities and many others in U.S. history. Since the time of John Winthrop, FitzGerald argues, and especially during the Second Great Awakening, people in the United States have created new communities—new movements both secular and religious in nature—intended for the betterment of themselves and their society.[4] In the 1960s, this tendency reemerged in force, but FitzGerald argues that it had changed along with the rest of U.S. culture: there was a new emphasis on pluralism rather than consensus and an intensified focus on remaking the individual that was related, in part, to the human potential movement. While these changes are connected to the religious individualism discussed in the previous chapter, most important in FitzGerald's eyes was not pluralism or individualism but a third factor: a reorientation of identity and community.[5]

From the early nineteenth century through the 1950s, ethnicity and religion were two major points of contention in the identities of European Americans: one was identified as Irish and Catholic, Anglo and Protestant, Polish and Jewish. But FitzGerald points out that in the 1960s, these identities blended together as new ones, ethnic and otherwise, gained cultural power: black, Latino, Native American, female, and gay. At the same time, economic and demographic shifts were changing the family structures and living situations of many in the United States, breaking up old neighborhoods and re-distributing their inhabitants across the rapidly growing suburbs. As the older residents left, young people filled the urban neighborhoods. In this way, Fitz-Gerald argues, the Castro district was born, not simply as a result of the gay liberation movement but because of fundamental changes in the nature of identity and community in American culture.

FitzGerald identifies Falwell's heterosexual Christian organization and San Francisco's secular gay community, normally bitter enemies, as having more in common than they might suspect due to their shared identity as new groups of the 1960s. As a group whose members were both Christian and gay, as an innovative religious community that gathered its membership from the population flooding the Castro district and other urban gay enclaves during the years of its formation, the early UFMCC is a compelling example of a group founded on the basis of old U.S. traditions and new U.S. communities.

During its first eight years as a denomination, the UFMCC grew at a rate of approximately ten congregations per year.[6] In 2002, thirty-four years after the first MCC service, the denominational Web site claimed approximately 300 churches and over 40,000 members in eighteen countries.[7] Clearly this is a denomination on the move. The pressing question, then, is: Why?

Explanations of UFMCC Growth: Previous Theories

To date, there have been only two published attempts by authors outside the UFMCC to address the question of the denomination's growth: Bauer's study of MCC Denver and Warner's article on the denomination itself.[8] Both authors provide valuable insights into facets of the UFMCC's success.

Bauer's 1976 article takes a decidedly internal approach to the question of the UFMCC's attraction for the LGBT community. Echoing many UFMCC publications,[9] Bauer suggests that "the MCC has grown so rapidly because it is a workable solution to the two major problems facing the homophile community: religious 'respectability' and social acceptance."[10] He views acceptance by God or Jesus as the critical factor in the UFMCC's solution to each of these problems, and argues that the gays and lesbians attending MCC Denver in the mid-1970s had been conditioned not to expect any social or political solution to their oppression; they turned instead to spiritual affirmation of their sexual identities.[11] Bauer also makes the important observation that MCC congregations create strong social communities that assist members in dealing with their struggles.

Bauer, like other scholars interested in MCC, is especially curious about the link between an apparently radical subculture and evangelical Christianity. His conclusion resonates with the deprivation theory of new religious movements that was current at the time: arguing that fundamentalism arises as the result of a group's isolation from the cultural mainstream, Bauer suggests that lesbian and gay communities, isolated by societal prejudice, have responded especially well to a fundamentalist religion. While this interpretation strikes me as being the key weakness of Bauer's argument—because of both his misapplication of the term "fundamentalist" to the denomination and his apparent assumption that the majority of lesbians and gay men actually are drawn to MCC or to organized religion in general—his observations regarding the affirmation of acceptance by God and the presence of a strong LGBT community in the church are of great use in understanding the rapid growth of the UFMCC.

Any attempt to address the question of who was drawn initially to the UFMCC brings a particularly sociological issue to mind: namely, the question of the religious market. This is one theme of Warner's work on MCC. Warner characterizes Perry as a "religious entrepreneur" in the tradition of such famous American evangelists George Whitefield, Charles Grandison Finney, and Oral Roberts, and notes that part of Perry's success has been due to the existence of a "cultural market" for his church.[12] In 1968, this market was shaped by the presence of a gay male subculture that had been growing since World War II in metropolitan areas of the United States and by the fact that many members of that subculture suffered from "long-frustrated religious yearnings."[13] Warner suggests that Perry's new market, which in 1968 was virtually untapped by religious groups, had two crucial but logical aspects: homosexual identity and Christian inclinations.

Every successful entrepreneur, however, succeeds not only by cornering a market but by providing that market with a well-crafted product. Ultimately, Warner argues, the success of the UFMCC is attributable to the fact that "it is an American church."[14] Warner points out that churches in the United States have the capacity to serve as subcultural social spaces as well as bases for social action. In taking advantage of this capacity, the UFMCC provides its members with a source of community and a chance to address the external oppression suffered by many of its members. Moreover, Warner suggests, since religion historically has been a major source of LGBT oppression, it is a necessary factor in the struggle against and the healing from that oppression.

Warner's work moves beyond Bauer's earlier arguments, addressing questions of both external factors (the available market) and internal factors (the product offered by the UFMCC) in the growth of the denomination, as well as the UFMCC's role as a church and the ever-present question of its Pentecostal roots. The picture that emerges from early denominational materials is even more complex, however, suggesting a greater range of both external and internal factors that may have helped the UFMCC to become what it is today.

External (Social) Factors

In exploring the social factors that underlie the growth of the UFMCC, it is necessary to elaborate upon Perry's assertion that the UFMCC's success was in part a matter of timing. The social and cultural milieu of the urban United States in the late 1960s influenced both the initial founding of the UFMCC and the denomination's growth and success. In addition to the increase in religious individualism, five aspects of that milieu have been central to Perry's work: the civil rights movement, evolving trends in theology, the growth of evangelical churches in the late 1960s, the responses of the mainline churches to homosexuality, and the gay liberation movement.

The Civil Rights Movement

The late 1950s and the 1960s saw the development of a political movement in which religious organizations were actively and visibly involved in the struggle for greater social and legal recognition of a group of people: the black civil rights movement. The efforts undertaken by African Americans not only inspired other groups, such as Latinos, Native Americans, and women, to action; they also provided a model for religious involvement in such movements.

The Metropolitan Community Church, like many of those struggling for lesbian and gay rights, identified from the beginning with the movement spearheaded by Martin Luther King, Jr. Understanding their sexual identity to be innate, many LGBT leaders from the 1960s to the present have described their oppression as being similar in nature although not in history to that of African Americans. Metaphors of chains and enslavement are not uncommon in early discussions of lesbian and gay oppression in the UFMCC newsletter, *In Unity*.[15] In the second edition of this newsletter, which was dedicated to King's memory, an article written by Perry presents King and the movement he led as role models for the homosexual community. Perry praises King's non-violent tactics, his focus on freedom, and his emphasis on integration instead of separatism. "Metropolitan Community Church is much more than some 'gay' organization," Perry exclaims, sounding a recurrent note in UFMCC literature, "we are born again believers!"[16] Despite the intrinsically political nature of the UFMCC, Perry points readers' attention past sexual identity to the denomination's Christian (and here, evangelical) identity. He makes his integrationist goals even clearer in another article: "I want an America that is free from prejudice; so that labels like Blacks, Chicanos, Homosexuals, etc. won't exist anymore. . . . There will be only one label and that is American."[17]

Other sermons and articles published in the early issues of *In Unity* show the authors' identification both with contemporary oppressed minorities and with the biblical people of Israel. One letter to the editor of MCC San Diego's church newsletter, in extolling the virtues of MCC, proclaims, "The words attributed to Jesus are full of glorious color. Then, as now, black, white, brown, yellow, red are all beautiful," and "the Message [of Jesus] must come through the familiar symbols of [each] culture."[18] The implication here is that Jesus' message must also come to LGBT people in their own terms. Another author, picking up on an ever-popular biblical theme, says the following with reference to her "circle of gay friends": "I promised them that God would surely send a leader or shepherd who would be strong enough to lead them out of this desert of despair even as Moses was chosen to lead his people out of Egypt."[19] In statements such as these, lesbian and gay people become one oppressed minority among many in world history, and the way to freedom for all of these groups is to be found in God.

Theological Trends

Despite the Pentecostal roots of the UFMCC, the denomination's foundation and growth have been affected not only by the strength of evangelical Christianity in the 1960s and 1970s but also by liberal theological innovations. Perry highlighted this combination in a recent interview, wherein he described himself as "a liberal evangelical."[20] The two liberal developments whose effects can be seen most strongly in the UFMCC are liberation theology and ecumenism.

Liberation theology began in the 1960s in the Catholic churches of Central and South America as a theological movement that stressed the rights of the poor. By the end of the decade, African American theologians had adopted liberation theology and altered it to fit the situations of their own communities. As with the civil rights movement on the political level, liberation theology set an example on a Christian theological level for other oppressed minorities who were working to gain their rights. Thus, in the United States, liberation theology can be said to have influenced not only Chicano, Latino, and African American theologians, but also feminist, womanist, *mujerista,* and LGBT theologians—including those of the UFMCC.

In a documentary video produced by the UFMCC in 1984, the denomination is described as espousing a "liberation theology."[21] Beyond this self-description, however, UFMCC literature contains many theological affirmations of the rights of all minorities. One example is the letter to the editor mentioned above, wherein the author emphasizes the multicultural character of Jesus' audience and goes on to applaud the appearance of "black Holy Families in African churches."[22] More than anything else, the effect of liberation theology on the UFMCC is apparent in the emphasis on political involvement among denominational leaders. It is possible to argue that this church makes a political statement simply by existing as an organization of "practicing" LGBT people who are also practicing Christians. As of 1996, UFMCC churches, including the mother church, had been the victims of seventeen arson attacks, one of which killed over thirty people; clearly, the UFMCC is radical enough to attract violence.[23]

On another, more activist level, Perry himself was involved in the struggle for homosexual rights from the early days of the church. Just six months after MCC began, Perry and other church members attended a demonstration in San Francisco. In 1970, Perry fasted for ten days on the steps of the Los Angeles Federal Building in order to publicize the demand for legal rights for homosexuals. In 1971, he led a march from San Francisco to Sacramento in support of a bill that gave homosexuals greater public freedom. The UFMCC staged a demonstration for gay and lesbian rights at the 1972 Democratic convention, and this kind of activism has continued steadily up to the present day.[24]

The increasing trend toward ecumenical activity in liberal denominations during the 1960s also affected MCC's development and self-understanding, albeit more indirectly than liberation theology or the civil rights movement. Following a time-honored tradition in the United States that includes the black churches, ethnic Catholic parishes, and even such recent newcomers as the Korean Presbyterian churches, the UFMCC organized around a subcultural identity more than a particular theology; thus, from the beginning, this particular denomination attracted participants from many different Christian backgrounds. Willie Smith, one of the founding members of the church, had been raised as a Seventh-day Adventist, while Reverend Richard Ploen, the first pastor to join Perry's team, had studied at a Presbyterian seminary. Reverend Arthur Green, founder of MCC Chicago, was formerly affiliated with the old Catholic Church. As Perry reflected in 1972, "I knew that I was not starting another Pentecostal church. I was starting a church that would be truly ecumenical."[25]

Ecumenicity and inclusivity also play a role in the UFMCC's vision of itself as a chosen group with a special mission; these factors are especially apparent in an article from an early issue of *In Unity.* After relating the ways in which three of her "circles of friends" (which she labels people of color, gay people, and "flower children") had been rejected by churches, the author describes her discovery of MCC as the fulfillment of her "impossible dream," implying that it welcomes all rejected peoples. She closes the article by stating that "Metropolitan Community Church . . . is truly God's home on this earth."[26] With more than a touch of hyperbole, during an interview for the denomination's documentary film, Reverend Elder Nancy Wilson called the UFMCC "the most successful grassroots ecumenical organization since the Reformation."[27]

Growth of Evangelicalism

In *American Mainline Religion,* Wade Clark Roof and William McKinney argue that the recent history of religious groups in the United States has been characterized by a "collapse of the middle."[28] While the mainline denominations have been losing members, they suggest, more radical religious groups and more conservative ones have grown. In the 1960s, "Protestant evangelicalism and fundamentalism, neo-Pentecostalism, and some splinter faiths . . . grew at rates often exceeding the nation's population growth rate."[29] As the UFMCC has roots in Pentecostalism and some of its churches have retained a certain evangelical feel, it is tempting to include it in this group. There are two potential problems with such an identification, however. First, the breadth of theological positions encompassed by the UFMCC make it difficult to classify. There are enough liberal theologians in the denomination to make its classification as conservative impossible. Second, Roof and McKinney note that all of the conservative denominations that grew during the 1960s were highly "exclusivist and antiecumenical."[30] Again, MCC does not fit.

How, then, is UFMCC's growth to be understood in light of the general situation of American religion in the 1960s? The denomination is liberal in some ways, but most liberal churches were shrinking while it was expanding rapidly; the more radical religions were growing, but its evangelical tendencies make it a somewhat unusual colleague for radical religious groups; and most conservative and evangelical churches were growing as well, but they were exclusivist and the UFMCC is not. The answer to this question, in fact, may lie in the denomination's hybrid nature.

Many people who hear of the UFMCC ask in surprise what an LGBT person might want with an apparently conservative religion. At a basic level, however, the UFMCC can be described as a hybrid organization. It embodies conservative elements in its affirmation of charismatic gifts, certain aspects of its theology, its emphasis on evangelism, and its Pentecostal roots. Yet the denomination's very existence as a Christian church that affirms and celebrates LGBT people is radical, and its membership includes pastors and congregations on the far left of the theological continuum. Alongside the conservative push of some for the traditional morality of monogamy and avoidance of premarital sex, UFMCC pastors regularly marry same-sex couples, and they speak radically of developing a new "theology of sexuality."[31] Perhaps, then, the UFMCC somehow benefited from both the conservative effervescence and the growth of radical religions in the 1960s. One might even hypothesize that the political voices that appear in *In Unity* are those attracted to the UFMCC's radical side, while those that insist on the primacy of Christian identification and a focus on God are those drawn by the denomination's conservatism. Indeed, as will be discussed in more detail below, these opposing voices are a part of what makes the UFMCC so diverse.

Mainline Churches and Homosexuality

The homosexuality debates were also an important external factor in MCC's development. Though these debates developed most rapidly in the 1970s, religion and homosexuality already had been at issue in minor ways for over two decades when MCC began.[32] In his 1943 work *On Being a Real Person,* for example, inspirational writer Harry Emerson Fosdick addressed the necessity of training clergy to respond to the issue of homosexuality.[33] In 1946, eighty-five people calling themselves the Eucharistic Catholic Church attended a Christmas Eve service in a gay bar, and in 1964 the Council on Religion and the Homosexual was formed in San Francisco. Gary David Comstock identifies the first "groundbreaking" publication on religion and homosexuality as Derrick Sherwin Bailey's 1955 book, *Homosexuality and the Western Christian Tradition.*[34] As the 1960s dawned, however, the issue received increasing attention, both from individual scholars and theologians and from religious groups. Thus, the UFMCC took root in a time of rapidly increasing concern with homosexuality among mainline religious groups; on the heels of its inception (but probably triggered at least as much by the gay liberation movement as by the nascent denomination) came a rush of official statements on religion and homosexuality, beginning a debate that continues today.

The Gay Liberation Movement[35]

Before 1969, the most well-known and active groups supporting homosexual rights were the Mattachine Society and the Daughters of Bilitis. The Mattachine Society, begun as a semi-secret fraternal group and named after an organization of unmarried men in medieval and Renaissance France, was founded in 1948 by Harry Hay in Los Angeles. As originally conceived, the group was intended to provide a central source of community for (primarily male) homosexuals and to foster discussion of homosexuality; to the latter end, Hay included heterosexual professionals as well as homosexuals in the group. Included on the initial roster were a sociologist, a psychologist, and a Unitarian minister, all ostensibly heterosexual but interested in promoting discussion of the issue of homosexuality. The Mattachine Society founded a magazine, *One,* which eventually became the independent group known as ONE, Incorporated. The Mattachine itself reorganized in 1953 to become a more visible but also more conservative group whose main goals were education and research on homosexuality.

Two years later, in 1955, two San Francisco women formed a similar women's organization, the Daughters of Bilitis. This organization took its name from a fictional contemporary of Sappho; the term "daughters" was employed to make the group sound like any other American women's club, such as the Daughters of the American Revolution.[36] The Daughters of Bilitis followed much the same path as the Mattachine Society, emphasizing community, education, and research. It, too, soon spread across the nation (like the Mattachine Society, its first East Coast outpost was in New York) and founded a magazine, *The Ladder.* In the 1960s, these two groups adopted the term "homophile," originally coined in the 1950s as a synonym for "homosexual," to describe the growing movement for homosexual rights.

The gay, or "homophile," subculture of Los Angeles in which Perry came out was thus the home of a major homosexual rights group, but as Toby Marotta argues, the sixties were also a time of reformist focus for such groups.[37] The homophile movement, Marotta points out, took shape during the McCarthy years, when homosexuality often was considered to be linked with socialism or communism. Thus, homophile leaders even in the sixties were careful to emphasize education rather than political activism, to work in concert with government groups, and to foster friendships among influential people. Moreover, the central homophile message, as exemplified by Bobby at the beginning of the chapter, was a normalizing one. As Harry Hay described it in a 1974 interview, "that position—'we're exactly the same [as heterosexuals]'—characterized the whole Mattachine Society from 1953 to 1969."[38]

One event in 1969, however, sparked a change that had been building for several years: the Stonewall Riots. On June 27, police raided the Stonewall Inn on Christopher Street in New York's Greenwich Village, intending to close down the bar and to arrest employees, patrons without identification, and suspected cross-dressers. This was not an unusual occurrence in any city that housed gay bars; the difference was that for various reasons, this time the victims resisted. The resulting crowd threw bottles, rocks, and anything else they could find at the building; some threw a trash can full of burning paper through a window. The uproar drew others, most notably gay members of New Left organizations who had been planning and agitating for a gay revolution. These people saw the riot at the Stonewall Inn as their opportunity.

Repeat riots at the same location followed for several successive nights, and hopeful new leaders began printing flyers and looking for further chances to organize. They initially attempted to work together with the homophile organizations already in place in New York. Both the Mattachine Society and the Daughters of Bilitis had already been under some internal pressure to radicalize their activities, but ultimately the radicals made little headway within the homophile movement. An alternative, more activist organization soon formed, known as the Gay Liberation Front; within a few years, most branches of the Mattachine Society and the Daughters of Bilitis had faded into the background or disappeared entirely.

Marotta sees the Gay Liberation Front, spearhead of the more commonly known gay liberation movement, as a combination of members he calls radicals and those he calls revolutionaries.[39] While the latter group was concerned with taking radical, primarily political measures to change the place of homosexuals in society, Marotta argues that the former took its cue from the Black Power movement and focused on creating a sense of identity and pride among homosexuals. It was out of this latter side of the movement that the now-common Gay Pride celebrations stemmed; the first were held in June of 1970 to commemorate the anniversary of the Stonewall Riots.

Lesbian Feminism

An overview of the changes in homosexual political and social action in the late 1960s and early 1970s would not be complete without a discussion of the feminist and lesbian-feminist movements. Awareness of the differences between lesbian and gay male experiences was present as early as the founding of the Daughters of Bilitis; the advent of second-wave feminism in the late 1960s and the movement of lesbians between feminist groups, homophile organizations, and gay liberation organizations indicated a testing and redefinition of boundaries. With the growing consciousness of the feminist movement, lesbians became increasingly aware of sexism within the homophile and gay liberation movements. They also began to make the related observation that due to differences in the lesbian and gay male subcultures, many of the issues crucial to the gay male population were of little concern to lesbians. The solution, however, was not simply to join the feminist movement, for while lesbians often experienced sexism in gay rights organizations, they encountered homophobia and heterosexism in feminist groups. Indeed, feminist leader Betty Friedan once referred to out lesbians within feminism as a "lavender menace" whose demands for rights as homosexuals could permanently damage feminist efforts toward (heterosexual) women's rights.[40] Lesbian activists, influenced by both the feminist movement and the gay liberation movement but fully comfortable in neither, thus founded their own organizations as well as a movement that became known as lesbian feminism —and this movement, too, came to have an impact on the growth and development of the UFMCC.

Troy Perry thus held his first service at an auspicious time. Influenced by his Pentecostal background, by the civil rights movement, and by the political activity of American churches, Perry served his first communion as the snowball of gay rights, lesbian feminism, and homosexual issues in religion began to roll. In addition to being background or external factors in the development of the UFMCC, the rapid growth of the movements for gay and lesbian rights provided Perry with a crucial internal factor: his market. Before turning to the question of Perry's clientele, however, it is important to examine two other factors internal to his organization: leadership and evangelism.

Internal Factors

Leadership

Warner points to the first crucial internal aspect of the UFMCC's success when he calls Perry a religious entrepreneur and classes him with men such as Whitefield and Finney. However, recognition of the important role played by individual leaders in the development of new religious movements also recalls to Max Weber's discussion of the prophet. For Weber, the prophet is a dedicated leader with a personal call; she or he is also a bearer of charisma and is often the founder of a religious group. Weber further distinguishes between the ethical prophet, who specializes in laws and doctrine, and the exemplary prophet, who leads by example.[41] Perry can be understood to be a bit of both.[42]

Certainly Perry fits the role of the prophet in general. Aside from the obvious fact that he successfully started a new Protestant denomination, Perry has been extremely dedicated to his church from the beginning. During MCC's second year, for example, Perry supported himself and his mother on a small salary that had to be supplemented occasionally with the congregation's food donations to the needy. "The success of the church," he relates, "brought . . . among other blessings, a steady income and hot meals on the dining room table."[43] This is perhaps a small factor, but it indicates the struggles Perry undertook to get MCC off the ground.

Perry's sense of a personal call was quite strong, as is his charisma. Every history of the UFMCC relates Perry's account of his conversation with God wherein he says he learned that God wanted him to start a church—*now*.[44] And although Warner is accurate in observing that Perry "is not a scholar, an intellectual, or even an eloquent speaker," Perry's sermons have all of the fire, vigor, and crowd-handling savvy of the best evangelical preachers.

While charisma is an important aspect of Perry's ministry, Perry also embodies aspects of Weber's ethical prophet. He began his work in the LGBT community with a new interpretation of old laws—an interpretation that defined homosexuality as innate and God-given—and he defined gay and lesbian Christians as people with a special mission in the world. Moreover, he led his congregation into its mission by example: by preaching, protesting, and ministering, Perry put his beliefs regarding the new law of God into action.

Evangelism

If Perry inherited his charisma and "fiery rhetoric," as the UFMCC documentary calls it, from his Pentecostal background, he also inherited another practice that was a powerful factor in the UFMCC's growth: evangelism, or aggressive religious marketing. MCC was making evangelistic efforts as early as July of 1969, when Perry began to hold prayer meetings in suburban Orange County at the request of an MCC Los Angeles deacon. That mission eventually disbanded because of a leadership conflict, but Perry learned from the experience and set requirements in place for greater organization of subsequent missions. MCC Los Angeles church members, including one member who lived in San Diego, also invited Perry and others to lead services in their hometowns. Perry's response to the San Diego invitation was to hold a weekend revival, complete with church choir. Sixty-nine people attended, and the San Diego mission developed shortly thereafter.

Once the UFMCC was formed, evangelism remained important. Sermons reprinted in *In Unity* often stress the importance of spreading the news of God's love to others in the gay and lesbian community, and a report at the second General Conference of the UFMCC "recommended that the Fellowship aggressively start establishing more churches across America."[45] Perry also was careful to attend to the needs of those from diverse religious backgrounds who were attracted to his church. In addition to recognizing the ecumenism of his new organization, he saw the importance of appealing to a wide variety of Christian sensibilities.

At the first meeting of MCC, for instance, at the suggestion of a Congregational minister, Perry preached in a robe instead of the typical Pentecostal minister's suit and tie. As the church developed, Perry relates, Reverend Richard Ploen's research efforts were "most helpful in gleaning what we needed from other denominations' ceremonies."[46] Perry was aware from the start that his mission field extended well beyond the boundaries of Pentecostalism, and he was prepared to adjust his church as much as was necessary to attract the LGBT Christians with whom he longed to share what he viewed as God's new revelation. Ultimately, however, no mission effort, no matter how carefully planned, can be successful without a receptive audience to missionize.

The Market

In 1968, lesbians and gay men in many metropolitan areas considered their sexual orientation to be a part of their identity rather than an aberrant behavior or an illness, and they were beginning to be aware of the possibility of increased visibility. Moreover, Perry began his work in the city that hosted the founding of both the Mattachine Society and one of the foremost gay news magazines, the *Advocate.* By the time the UFMCC was organized in 1970, the Stonewall Riots were last year's news and the first Gay Pride celebrations had already taken place. The Gay Liberation Front had formed in New York and was busy demanding gay rights and fostering gay pride, and New York's Radicalesbians had just come into existence. When the UFMCC dedicated its Los Angeles mother church in February of 1971, Perry noted the attendance of representatives from the Daughters of Bilitis and the Mattachine Society; ONE, Incorporated; the Gay Liberation Front; and the Society for Individual Rights, a San Francisco–based gay group.[47]

Many lesbian, gay, bisexual, and transgender people no doubt watched these events from afar, held back by still-extant sodomy statutes; by the threat of job discrimination, excommunication, or family rejection; or simply by the fact that they were not inclined toward radical social action. Nevertheless, the growing visibility and self-acceptance of LGBT people across the country surely had an impact even on those who did not participate.

The one missing component in the new movement was an organized religious base. Granted, the Marxists in the movement would have been little interested in such an addition, but it is a fact of U.S. history that for every Marxist facet in movements of the 1960s and 1970s, there was a matching, overtly religious one. Moreover, liberation theology itself contains more than a dash of Marxism. If self-conscious religion had joined Marxism in all of these other movements, the gay liberation movement was unlikely to be different.

In 1968, however, the LGBT religious market had not blossomed fully, and no one had yet emerged to corner it. Perry's product, to use a purely economic metaphor, was the first to appear on the market. Not that the situation remained that way for long: within a few years, three other major LGBT religious groups appeared on the scene. These were Dignity, a gay and lesbian Catholic group; Integrity, a similar group within the Episcopalian church; and the first LGBT Jewish synagogue, Beth Chayim Chadashim in Los Angeles. All three are still in existence today, along with many other LGBT synagogues, Buddhist and Muslim groups, pagan circles, organizations for LGBT people in most mainline Protestant denominations, a growing African American gay and lesbian church movement, a Mormon group, a Seventh-day Adventist group, an Orthodox Christian group, a Southern Baptist group, and an umbrella organization for evangelicals (among others).[48]

Why Pentecostal?

Discussion of the UFMCC's development cannot be closed without returning to the question that intrigued Bauer and Warner, the juxtaposition that never ceases to startle those who have not yet heard of the UFMCC: Why on earth would "the lesbian and gay denomination" be one founded by a former Pentecostal minister, complete with outbreaks of charismatic gifts and, on some issues, a fairly conservative official theology?

While Bauer's thesis that lesbians and gay men are drawn to Pentecostalism as a result of their social isolation remains unconvincing, Warner's argument regarding theology and divine acceptance is stronger. The argument can be pushed further, however, because Warner's analysis does not fully account for the fact that not all LGBT people, or even all LGBT Christians, have joined MCC. It is to be expected that many have refrained from joining because of a disaffection with religion in general or a dislike of Christian language in particular. However, if a powerful affirmation of identity was the central factor at stake in the UFMCC's appeal, why is it that neither UFMCC publications nor my own research indicate any significant percentage of previously non-Christian converts? There are no solid data available on this issue, but all published material on the UFMCC, as well as the present study, suggests that the majority of those attracted to the denomination have come from Christian backgrounds. Many seem to have been disaffected with the organized churches, to be sure, but the indications are that most were fairly religious at least in their youth.

The clue to this puzzle lies in a tension suggested by my earlier characterization of the UFMCC as a hybrid organization. The question of which of the denomination's identities should be foremost exists in large part because of the UFMCC's hybrid nature, and it is clearly present in the early editions of *In Unity*. While no actual arguments take place around the question, even articles within the same issue of the newsletter often stress very different aspects of the denomination, and each explicitly downplays the other aspect. The crucial question for these early members of the UFMCC seems to be: "Are we gay and lesbian Christians or Christian gays and lesbians?"[49]

Articles and columns from *In Unity*, especially in the first year and a half of publication, repeatedly emphasize the importance of gay liberation, gay pride, and gay activism. Printed sermons explain the necessity of evangelism in order to spread the message of divine acceptance to those who still labor under misconceptions forced upon them by unsupportive churches. In contrast, interspersed with these political pieces are sermons and articles that barely mention homosexuality at all; as one columnist advises her readers, "let us get off of the 'soapbox of sex' and climb aboard the 'bandwagon of Christ.'"[50] Another article in a later issue demonstrates the ways in which traditional Christian morality can be applied to the lives of homosexuals. Entitled "Ten Golden Rules for a Happy Gay Marriage," the article stresses such timeworn values as love, loyalty, "abstain[ing] from the angry word," family prayer, and loving one's neighbors.[51]

Articles that promote a same-sex version of traditional Christian life, as well as other early pieces that celebrate MCC's importance in bringing a Christian standard of morality to the chaotic gay male world of the late 1960s, suggest one role that MCC and the UFMCC might have played, and perhaps still play, for those who join. In a milieu of rapidly expanding LGBT activist groups, social clubs, and other secular organizations, not only did Christian LGBT people want an affirmation of their identity before God, they also sought a place where they could be both lesbian, gay, bisexual, or transgender, *and* Christian.[52]

It is already clear that few LGBT people in the late sixties and early seventies would have found their sexual orientation or transgender identity unequivocally affirmed in mainline churches; though such churches have become important sources of support and community for some, others still do not find that affirmation today. In addition, however, the long history of religious repression of homosexuals and other "sexual deviants" has resulted in a particularly hostile attitude toward organized religion, especially Christianity, among many LGBT people. LGBT Christians, therefore, are caught:

while many churches still reject their sexual or gender identities, many LGBT communities scorn their religion. In 1997, I heard an MCC pastor relate that at a recent Gay Pride parade she had "come out as a Christian" to the other lesbians with whom she was marching. Many of those present at the service laughed and nodded, clearly identifying with her experience. Thus, these tensions continue for some today.[53]

Beyond the Roots

By the mid-1970s, the UFMCC once again had new concerns. It was grappling, as was the gay liberation movement, with the demands of women for equal access and representation. The denomination's first woman minister, Freda Smith, was licensed in 1972, and she immediately began to agitate for change. Her first step was to demand at the General Conference that the male pronoun used to refer to ministers throughout the denominational by-laws be changed to "he or she" and other references be changed to "man or woman." This took a considerable amount of effort, she explained in one interview, because she had to make a new motion for every single sentence.[54] Women's influence in the denomination grew slowly; Perry and Swicegood claim that in 1973—five years after the church was founded—approximately 10 percent of UFMCC members were women.[55] Today, however, the number of female members has increased significantly and there are many more female ministers than were licensed in the early seventies. The UFMCC also encourages the use of inclusive language in all of its services.

The denomination's other major move by the mid-seventies was a step across the Atlantic Ocean in order to begin an international outreach. The first church to be chartered outside the United States was MCC London, which became official in 1973.[56] A congregation in Toronto followed in short order, then a group of Biafrans, an ethnic minority in Nigeria, started a church.[57] An Australian church was underway in Sydney by 1975. Currently, Australia holds the record for the greatest number of MCC congregations outside the United States, and it recently hosted the first UFMCC General Conference to be held outside the United States. More than three decades after Perry held the first MCC service, the UFMCC's rise to success has not yet reached its apogee.

Success, however, is a complex phenomenon. As discussed above, the UFMCC took many of its cues from the social currents of the 1960s: the civil rights movement, liberation theology, the homophile movement, and the growing interest of mainline churches in the issue of homosexuality. It also benefited from the growth of religious individualism during this period. Additionally, Perry caught the wave of new gay and lesbian (and eventually

LGBT) movements that began to rise less than a year after MCC began. Yet Perry's success also rests on internal factors, such as his own charisma and organizational abilities and the abilities of those who helped to found the church. Furthermore, his sensitivity to the needs of his ecumenical market can only have helped matters. The UFMCC's message provided a powerful affirmation of LGBT identity, while the uniqueness of a gay and lesbian Christian organization (or a Christian gay and lesbian organization) drew those who were struggling to find a home where both identities would be accepted and nurtured.

In the end, however, factors specific to MCC cannot offer a complete explanation for its continued survival and growth. FitzGerald, examining four communities that were contemporaries of MCC, sees a similar combination of internal and external factors. Of the thousands of experimental communities founded during the 1960s and 1970s, many lasted only a few years, and only a handful actually grew in addition to surviving. Making an argument that harks back to Weber's concept of the routinization of charisma, FitzGerald suggests that the successful communities were those that developed structure in addition to continuing to respond to changes in the surrounding culture.

The UFMCC, in fact, displays both of these attributes. A denomination by the end of its second year, it attended to the question of structure from the founding of its first mission. Moreover, UFMCC leaders have continued to press for inclusion in the ecumenical movement and have attempted to address changing issues of concern in LGBT communities, such as AIDS, transgender issues, the full inclusion of people of color, and marriage rights. Perhaps most important to the survival of the UFMCC, however, is the failure of Perry's original goal of assimilation.

Rather than becoming obsolete through the integration of LGBT people into mainstream America, the UFMCC has survived and prospered because of the survival of its form of community. As FitzGerald argues, Sun City and other retirement communities remain successful not only because of their structure but also because of the continuing tendency in American society to form what FitzGerald calls "age-segregated communities."[58] Falwell's church and the Moral Majority grew astronomically because of the addition of political structure but equally because of the ongoing tradition of evangelical community in the United States. Like these and many other organizational children of the sixties, Perry's mission in the LGBT marketplace is a continuing success not only because it took on denominational structure but, more important, because the formation of community around minority sexual or gender identity continues to be a valid and popular practice in American culture.

But what leads people to MCC today? Organized religious options for LGBT people are on the increase in both number and variety, so this question is becoming increasingly pressing. When study participants faced the apparently diverging roads of Christianity and LGBT identity, they took it upon themselves to alter the geography by turning divergent paths into convergent ones. In the same way, when faced with old worlds wherein LGBT identity and Christian belief cannot coexist, MCC churches create a new world in which LGBT Christians are the norm—and this may be another reason for MCC's continuing popularity in the LGBT religious market.

4 Creating New Worlds

During an interview early in September 1998, I asked Reverend Patrick what brings people to his church. "I think the reason people come for the first time," he responded, "is they've either heard something about this church or they're curious about religion in general, or spirituality, and wonder—because I think we're identified as a place where gay and lesbian people go—'Maybe this is different than the kind of religion that I've learned not to like. . . . So I'll check it out, and see if it lives up to my expectations.' Or just sort of like, 'I can't imagine what this would be like.' That's what I felt before I ever went to MCC: 'I can't imagine what this would even look like.' . . . I was curious. And I think a lot of people come out of a kind of curiosity like that." When I asked why people continue to attend, he speculated, "I think . . . the reasons that people stay—is they find spiritual nourishment, intellectual stimulation. . . . I think music and connection with people that . . . how do I want to say— feeds the soul. . . . And I think the sense of community that people get. . . . They like being a part of something where people have some vision for correcting major injustices in the world, and they want to be a part of a community that's making a difference. . . . People learn something. I think the main reasons, really, that people come—keep coming back here is that they learn something that they value." He later added that his own early experiences in MCC had offered him a strong community but had not been fulfilling religiously. "I would like for this church not to be like that," he told me. "I would like for it to be something that challenges people in a forward-looking way."[1]

Robert left the Catholic church and the seminary in the early 1970s. As he explained in the survey: "I knew I was gay and that I would not be able to lie about it *and* be a priest. So—I left." He did not set foot in a church for twenty years, but in 1990 he decided to try MCC. When we talked in August of 1998, I queried Robert about his experience that first day back in church. "What made you decide to come back?" I asked. "Spur of the moment," he said with a smile. "Sunday morning—nine-thirty—and I've never forgotten it. I just decided . . . I had ended a twenty-year relationship, was living by myself and having a hard time . . . it did not end nicely. So I was . . . just a wreck. And so . . . one morning—it was Sunday morning . . . and I decided, 'I think—I think I want to try it.' I'd never been to one [an MCC church]. So I called the church, liked the recording, got directions, and just decided to go. And the service started at ten-thirty. And I came run—I was late—came running up, and the pastor . . . was standing at the door, waiting to process in and start church. And I came running up, and he stopped me, and he said, 'Slow down,' and he just put . . . his hand on my shoulder, and he says, 'You're home now. You don't have to run anymore.' And I went, boing!" Robert laughed. "Lightning strikes! So I went in and sat down. And I've never left."[2]

Sharla's connection to MCC began in another state in a congregation well known for its innovative theology and services. This suited her well, as Sharla is more interested in spiritual exploration than in Christian teachings. "I was drawn to MCC," she wrote, "*because* I was coming out. I was looking for people I could feel comfortable being with and coming out to. I didn't have any negative feelings about homosexuality, at least not any brought on by my religious beliefs. Finding MCC at the right time was very important to my acceptance of my being lesbian, and I found my sense of faith and spirituality also heightened (probably a combination of my coming out to myself and the peace that brings and the MCC community I found)." Later in the survey, she added: "Coming out was a very spiritual experience for me and it felt natural to share that time with spiritual people. About 1½ to 2 years after I first walked into MCC, my interest faded a bit. The messages didn't seem so poignant, so maybe it was just time for me to look other places for spirituality, including within (which probably would not have been possible without my MCC experience)." She has attended MCC Valle Rico "occasionally, but the energy is a little different there and perhaps I am not in a frame of mind to enjoy organized religion right now."[3]

Sue, who attends Oceanfront MCC when her work schedule allows, came to the church not because of rejection but because her children and ex-husband attended the Methodist church she was accustomed to attending. Sue wrote that although her husband was very supportive, when she entered into a relationship with another woman, "going to the Methodist church became not an option. I . . . would not put my children and ex husband in such an uncomfortable position. So we started to look for another church to attend and came across MCC through an ad in the local Gay newspaper. I have never had any doubts that God loves me as I am. But to be able to express my love for another woman in church by holding hands or a light kiss was such a joyous thing for me. For although we could attend the Methodist church and did so on Christmas etc. with my children, any outward physical display of affection for one another would have made those around us very uncomfortable. But even now that I am single I attend [OMCC] whenever possible, for I know that the Holy Spirit is working there. That is why I attend, not because it is a 'Gay' church. But for the blessing my spirit receives and the message my heart hears. God loves me. As much now as the day I was born."[4]

What brings people to MCC churches, what makes them stay, and why do they leave? As the words of Reverend Patrick, Robert, Sharla, and Sue make clear, people come to MCC congregations in a variety of ways and for a variety of reasons. In an earlier decade, the central reason for MCC attendance would have been obvious: it was one of the only organizations in which LGBT Christians could be open about both aspects of that identity. But such is not the case today—and even if it were, it is not necessarily self-evident that people would choose to give up their home churches for the sake of being out.

This chapter begins with an overview of the wide variety of religious options available to LGBT Christians today—including everything from highly conservative churches wherein LGBT Christians must pass as heterosexuals to LGBT religious organizations other than MCC. While Comstock has found that non-LGBT religious groups attract reasonably large numbers of lesbians, gay men, and bisexuals,[5] many of the participants in this study draw a clear line between LGBT congregations and those that are accepting of LGBT people but are predominantly heterosexual. The difference, for such respondents, lies in the fact that non-LGBT religious groups, whether accepting or not, still function within the rubric of an old world in which LGBT and Christian identity are divergent. Even accepting congregations often have members who disapprove of the presence of LGBT people in the church, and even when such people are not vocal, the minority status of LGBT church members speaks volumes in itself. Welcomed and celebrated they may be, but in non-LGBT religious organizations, LGBT Christians remain a small population. Some of the participants in this study consider such situations to be opportunities for the education of heterosexual Christians. Many others, however, prefer a group wherein their status as "true" Christians not only is affirmed but is never even questioned. This is the new world offered by MCC.

Traditions, Tensions, Innovations

LGBT people who choose to stay within the "straight" churches experience a wide range of reactions from others in their congregations, including enthusiastic welcomes, acceptance, indifference, sympathetic if misguided attempts at healing, fear, and revulsion. Correspondingly, they have a wide range of options for self-presentation, from being completely closeted to openly affirming their sexual or gender identity. Because understanding why people choose to attend MCC also involves understanding why they do *not* choose other churches or groups, this chapter begins with a discussion of the options available to LGBT Christians in the United States at the turn of the millennium.

For the sake of simplicity, this section is divided into three categories: churches where LGBT people tend to be closeted, accepting congregations, and LGBT Christian groups other than MCC. For the most part (but there are notable exceptions), such categorizations follow denominational lines. In conservative denominations and within Catholicism, out LGBT people are more likely to face concerted hostility, while it is more often within the mainline and liberal denominations that active movements may exist to welcome LGBT Christians. It should be said at the outset, however, that reality is nowhere near as simple as such groupings might suggest. Interview participants often mentioned, for instance, that personal contact with even the most conservative of Christians could lead to acceptance or at least a grudging tolerance.[6] Region, too, can make a difference in the attitude of a church and its congregants toward LGBT members, as the mainline denominations have painfully discovered during divisive battles over the status of LGBT Christians.

The individual nature of a congregation and its leaders also can foster approaches to LGBT members that fly in the face of denominational attitudes. For instance, shortly before the Southern Baptist Convention's infamous boycott of Disney, one Southern Baptist church in North Carolina performed a commitment ceremony for two gay men and another licensed a gay minister.[7] The two churches were later expelled from the denomination, but the fact remains that they undertook these actions while still a part of it.

Ethnicity, too, can play an important role in determining the nature of a congregation's attitudes toward its LGBT members. Traditional ideas about gender and family in many Latino communities, for instance, reinforce the conservative teachings of many Catholic and Pentecostal churches. Asian American LGBT people often report similar experiences. And in African American churches, LGBT people are sometimes attacked as a threat to the ongoing struggle to strengthen the black family.[8] Yet some heterosexual members of these communities have noticed a similarity between the experiences of LGBT people and their own experiences as ethnic minorities in a white world and have become strong allies in the struggle for LGBT affirmation in the churches. The Progressive National Baptist Convention, for example, took a stand in 1994 against discrimination on the basis of sexual orientation, and Jesse Jackson's Rainbow Coalition recently formed ties with the UFMCC in the fight against hate crimes.[9]

Traditions: The Christian Closet

In November 1990, *Christianity Today* ran a brief article entitled "The Evangelical Closet." Set off by a large photograph of a young man gripping the edges of an upper-story window, the article suggests that there may be as many people "struggling" with homosexuality in evangelical churches as there are in the broader population. After brief and polite attention to the argument that homosexuality is innate, the author devotes the final two-thirds of the piece to contentions that it is a curable condition and notes the importance of making homosexuality visible in evangelical circles for the sake of those "struggling" in silence.[10]

In her study of *Christianity Today*'s portrayal of the LGBT community, Didi Herman notes a decided shift toward extremism in the early 1990s. Concomitant with a marked increase in discussions of evil and the demonic, discourse on lesbians and gay men moved from a focus on healing to dire warnings about the growth of "gay power." Although the publication was inching back toward a centrist position by the mid-1990s, Herman notes, it remained well aware of, and distinctly disturbed by, the growing visibility of LGBT people in mainstream U.S. culture.[11]

Within the culture of conservative and evangelical Christianity, those LGBT people who do not wish to be "healed" often are forced to keep a very low profile. That they are indeed present, however, is attested to by the existence of the LGBT support network known as Evangelicals Concerned and by the gay conservative Christians studied by Edward R. Gray and Scott Thumma.[12]

It is not only within such virulently anti-LGBT circles that LGBT people must remain quiet about their sexual or gender identity, however. The stance of both the Vatican and U.S. bishops on homosexuality, for example, emphasizes celibacy and considers acting on one's same-sex desires to be sinful. To many of those I interviewed who had been involved in Catholicism, the idea of regularly confessing activities they did not consider wrong was ludicrous; therefore, unless they had access to supportive Catholic congregations, the closet was the only viable option.[13] Similar cases also exist among the more conservative congregations of the mainline churches.

Tensions: The Affirming Movements[14]

The mainline and liberal denominations are an increasingly viable alternative for many LGBT Christians, but the path to complete acceptance is not an easy one in most of these groups. Aside from MCC, for instance, the only major religious organizations in the country that officially bar anti-LGBT discrimination in ordination are the United Church of Christ (UCC), Reform and Reconstructionist Judaism, and the Unitarian Universalist Association. As with the Southern Baptist church in North Carolina, other denominations have gained LGBT clergy through the actions of individual congregations or bishops. However, openly LGBT clergy in many of these denominations constantly run the risk of being stripped of their credentials by the denomination's governing body.

Though no major religious group has yet agreed to marry same-sex couples in the same way as it marries heterosexuals (and even the UFMCC is careful to call such ceremonies "unions" rather than "marriages"), the status of "commitment ceremonies" for same-sex couples is similar to that of LGBT ordination. A couple seeking an officiant from a mainline or liberal group to perform such a ceremony would have the most luck in the UCC, a Unitarian Universalist congregation, or Reform or Reconstructionist Judaism. With some searching, however, they could probably find a willing minister and congregation in most of the mainline denominations and even, as mentioned above, among the Southern Baptists.

It is a more theological question that currently divides the mainline and liberal churches. As evidence has mounted to support the claim that homosexual, bisexual, and transgender identities are inherent and may be genetically determined, most mainline organizations have accepted this theory and have gone on to advocate civil rights and anti-discrimination protection in non-religious contexts, at least for lesbians and gay men (as with many other discussions, bisexuals and transgender people often have been excluded from these policy statements). Yet conservatives and many moderates in these denominations have found biblical anti-LGBT arguments too strong to ignore and have refused to back statements that affirm the acceptability of *acting* on one's sexual or gender identity.[15] Celibacy, therefore, can open doors that remain shut to LGBT people with life partners. In these denominations, the best homosexual is one who is publicly indistinguishable from (single) heterosexuals.

Policy statements, though, are far from being the end of the story. During the 1990s, movements began in six different Protestant denominations to identify individual congregations as safe places for lesbian and gay churchgoers. These movements are known by various names. Presbyterians have the More Light movement, Disciples of Christ and United Church of Christ the Open and Affirming movements, Lutherans the Reconciled in Christ movement, United Methodists the Reconciling movement, and Baptists the Welcoming and Affirming movement. In each case, a congregation that wishes to work toward self-identification as More Light, Reconciling, and so on goes through a process of education, discussion, and meetings before voting as a group on the issue. The movements have been growing rapidly, and today it is possible in most metropolitan areas of California to open a telephone book and find several churches advertising such status.[16]

After the dismissals and ambiguous acceptance offered by many churches, the accepting movements have been welcome indeed for LGBT Christians and for their families and friends; some of the participants in this study eventually left MCC for accepting congregations within their childhood churches. Though MCC fills many needs, the accepting churches offer familiar hymnals and liturgies learned by heart, and sometimes the comfort of tradition can be a powerful call.[17]

Working from Ralph McFadden's brief article on lesbians and gay men in the Church of the Brethren,[18] Comstock identifies three main themes in the reasons given by lesbian, gay, and bisexual people for choosing to remain in conservative or mainstream churches. The first turns on the meaning of suffering in Christianity and associates the suffering of closeted or beleaguered LGBT people with the suffering of Jesus. The second Comstock describes as risking: a belief that only by taking the risk of staying within one's own church can one hope to impact that church. Finally, a stronger version of the same theme is embraced by those who are fighting. These people believe that leaving their churches means turning over denominational control to anti-LGBT conservatives. To leave is, in effect, to capitulate.[19] These reasons, and probably more as well, account for the considerable (though to date uncounted) number of LGBT people who remain—closeted, open, or activist—within conservative and mainstream denominations.

Despite the efforts and heartfelt convictions of accepting churches, however, and despite the potential persuasiveness of these reasons for staying, sometimes openness and activism are not enough. For transgender Christians, the problem often lies in the fact that mainstream culture is becoming open to sexual minorities far more rapidly than to transgender women and men. An accepting congregation may be ready for Kim and Carla, but it may struggle to open its arms to Maureen who was christened as Marcus.

A second problem may lie with the outvoted minority in the congregation, who continue to believe that there is something intrinsically disordered about LGBT people. One woman who currently attends Oceanfront MCC wrote the following in the survey: "The minister from the Methodist church was very accepting as were many of the congregants. The minister in fact had a commitment ceremony for my partner and I at a later date." However, such support was not enough because it was not unanimous; in this case, there were children to protect. "Some people in the . . . church were bothered by lesbianism. I had children going to that church and to protect them from some hurtful gossip I started going to an MCC where we all felt very comfortable."[20]

While some respondents want simply to be accepted as members of the congregation, for others this is insufficient. LGBT people, they say, face particular difficulties in the world, and any congregation that pronounces itself an ally of LGBT people must also be prepared to address these difficulties on both a public and a personal level. One man told me, "I've seen some embracing churches, but very few of them will go out of their way to address the specific problems that gays and lesbians, bisexual and transgender have."[21] Robert, whose story appears at the beginning of this chapter, holds a similar position. "There are a number of Christian churches I can go to that are even supportive," he explained, "but none that embrace the community quite so broadly [as MCC]."

I clarified: "You choose not to go [to accepting churches] because of the community?" and Robert responded, "I just think there's more work for me to do in a gay and lesbian church like MCC. I could go and I could become a member of a Unitarian church or Unity church and probably be comfortable there just as a member. But that's not what . . . I've got more work to do than that. So I think my own personal ministry is with MCC."

"What do you see yourself doing?" I asked. And Robert, who had left the seminary nearly thirty years before, replied, "I'm moving towards being licensed."[22]

Innovations: LGBT Groups

As the debate over LGBT people in the churches has become increasingly heated, more and more groups welcoming only LGBT people and their allies have formed within these denominations. Some groups, such as the UCC's United Church Coalition for Lesbian and Gay Concerns and the Unitarian group Interweave, are supported both officially and financially by their denominations. Others, such as Presbyterians for Lesbian/Gay Concerns and American Baptists Concerned, operate independently. But today organizations exist that support lesbian, gay, and sometimes bisexual and transgender people in nearly every major faith in the United States, from the National Gay Pentecostal Alliance to AXIOS (a group for Orthodox Christians), the Muslim organization al-Fatiha, and the Mormon group known as Affirmation.[23]

While many of these organizations exist only for the purposes of support and sometimes activism, one is notable in offering religious services as well. Dignity, an organization for LGBT Catholics, was the second major LGBT Christian group to form in the United States; it was founded in San Diego shortly after MCC began. A national organization with a sister group in Canada, Dignity listed sixty chapters in its online directory as of August 2002.[24] Although Dignity's masses are not officially Catholic masses because Dignity has been banned by the church hierarchy, Leonard Norman Primiano notes that at the masses he attended, "the powers bestowed at priestly ordination were all the legitimacy Dignity's priests needed."[25]

In addition to denominationally affiliated groups, there are independent organizations other than MCC that serve the LGBT Christian community. The number of black lesbian and gay churches, for example, is small but growing, spurred in part by the efforts of James S. Tinney in Washington, D.C., and Carl Bean in Los Angeles.[26] Evangelicals have access to a number of local groups across the country in addition to the national organization, Evangelicals Concerned.[27] Even locally, a group with evangelical leanings meets weekly at the LGBT community center in Valle Rico, just a few miles from MCCVR. This group, in fact, tends to attract some of those for whom MCCVR is too liberal, and MCCVR appeals to those who find the evangelical group too conservative.

The question remains, however: Why might some people choose MCC over these other LGBT groups? Comstock suggests that inclusion of women, bisexuals, and ethnic minorities is often a stumbling block for such organizations.[28] It could be argued, however, that similar issues might be at stake in some people's rejection of certain MCC congregations. In other cases, an individual factor may be at work: the local chapter of one group may be more inclusive than the local chapter of another, even though on a national level the groups work hard to be inclusive.

Though Primiano also points to the issue of gender as a problem in Dignity, he adds a helpful nuance. The concern of women in Dignity, he suggested in 1993, was not only that they felt excluded because services were directed at men; it was also related to their perception that Dignity refused to challenge the Catholic church on any issue other than homosexuality—including women's ordination.[29]

Because of the unusually high proportion in this study of people who were raised Catholic, I was curious about why so many of them had chosen MCC over Dignity. For several, the issue highlighted by Primiano was exactly the problem: aside from its acceptance of gay men and lesbians, they claimed, Dignity followed Catholic teachings uncritically. Becky, a white lesbian who attended twelve years of Catholic school and spent ten years married to "a good Catholic boy," was one of these people. She told me: "I didn't really know where I needed to be, but I knew I didn't want—didn't need to be at a church that wasn't very supportive of women in general, that was very dogmatic and didn't allow women to celebrate Mass and do a lot of other important things." After avoiding churches for a while, she began attending MCC with her partner but found that Christianity no longer resonated with her; she currently considers herself New Age.[30] Others found MCC first or harbored negative images of Dignity that discouraged them from attending.[31]

Although few people in the study discussed involvement with LGBT religious groups other than Dignity or MCC, one woman did share with me her recent experiences with Integrity. Diane, a white lesbian who has just begun attending MCC, continues to be involved with a local Episcopalian congregation. She is not generally out at the latter church, although she believes that most of her friends know she is a lesbian. She told me that at the beginning of the summer of 1998, "one of our members at church . . . started the Integrity . . . group." "And," she continued, "there were probably about . . . five or six couples—adult . . . heterosexual couples, who came to the meeting. And . . . at least five or six of us who were single . . . or our spouse was not there. . . . I and the organist were the only gay people. And we got . . . six people to sign up as members of Integrity."[32]

While the high turnout for this initial meeting is promising, the fact that only six of the fifteen to eighteen people attending were willing to join the group officially is a less positive sign. Moreover, roughly 12 percent of those at the meeting and one-third of those who signed up as members are gay or lesbian (assuming that both Diane and the organist enrolled). As a group concerned with working to support LGBT people in the Episcopalian church, this chapter of Integrity will probably be a fine grassroots organization, but as a support group and a source of community for LGBT Episcopalians, it currently leaves something to be desired. Diane instead finds community at MCC.

Certainly there are many LGBT people involved in all levels of the major Christian organizations of the United States. Because they are not involved in MCC as well, they are not represented in this study. Among those studied here, however, there is a wide range of responses to mainstream religious groups. Like Becky, some of the participants in this study rejected such organizations entirely. Others, such as Diane, chose to attend both a mainstream group and MCC. The common denominator, however, is that all, at some point, found MCC attractive. Why? The key factor seems to be that rather than attempt to change the old world, in which LGBT identity and Christianity are still seen as incompatible, MCC creates a new world wherein such a combination is the celebrated norm.

The Old World: Two Roads Diverged

Alicia was deeply involved in a fundamentalist church when she first realized she was a lesbian. In addition to being summarily evicted from both church and home when she revealed this identity to someone, Alicia had her undergraduate degree revoked by the church-run college she had attended. The message, in this case, was quite clear: lesbians are not, and never can be, Christians.

Alicia has recovered from these experiences to the point that she is able to joke about them from time to time, and her comments provide an apt introduction to this discussion of the old world in which LGBT identity and Christianity appear irreconcilable. When I asked her how straight Christians respond to her as a Christian who is also lesbian, Alicia answered wryly: "All my old church friends and colleagues are really convinced that I'm the Antichrist." Later, I reversed the question and asked how non-Christian LGBT people respond to the fact that she is lesbian and also Christian. With a twinkle in her eye, she responded promptly: "I'm the anti-Goddess!"[33]

In this old world, it is not only Christians who view LGBT identity and Christianity as divergent, but also the LGBT community itself—though for different reasons. This may be more true in a religiously diverse state such as California than in more exclusively Christian areas of the United States, but the old world is also undergoing significant changes. While there is still a strong awareness among interview participants that their religious and sexual identities are seen as incompatible by others, participants also report that this message no longer comes across loud and clear. Instead, it is becoming garbled as an increasing number of people acknowledge the validity of LGBT Christian identity.

"You're Christian and WHAT??"

Few people went so far as to say, in jest or seriously, that heterosexual Christians viewed them as the Antichrist. In fact, only around 15 percent of those I interviewed reported entirely or mostly negative responses from straight Christians. Occasionally someone reported incredulity, but the positive responses were much stronger: around one-third reported entirely or mostly supportive attitudes from straight Christians or said that their LGBT identity was never an issue for their straight Christian friends and acquaintances.

Often these positive responses are the result of careful screening. Many of those I interviewed, for instance, rarely form close connections with straight Christians or they avoid coming out to such people. Others qualified their remarks on the subject by telling me that the only straight Christians they knew were those who are already allies of the LGBT community. Sometimes this is because they belong to groups such as Integrity, Lutherans Concerned, or the secular organization called Parents, Families, and Friends of Lesbians and Gays (PFLAG). Others are selective about their heterosexual social contacts. Ken, a white gay man in his 30s, explained: "Most of the people in my life . . . are open and accepting, and it's something that most people don't even think about . . . because I have put myself in a situation where I am mostly meeting and interacting with those kind of people. You know, my housemates, my friends . . . colleagues that I'm close to." He acknowledged that the situation might be very different were he to return to his home state of Alabama.[34]

Over half of those I interviewed reported a mixture of reactions from straight Christians. Ken's story suggests one determining factor in these reactions: region. As might be expected, another factor is the denominational background of the straight Christian in question. Terry reflected that while most fundamentalists have been very negative toward her self-identification as a lesbian Christian, the reaction from the mainline denominations seems more mixed. However, she noted that in her experience it was the pastors who were pushing these congregations toward acceptance, and overall the church members were less inclined to respond favorably to her than were their leaders.[35]

In addition to region and denomination, a third factor affecting the responses of straight Christians to LGBT Christians is one that many LGBT people emphasize as an important route to social acceptance: personal interaction. In some cases, even conservative Christians can come to a point of tolerance or acceptance of their LGBT Christian friends and acquaintances.[36] Walter's parents, for instance, attend a Mennonite church and a non-denominational conservative church. Others who attend these churches know that Walter is gay and that he has AIDS. And Walter did tell me that "there have been times in [the non-denominational church] that people have mentioned some things about—they were grateful that somebody they knew had renounced their homosexuality, and I kind of bristle up the back, keep my mouth shut about it since I'm only there a few times a year. But," he continued, "I actually haven't heard that . . . for quite a long time." In fact, when he attends now, "people always ask about my health, what I'm taking, they've heard this in the news and they heard that on the news, what I'm doing, very interested in me and how I'm doing. . . . It's a very good relationship."[37]

In the old world of heterosexual Christianity, the once clear divergence between Christianity and LGBT identity is becoming increasingly blurred. Ironically, although such blurring is taking place in LGBT communities as well, it is these communities more than Christian ones that seem to reinforce identity separation for the participants in this study. As Abigail told me: "In my own life it's been easier to come out about being a lesbian than it has been to come out about being Christian."[38]

"You're Lesbian and WHAT??"

When I asked how non-Christian LGBT people responded to them as LGBT Christians, those I interviewed offered a wide variety of responses. As with the attitudes of straight Christians, "mixed" was a common answer. Yet unlike the previous category, with this audience several other responses were also strong.

Incredulity was one. Jason, a gay man in his 40s who is himself somewhat uncomfortable with Christianity at the moment, explained, "A lot of lesbian women and gay men that I know think [being gay and Christian is] pretty crazy." He chuckled. "And sometimes I agree with them." Few people, he said, are outspoken about their opinions, but "if you talk with them about it, you may find that . . . you get a confirmation that they think this is very strange."[39]

Outright negativity, ranging from discomfort to anger, also ranks high on the list of responses from non-Christian LGBT people. "They use terms like 'hogwash,'" Bill told me, "and 'religion is bad.' They're very hostile toward the whole idea of religion. They find the idea of a gay Christian almost as contradictory as a gay Republican."[40] Carrie, who pulled herself out of drug and alcohol abuse before she discovered MCC, told me with frustration: "They won't go into MCC. They'll put everything into their system but the Word. They'll take any pill. . . . But if you ask them to go to church with you, no, they don't want to. Why? Because they feel that they'll have to change. But, see, that's our old thinking. You don't have to change—nothing!"[41]

For a number of respondents, the question of religious beliefs simply does not come up with non-Christians. Many of those I interviewed manage potentially unpleasant situations in the same way as they do when interacting with straight Christians: they restrict their social contacts to other LGBT Christians or consciously avoid bringing up the topic of religion. For some, the latter strategy is a natural outgrowth of the policy that religion and politics should not be discussed in polite company. Others avoid the subject out of sheer self-preservation.

It is interesting that just as there is a mitigating factor in the reactions of heterosexual Christians to LGBT Christians—personal interaction—there is also such a factor in the reactions of LGBT non-Christians to LGBT Christians. In this case, the reaction hinges on one crucial word: spirituality. While non-Christian LGBT people are generally hostile toward Christianity, they are apparently much more accepting of and interested in spirituality. Those respondents, for instance, who identify themselves more as spiritual people than as Christians tend to report fewer negative reactions toward their religious beliefs than do those who identify explicitly as Christian. Joe, who attended MCC for a few years but is now heavily involved in Unity, explained to me how this works in his own life. "I believe that Christ was here as a way-shower," he explained.

> Unity says—at least, this Unity does at the beginning of every service . . .
> "As Christ has said, the things I do, you can do, and even greater things."
> Well, the only way we can do any of that is if we tap into the source of the
> Christ consciousness. . . . So that's where my Christianity is kind of based—
> it's more spirituality. So people that are friends of mine that aren't neces-
> sarily churchgoers don't really have a problem with any of that. In fact,
> they're quite the same.[42]

The types of Christianity to which non-Christians in the LGBT community seem to object most strongly are those that sound conservative or evangelical and those that smack of organized religion. LGBT non-Christians appear to be far more comfortable with individualized belief and practice, Christian or not, that utilizes a language of instruction and self-improvement rather than obedience and control. Given the ways in which many religious organizations continue to demand obedience of them and to refuse their efforts at self-definition, such reactions are unsurprising.

This, then, is the old world inhabited by some LGBT Christians. It is currently a world of mixed reactions—whereas just a few decades ago it was nearly unthinkable to be LGBT and Christian—and that is often a source of hope. It is a world in flux that includes passionate supporters, outspoken LGBT activists, virulent detractors, and others who seem to wish that the whole issue (and the people who have brought it to the table) would silently disappear before their denominations are permanently rent. Despite the presence of welcoming, supportive places and people, it is a world in which LGBT

Christians often must look before they leap, a world where they choose their friends carefully in order to avoid painful rejection from Christians or from other members of the LGBT community. For these reasons, the safety and comfort of a new world may be highly attractive.

A New World: Two Roads Converge

The world that MCC offers to its participants is one in which, at least for a few hours on Sundays, being Christian and lesbian, gay, bisexual, or transgender is something to be celebrated or perhaps is something completely unremarkable. While at accepting churches people often must remind themselves to include their LGBT members in broad statements, at MCC it is the heterosexuals who are not normative and thus are sometimes overlooked. After years of making daily decisions about wording (Do I introduce her as roommate or partner?) and behavior (Is it wise to hold his hand here?), for many who attend MCC it is a relief to be freed from such choices in church.

But MCC now has some competition. Only a few competitors—the other independent LGBT organizations—offer a change from the old world. However, accepting churches and denominational organizations are also a viable and often valuable alternative, despite the disadvantages discussed above. Why, then, do people come to MCC, and how do they get there?

Routes to MCC

Study participants followed four major routes from their religious upbringing to MCC (see Figure 4.1). The first route is the simplest: just over 40 percent went directly from their childhood religion to MCC (this includes those who attended more than one church or denomination but remained in the same general category of liberal Protestant, conservative Protestant, and so on). However, nearly 16 percent followed a different path, shifting from their childhood religion to liberal Protestant, metaphysical, or New Age groups before coming to MCC. Another 10 percent, perhaps seeking to combat their growing awareness of LGBT identity, moved into conservative Protestant churches first. Finally, 10 percent became religious seekers after leaving their childhood religious organizations, trying many different organizations but committing to none.[43] For this latter group, MCC is often another brief stop on the journey; they rarely attend for long or with great frequency.[44]

By far the largest percentage of Catholics, mainline Protestants, and liberal Protestants went directly from their religious upbringing to MCC. However, nearly 17 percent of mainline Protestants shifted first to conservative Protes-

---

Figure 4.1. Routes to MCC

Childhood religion → MCC (41.7%)

Childhood religion → Liberal Protestant, Metaphysical, or New Age → MCC (15.9%)

Childhood religion → Conservative Protestant → MCC (10.6%)

Childhood religion → Seeker (10.6%)

---

tantism before coming to MCC, whereas just under 9 percent of Catholics and no liberal Protestants took this route. Given the wide range of positions on LGBT identity held by the mainline denominations over the years, it would not be surprising if a certain number of people raised within those denominations sought a more rigorous atmosphere in which to eradicate same-sex desire or transgender identification. Stories told by those I interviewed suggest that this is one likely explanation for such a move. However, there are other reasons that have little to do with LGBT identity. A shift in religious beliefs or a change in friendship patterns, for instance, might lead to denominational switching.[45]

Among conservative Protestants, 21 percent became seekers; 14 percent of liberal Protestants also followed this path. The reasons, however, are likely to be different for those from these two backgrounds. While the broadly inclusive theology practiced in some liberal Protestant churches could easily encourage a tendency toward religious seeking, a similar process is less likely in conservative Protestantism. Indeed, Roof and McKinney suggested in 1987 that those who leave liberal Protestantism are most likely to switch to no affiliation, while conservative Protestantism tends to lose its members to the mainline and liberal churches when it loses them at all.[46] The complicating factor in this study is the LGBT identity of these conservative Protestants. LGBT Christians are likely to receive less sympathetic treatment in conservative churches than in mainline or liberal ones (remember Suzanne's story of exorcism, Carrie's belief that she had a demon, and Alicia's loss of her bachelor's degree). As a result, LGBT Christians from conservative backgrounds might also be more likely to leave religious affiliation behind, choosing instead either to ignore religion or to avoid risking commitment to a single group or leader.

The final well-represented pathway leads from childhood affiliation to liberal Protestant, metaphysical, or New Age groups and then to MCC. Again, conservative Protestants show up in respectable numbers: 21 percent of respondents from conservative Protestant backgrounds followed this pathway. Among Catholics, 14 percent took this route, as did 14 percent of liberal Protestants.[47] For the liberal Protestants, as with those who became seekers, this latter move is not particularly surprising. For some, perhaps, it took place because their congregation was not as accepting of LGBT people as others have been known to be and the metaphysical or New Age group was more open. For others, however, it is just as likely that the move was the result of a shift in religious interests.[48]

For the Catholics and conservative Protestants whom I interviewed, the move to liberal Protestantism was made for different reasons than the move to metaphysical or New Age organizations. In the former case, the shift was usually due to a change in theology, often but not always prompted by a reaction against the anti-LGBT teachings of most conservative Protestant and Catholic congregations. While the people in question remained Christians, they no longer felt able to espouse the beliefs of their religious communities, and they sought a less strict forum in which to learn and practice their Christianity. One bisexual man, for instance, was raised in the Lutheran Church–Missouri Synod (a conservative branch of Lutheranism). In his survey he wrote that in college, "I became an Anglican (Episcopal) because the Missouri Synod was too conservative." Yet he remained deeply involved in Christianity, becoming an Episcopal priest and eventually an MCC pastor.[49]

Those who switched from Catholicism or conservative Protestantism to metaphysical or New Age groups made a shift that was often similar to the one made by seekers. Rejecting more than just biblical literalism and adherence to doctrine, these people might have retained a connection to Christianity through the teachings of Jesus, but they questioned church teachings regarding his uniqueness and divinity, not to mention such Christian staples as sin and salvation. Becky, who was raised Catholic, tried a shift to metaphysical Christianity in the form of MCC Valle Rico, but even that church was still too conservative for her:

> I still had issues with the dogma of the church [the UFMCC] . . . in terms of the biblical structure. And I became very much out to the left as far as any dogma when it came to questions like 'Have you been saved,' 'Christ is my savior,' 'We must pray for the forgiveness of sins.' I just kind of let go of all of that and became more of a real far out New Ager.[50]

Becky stressed that she respects the importance of Christianity in the life of her partner, but added that although she might attend services with her partner, she no longer believes in the teachings promoted at MCC churches.

Why MCC?

It is clear that participants in this study arrived at MCC through a variety of different routes. But the question remains: Why did they choose MCC? In the opening passages of this chapter, respondents mentioned a number of different reasons for attending. This diversity is evident among study participants as a whole, but the underlying theme that ties together many of these responses is once again the idea of a new world: participants felt that MCC offered an unusually powerful answer to their needs as LGBT Christians. Yet this belief in MCC's exceptional difference from other churches had negative as well as positive consequences: it also led to mistaken preconceptions about the denomination.

In two recent ethnographic studies of LGBT congregations, the authors mention their initial apprehension or misconceptions regarding the communities they studied.[51] Surprising though such admissions may be, coming as they do from scholars who had become thoroughly familiar with their proposed research topics before beginning fieldwork, they betray the tenacity of prejudice and of that old world in which "the gay [male] culture"—as if there were only one—is considered to be thoroughly incompatible with the quiet dignity and sanctity of a religious service. Nevertheless, even more surprising, and perhaps disturbing as well, is the fact that these heterosexual scholars are not alone in their pre-attendance jitters. Some of the people I interviewed related that they, too, were initially wary of attending "the gay church."

It is interesting that preconceptions of MCC among interview participants stemmed from stereotypes about two separate aspects of its identity. Reproducing the old-world biases of heterosexual Christians and LGBT non-Christians, some people feared either that MCC would be overly gay or that it would be overly Christian. Lurking in the former category are images of stereotypical gay culture run amok. Andrew, for instance, told me that his expectations of MCC were the same as his preconceptions about gay bars, which also proved incorrect: "I expected . . . the people would be a lot more flamboyant than they were," he told me. "I expected, you know, there to be pink walls, and chiffon all over the place, and . . . outrageous rituals—and [there was] none of that, you know, [it was] just a church. . . . Which is what I was looking for."[52] It is telling that both men and women who held preconceptions like Andrew's based those images on stereotypes about gay male culture—perhaps because the stereotype of lesbians as unshaven, braless, man-hating Amazons is even less compatible with church than are pink chiffon, stiletto heels, and interior decorators.

On the opposite side, however, some people's fears focused on MCC's Christian identity, drawing especially on the fact that it was founded by a former Pentecostal minister whose booming voice can still fill some of the largest churches in the denomination. Matt recalled: "I was really very nervous the first time I went there [to MCC]. And I wasn't sure . . . would there be, like—you know—fire and brimstone from . . . the pulpit?"

I clarified, "So—you were nervous partially because you were afraid it might be . . . a traditional or conservative Christian church?"

"Well," Matt answered, "I mean, it couldn't be too conservative—obviously. But it could still be a conservative message. It could still be an evangelical message."

"What gave you the idea that MCC might have been like that?" I asked.

"Oh—it's church," he responded. "It's religion."[53]

MCC did not turn out to be what Matt expected, though; in fact, MCC Valle Rico fit right in with his previous background in Unity. When we spoke, he had been attending for roughly two years and was currently quite active in the church.

Individual reasons for attending MCC varied widely. Some people began attending because a partner or friend was going; a few hoped to meet a Christian partner. Many sought social interaction and emphasized the value of MCC as a source of community separate from the bar scene. This latter reason was especially crucial for those recovering from addictions, but it was also important to people who disliked the noise, late nights, and emphases on youth and beauty that are prevalent at straight and LGBT bars alike. Reverend Sharon, for instance, told me that when she found MCC shortly after the denomination began, "it was the first time I'd ever seen gays and lesbians together not in a bar scene. So it was pretty exciting, actually."[54]

Inclusivity was a driving factor behind many respondents' exploration of MCC. As Suzanne put it with a grin: "Where else can I be a charismatic, evangelical, Catholic, liberal, feminist, metaphysical person?"[55] Where else, one might add, could she be all of these as well as a transgender lesbian and be ordained? Theological inclusivity, then, is one aspect that drew people to the two churches in this study. Human inclusivity is also important in a broad sense. Not only are respondents concerned with being included as LGBT people; they also value the inclusion of all people that they believe MCC offers. Although this belief ironically flies in the face of some of the demographic imbalances at both of the congregations in this study, several respondents mentioned that attending MCC had brought them greater understanding of people with whom they might not have had contact otherwise. One gay man told me he valued the interaction he had with lesbians through MCC;[56] another gay man and a bisexual woman both told me they had learned a great deal about the experiences of transgender people through attending MCC Valle Rico.[57]

Inclusion of LGBT Christians is of course another major reason for which participants in this study attend MCC. However, relatively few people reported that they began attending MCC in order to reconcile LGBT identity with Christian belief. Those people are present, to be sure, but only five respondents specifically cited reconciliation as their reason for attending. A much larger number—the largest, in fact, to support any single reason for coming to MCC—gave an explanation that differs in one subtle but important way. Rather than seeking reconciliation, they sought *support* for their combined identities. These people attended MCC because, in their words, it is a gay, gay-friendly, or gay-positive church and because they could be both LGBT and Christian there without anyone showing surprise or discomfort.

A related issue was the importance of not needing to guard one's words or actions, of being able to be out in church. "To be able to express my love for another woman in church . . . was such a joyous thing," wrote Sue, whose story appears at the beginning of this chapter. Many others agreed with her. One lesbian wrote: "I feel that church is not a place where I want to have to be in the closet or to downplay my identity, and MCC lets me be myself."[58] And the same consideration was relevant for a gay man who is entering a multidenominational seminary. Although he comes from an Episcopalian background and spent some time "soul-searching" about the denomination in which he wanted to be ordained, Chris finally chose MCC. "Especially with what's going on in the Episcopal church nowadays," he told me,

> I just couldn't see joining an organization that doesn't want me. I certainly can't go back in the closet at this later age. Also, you know, as a minister I would want to . . . be very honest about myself, and I just couldn't . . . I know that there are a lot of people who just keep their private lives private . . . but I just can't live that way.[59]

Unlike the old-world churches, the new world of MCC is a place where the congruence of LGBT identity and Christianity is never in question, where the identity of LGBT Christians never needs to be negotiated but is simply taken for granted.

Just as pathways into MCC are not necessarily related to LGBT identity, however, the primary reasons for attending also may be unrelated, or tangentially related, to that identity. For some respondents, the aspect of MCC that proved most attractive was its potential for furthering their own spiritual development. "MCC meets my mental/emotional/spiritual needs," wrote Wayne in his survey. "As an organization it affirms my total be-ing."[60] And his partner Robert wrote: "MCC was a church of *inclusion* not exclusion. This was a place where I knew I could find my spiritual journey (faith) and follow it."[61]

Perhaps Abigail said it best, though, when she explained why MCC's inclusion of LGBT people was essential but was not the sole aspect that made the church valuable to her. "There are zillions of Christian churches out there," she told me.

> To sift through them to find the ones that are not going to either react with outward hostility, or just quietly try to suck you in so they can change you . . . you don't need that. What I think people really need is an honest and real connection to God. There . . . are other churches that offer that, but they're few and far between.[62]

Seeking churches in the old world is not an attractive option for Abigail because to her it is a waste of time and energy that would be better spent with God.

Before leaving behind the question of why people attend MCC, it is worthwhile to explore two final categories, both of which are exceptions to the rule: non-Christian supporters and converts. Both are rare in Oceanfront MCC and MCC Valle Rico, although the latter does have a handful of adherents who are hesitant about calling themselves Christian. Supporters, however, make it clear that they do not attend MCC for the spiritual value of the services. Rather, the two supporters I interviewed believe that MCC is an important institution in the LGBT community, and they attend occasionally in order to demonstrate this belief. As one woman told me: "I suppose I get a kick out of it [MCC] because the right-wing Christians go nuts. . . . So it's sort of a 'tweak . . . the beard of the right wing.'"[63]

Converts to Christianity are just as rare among participants in this study as are non-Christian supporters. There are a few current attenders, though, who were raised with no particular religious affiliation. They began attending MCC only because a friend or partner was going, but over time they came to appreciate the church's message. Both of the converts whom I interviewed continue to espouse an extremely broad and inclusive theology, but both would call themselves Christian today. Reverend Sharon's partner June is one of these people, and her comments on the role of the church in her life are a suitable conclusion to this section. In the survey, she wrote:

> I am totally "out" in all aspects of my life, and I can do that more easily because I know that God is always walking beside me. At one time it was harder for me to come out as a Christian than it was as a lesbian. Today, I am very proud to share with anyone how important God has been in my life. It is because of MCC, and the liberalism of Rev. Sharon's theology, that I have reached this point. I thank God!![64]

Leaving MCC

As with any religious organization, some of the people who join MCC eventually decide to leave. For the most part, patterns of leaving MCC are quite comparable to those for other religious organizations in the United States.[65] Some respondents, for instance, are former members of MCC Valle Rico or Oceanfront MCC who have moved to an area with no MCC nearby. Others belonged to MCC congregations in another city and have found that MCCVR and OMCC do not meet their needs as well as their former congregation did. Sharla, who spoke at the beginning of this chapter, is one example of this latter group.

Sometimes people attend MCC out of a desire for LGBT Christian community but discover that the church's theology is too divergent from their own. More traditional or conservative Christians, for instance, tend to find MCCVR incompatible with their beliefs because of its metaphysical tendencies. In fact, Miguel, who was raised in the Salvation Army, told me that when he called MCCVR for information, the pastor with whom he spoke made it clear that the church's theology probably would not suit him. "So," Miguel said, "I let it go at that."[66] He continues to search for a gay-friendly group that will resonate with his own theology.

Andrew is another example. He no longer adheres to the fundamentalist beliefs with which he was raised, and he sees no conflict between being gay and being Christian. However, as he wrote in the survey: "I stopped attending MCC and joined an affirming Baptist congregation eventually because I didn't feel my beliefs were allowed." When we spoke in person, I asked Andrew to explain this further, and he responded with the example of "Amazing Grace." This hymn, in its original wording, speaks of grace "that saved a wretch like me." Liberal congregations, disaffected with the self-abasement implied in this phrase, often change the word "wretch" to "soul," and MCCVR is one such congregation. Andrew, though, objects to the change: "I think spirituality has to speak to the person who feels like a wretch, instead of denying that." This is not to say that Andrew left MCCVR over a word in a hymn; his objection was that in promoting what he sees as an overly positive view of human nature, MCCVR fails to address the negative tendencies that are also present, leaving congregants without spiritual resources in their moments of failure and self-doubt.[67]

A more unusual case is a lesbian couple whose strong involvement in Oceanfront MCC eventually led them into activist work in a local mainline congregation. One of the two wrote that although she and her partner had been heavily involved in MCC, "we have mostly withdrawn . . . on a temporary basis because we feel compelled to show mostly straight people in the local Methodist church that gays & lesbians can be fine upstanding, compassionate people and that we can truly be Christians."[68]

A fourth pattern is the most disturbing one for some MCC leaders despite the fact that it is compatible with Perry's original vision for the church. A number of people find MCC to be an invaluable source of support while they are first coming out but discover after a few years that they no longer need the church's message of acceptance. Finding no other direction in which to go, they switch out of MCC and explore their options in accepting churches and other religious organizations.

Reverend Patrick is clearly aware of this problem and has worked to prevent it in his own church. In fact, among former affiliates of MCC Valle Rico I did not find lack of spiritual growth as a reason for leaving—if anything, it was the opposite. Those with whom I spoke described having learned a great deal about metaphysical beliefs during their time at MCCVR; most who left had decided to move entirely beyond Christianity and found that MCCVR was now slightly too conservative for their tastes. Others preferred the integration of heterosexuals with LGBT people that they could find in accepting metaphysical and New Age organizations.

On a broader scale within MCC, however, I have heard the "revolving door" problem mentioned quite often. One woman who has been involved with the denomination on a national level has both experienced the problem herself and seen it in other congregations. Explaining her journey through MCC, Melanie wrote the following in the survey:

> The message of "God Loves You As You Are"—saved my life as far as I'm concerned. I owe my healthy self-esteem to MCC and my God-centered life today. Though developmentally what I need spiritually isn't available in MCC (much to my great dismay and wish it were), I am beholden to MCC for its basic message of truth that really set me free.[69]

Speaking as an observer of the denomination, however, she referred to this "basic message" as "Spirituality 101." While affirming the importance of this message to MCC newcomers, Melanie believes that MCC congregations need to offer more. When she talks with others who have left the church, she explained, "Always the story is somewhat, 'I got that God loves me, but I want to do something more than that.' . . . Another way they say it is, 'I got Spirituality 101; can I get 102 here?' You know, 'I want to move on.' They sense this calling from within for something deeper." At present, Melanie says, "Spirituality 102" is not offered in many MCC churches, and people seeking this kind of spiritual development are reluctantly leaving the denomination.[70]

Current MCC attendance among survey respondents averages slightly higher than once a month, with the most common attendance rates being weekly (12 percent), once a month to several times per year (32 percent), and less than once a year (29 percent).[71] In addition, 49 percent of survey respondents report attending another religious organization along with MCC; average attendance at these groups is also just over once a month. The organizations represented include metaphysical, New Age, or meditation groups (26 percent); liberal or mainline Protestant churches (11 percent each); Catholic or Orthodox churches (9 percent); other LGBT religious groups (9 percent); and twelve-step programs (5 percent).[72]

Partners are also an important factor in MCC attendance patterns. Within the survey sample, just over half of the respondents answered questions about partners. Of this group, 67 percent reported that their partners attend MCC, and 37 percent have partners who attend other religious groups in addition to MCC. For the most part, the other groups that partners attend are similar to those attended by respondents themselves.[73]

These figures suggest that MCC involvement varies widely within this sample. Moreover, just as religion in general has become a resource rather than a requirement for many of the participants in this study, it appears that MCC itself has suffered the same fate. The wide range in attendance and the high number of respondents and their partners who also attend other religious groups suggest that MCC is but one source of religious fulfillment for many who attend its services. However highly participants value the unique assets of MCC, some also have needs that are not met at MCC, and they turn to other religious groups to fill in the gaps.

Involvement and commitment also affect respondents' exposure to MCC's new world. For instance, despite the fact that nearly 80 percent of respondents currently attend MCC, only 44 percent are members. This in itself, however, is not all that unusual; as Robert Wuthnow has remarked, in the United States, the tendency to join religious groups has declined in favor of more independent piecemeal approaches to religion.[74]

Average length of attendance is also low: three to five years. This appears to support the assertions of those who describe MCC as a "revolving door" for people who need healing from religiously inflicted wounds. Yet there are in fact two peaks in attendance, and the second peak is at the high end of the scale. While 20 percent of respondents have attended MCC for three to five years and 13 percent have attended for five to seven years, a full 27 percent have attended MCC churches for more than ten years. Like many other religious organizations in the United States, these congregations seem to experience a high number of short-time affiliations but also apparently have a core group of "old-timers."

Involvement in MCC remains sizeable among this sample when measured by factors other than attendance.[75] Current or former board members make up 21 percent of the survey sample, and 14 percent have been or currently are deacons. Acolytes, who are a loosely defined and largely unofficial group in these two congregations, make up 17 percent of the respondents, and nearly one-third have been involved in ministries such as music, education, and healing.

Effects of Involvement in MCC

The effects of MCC involvement on the lives of those who attend are difficult to measure or to describe accurately. This section therefore takes two different approaches. It begins by exploring conclusions suggested by the survey about the effects of MCC attendance on self-acceptance. Using these findings as a springboard, it moves on to discuss the ways in which study participants felt that MCC had affected them.

The survey took two different approaches to measuring changes in respondents' lives during their time at MCC. The first continued measures that were utilized in other sections of the survey: attitudes toward organized religion, spirituality, and homosexuality. Current attitudes toward both spirituality and homosexuality were highly positive, with both averaging 4.6 on a scale from 1 to 5. Attitudes toward organized religion were cooler, with a mean score of 3.0 on the same scale. It is important to note, though, that a number of respondents specified that MCC did not count as an organized religion in their eyes. Therefore, it is not surprising that its effect on this measure was negligible.[76]

The second set of questions designed to measure MCC's effect asked respondents to rate their level of agreement with three statements: "MCC has helped me to reconcile my religious beliefs with my sexual identity"; "MCC has increased my pride in my sexual identity"; and "MCC has increased my pride in myself as a human being."[77] Ratings used a five-point scale, with 5 indicating strong agreement and 1 indicating strong disagreement.

While there was overall agreement with all three questions, the one on reconciliation garnered the least agreement, with a mean score of 3.85. Pride in sexual identity scored 4.02, and pride in self nearly tied with a mean score of 4.08. Like the questions about organized religion discussed above, the slightly lower mean of the reconciliation question may be due in part to the opinion of some respondents that it is inapplicable. Recall from Chapter 2 that a number of participants felt that religion and sexuality were unrelated in their lives and that many others began the reconciliation process before coming to MCC. As a result, and as some respondents pointed out in the margin next to this question, MCC did not help to reconcile religion with sexual identity because such reconciliation was never (or was no longer) needed.

The effects of religious attendance, however, can hardly be reduced to a series of statistical measures; the narrative accounts provide a more complete and accurate picture. In both the surveys and the interviews, spiritual growth and self-acceptance were the two main themes in stories of MCC's effects on people's lives. There are several variations on each theme, however.

Self-acceptance, first of all, encompasses a wide range of actual effects. On the one hand, several people wrote or told me that MCC had literally saved their lives. For the most part, these were people who were unable to begin reconciling religious and sexual or gender identity without the assistance of a supportive religious organization. Having reached a point of crisis, they had considered suicide before discovering or approaching MCC. But despite the power of their stories, these people are in the minority.

A more common role for MCC is to *assist* in the process of self-acceptance, supporting LGBT Christians and providing them with positive role models as they solidify the integration of their formerly divergent identities. Jeffrey, whose theological disagreements with MCCVR prevent him from attending services, nevertheless wrote in his survey that "simply because MCC exists it conveys to me that others also are dealing with same sex attractions and desire for love and acceptance by God without having to change or try to change."[78] And Carrie, who struggled through the reconciliation process on her own, wrote, "[I] so wished I had this support system while I was growing up and coming out."[79]

When Melanie, who spoke above about the need for more spiritual depth in MCC, describes her early years in the denomination, it is clear that her experiences span the spectrum of self-acceptance. Although she does believe that MCC's message of self-acceptance saved her life, she also feels that at a deep level she knew of God's acceptance before coming to MCC. "I think I knew in the marrow of my bones," she explained in an interview,

> that love wasn't in question. However . . . my social and cultural under-
> standing was, that was not what—the picture people were giving me. . . . I
> think that's why I was attracted to and eventually found MCC—I found
> a place where the two could go together. And I—I heard that message of
> truth that was in my bones being spoken out loud.[80]

For others, MCC's greatest impact has little to do with LGBT identity and much more to do with its identity as a church in which they feel they can pursue spiritual growth and experience closeness to God. While this is related to LGBT identity in that prejudicial treatment can detract from one's sense of connection to the divine, it is also much more similar to the goals of non-LGBT people in religion than prevalent images of MCC might lead one to expect.

Community is also important, as Cynthia indicated on the survey. "For me," she wrote, "participating in MCC is not a way to affirm myself and my sexuality in the eyes of God—that has not been an issue. But I love to fellowship with other g's [gays], l's [lesbians], b's [bisexuals], and t's [transgender people] because they too *practice* openness and I feel *safe* there."[81]

For Walter, spiritual growth and community have meant support and strength in times of trial. "Before I started to develop the symptoms of AIDS," he wrote,

> my brother was killed in a fire overseas. Then I started to develop the symptoms of AIDS, with 4 hospitalizations, about one a year. [MCC Valle Rico] and Rev. [Patrick] were a great support to my family through all of this. My faith was growing at the same time. . . . I had done so much with the tools that [MCCVR] showed to me that it all kicked in during these crises in my life.[82]

Others emphasize religious learning, spiritual insights, emotional healing and openness, and a sense of wholeness as aspects of MCC's legacy.

Components of MCC's Influence

What does affirmation look like in action, and through what media does MCC have its greatest influences? The most obvious answer, especially in logic-driven Western culture, is the messages carried by the sermons. Yet things are not so simple. In the survey, I asked two questions that attempted to pinpoint the most influential parts of MCC involvement. The first asked respondents to rate several church activities on a scale of zero to seven with respect to "their positive effect on your life" (seven indicated the weakest effect, one the strongest, and zero no effect). The second question asked respondents to write down which part of the weekly Sunday service had "the greatest impact on you or your life." The strongest-scoring activities on the first question, in order, were weekly services, special or holiday services, fellowship after service, life-ritual services such as commitment ceremonies and funerals, study classes, and community service activities.

On the second question, responses were surprisingly consistent: most included communion, sermons, and music either singly or in combination. Sermons and communion, in fact, tied at 33 percent for the greatest number of votes, and music was listed by about one-quarter of the respondents. Also included, but distinctly less popular, was the experience of community in weekly services, and twelve people answered that multiple parts of the service have a strong impact or that the most influential part varies from week to week. Several answers that cited music and worship may be related to the presence of people from charismatic backgrounds in both congregations, but for others the music brought back memories of childhood church services, building a connection between the new world and the old one. Additionally, several single people mentioned in surveys or interviews that the physical contact at services is extremely important to them.

In summary, MCC does play a role in identity integration, and the specifics of this role vary greatly according to an individual's needs and the route that person has taken toward self-acceptance. Study participants also suggested a number of different sources for MCC's impact, although it is unclear whether these sources affect self-image and identity or other things entirely. Chapter 5 fills in this sketch by focusing more closely on the symbolic, mythic, and ritual aspects of MCC services: the tools with which MCC and its partici-pants re-create the world.

5 Re-Creating the World

Jane is a lesbian in her early 30s whose parents are from different Christian backgrounds: her father was raised Baptist and her mother, Catholic. She and her siblings were baptized Catholic at the insistence of her grandmother, and Jane attended mass regularly for a few years while she was in college. She still goes to church with her grandmother on major holidays such as Christmas Eve. Like Robert in the previous chapter, Jane came to MCC shortly after she had ended a relationship. Feeling "a little bit of a spiritual hole," she decided to go to church but knew that she did not want to reestablish close ties to Catholicism either through attending a traditional church or through becoming involved with Dignity. When we spoke at her house one hot summer afternoon, I asked Jane why she had chosen MCC over all of the other churches in her area. She explained that during that time, her job as a schoolteacher in a small town had forced her to keep her identity hidden most of the time. "And I think," she continued, "I wanted something in my life where I didn't have to worry about that, have to hide anything." She chose a large and active MCC in a nearby city. When she first attended, she told me, "It was quite an interesting experience." My curiosity piqued, I asked: "In what way?" Jane responded by asking me if I had ever been inside this particular church. When I answered in the affirmative, she continued: "[You] see all the rainbow flags on the walls, and hanging from the ceiling, and . . . they do that right around June for Pride, then they leave them up till Christmas. And . . . they also have an American flag and a California flag hanging in there. And I remember being sort of, I think, stunned by this. . . . It was things hanging in a church, which have a lot of . . . power, you know, saying, 'Yes, we're gay; yes, we're Americans; yes, we're Californians; and yes, this is our church,' and it was all of those things in one place, I think, that really moved me."[1]

Coincidentally, it was at this same large church that Reverend Dean began his association with MCC. Raised with no "formal religious affiliation," Reverend Dean began attending church on his own when he was in high school. For reasons of distance (he could walk there) and aesthetics ("it was probably the most quaint and attractive church in our little town"), as well as on the recommendation of his grandfather, he chose the Episcopal church. Although he attended services while he was in college and for a few years after graduating, when Dean started coming out as a gay man in the early 1970s he became acutely aware that his church responded to LGBT people with either negativity or silence. He left the church and made a firm decision not to return. Eventually a friend talked him into attending MCC, and he has rarely missed a Sunday service since then. Like many others in this study, Reverend Dean had begun to reconcile the Christian and gay facets of his identity when he started attending MCC, but that process was far from complete. "I think a lot of the heaviest part was over," he told me. "But . . . I had not come to a joyful acceptance; I had come to a deep resignation that this is how it was." "So," I asked, "was there anything in particular that took you from the point of 'deep resignation,' as you said, to a point of acceptance?" Reverend Dean's answer included many of the different ways in which MCC communicates affirmation of LGBT Christians. In particular, he told me of an influential sermon during which a simple shift of viewpoint yielded a radically different interpretation of a familiar biblical story. "I will never forget," he said, "the Sunday that the pastor . . . stood up and preached on Job but made it a gay story. That Job lost his lover. . . . It was just incredible that you could talk about God this way and God didn't destroy the building and the people that were in it. . . . That this was okay."[2]

For Reverend Sharon, the expression of the integration of LGBT and Christian identities during Sunday services is an explicit priority. She frequently relates the topics of her sermons to the struggles of LGBT people, and subtle additions to the Oceanfront altar quietly proclaim LGBT pride in the midst of Christian ritual. In addition, however, she believes the integration should be even more explicit. Although sermons and altar decorations were the only media though which her church affirmed LGBT Christian identity while I was in regular attendance, Reverend Sharon told me before I left that she had been particularly tired over the past several months and as a result had not done anything unusual or creative. She had some ideas, though, for future services. For instance, she felt that the church ought to treat National Coming Out Day (October 11) as a major holiday, or "holy day," thus foregrounding LGBT pride while celebrating it in a Christian way.[3]

A sizable majority of survey respondents named sermons, music, or communion as the part of the weekly church service that had the greatest effect on their lives. Since the term was undefined in the survey question, it would be shortsighted to assume that "effect" refers solely or even mostly to the affirmation of LGBT Christian identity. The overwhelming importance of these parts of the service does suggest, however, that they are the most likely sources of effective affirmative messages. Moreover, although few people gave detailed explanations of how MCC had affected their self-understanding as LGBT Christians, those who did elaborate point in the same direction. This chapter explores some of the explicit and symbolic ways in which MCC Valle Rico and Oceanfront MCC deconstruct the world of diverging roads and reconstruct a world of converging ones in which the adjectives "lesbian," "gay," "bisexual," "transgender" and "Christian" can be spoken together.

Symbolic processes of meaning-making have been of interest to analysts in fields ranging from cultural studies to psychology. Bruce Lincoln's work in comparative religion—most notably his *Discourse and the Construction of Society*—provides part of the organizing framework for my analysis.[4] Defining the term broadly as a form of communication evident in myth, ritual, and classification systems, Lincoln argues that discourse is a central element in the construction, maintenance, and deconstruction of social orders. His case studies span two continents and several centuries; they also vary considerably in the amount of explicitly religious material involved. Although Lincoln focuses primarily on conflicts at the national level, such as the St. Bartholomew's Day massacres in France and the Spanish civil war, much of his analysis deals with concepts of identity—both one's own and that of the "others" against whom one is contending. He argues convincingly that just as myth, ritual, and classification systems can help to legitimate an existing social order, in the hands of dissidents they can be altered to challenge or even undermine that order, replacing it with a new one that is in turn legitimated by new discourses or by reinterpreted versions of the old ones.

Delegitimation of an old social order and legitimation of a new one are also the processes through which MCC supports the integration of Christian and LGBT identities. Moreover, although classification systems hold less relevance for this study, myth and ritual are both central elements in most religious services; MCC is no exception to this rule. Every Sunday, MCC church services construct a world of convergent identities through dress, décor, liturgy, music, and social legitimation.

Discourse

Symbolic Discourse

Clifford Geertz defines cultural analysis as the study of symbol and meaning.[5] Although the focus here is subcultural, a similar definition applies, and subcultural analysis is an important tool with which to explore the sources of affirmation. While Geertz uses symbolic analysis to clarify the underlying dynamics of consensus or conflict within a culture, here I adapt his approach to make inferences about subcultural values and their expression through the creative use of symbols. Indeed, the work of Pierre Bourdieu points in exactly this direction and adds to Lincoln's argument about discourse and the social order. Effective symbols, Bourdieu writes, "can help to conserve or subvert the established order, that is to say, reality."[6] It is my contention that such symbols, subtly deployed, are an important part of the message of support and affirmation offered at MCC.

Because it is the weekly Sunday services that most people are likely to attend, and because it is often these services that give newcomers their introduction to the denomination, in this section I focus on the forms of symbolic communication evident in the sanctuary. Beginning with decorations in the building itself, the analysis moves on to consider altar design and the role of the clergy. For the most part, these messages are not blatant. Some are easily visible but symbolic, while others are even more subtle. None spells out acceptance explicitly, and most require some basic knowledge of LGBT cultural symbolisms in order to be comprehensible.

When she first entered an MCC church, Jane was strongly impressed by the omnipresence of rainbow flags, which are widely used in LGBT communities as an expression of pride. More than U.S. flags, rainbow flags are unusual elements of church decoration. Their assertive, almost defiant claim to visibility in a world of closets and hidden identities makes them popular as bumper stickers and themes for T-shirts and jewelry, and they sprout from windows and doorways during the month of June, when Gay Pride celebrations take place across the country. However, in an era when even the more liberal denominations continue to be uncomfortable with highly visible LGBT people, and at a time when Christianity is still a dirty word in many LGBT communities, rainbow flags and churches simply do not seem to go together.

Jane's church, however, was neither the first nor the last MCC to decide that the two can indeed be combined. At both of the churches in this study, the rainbow theme appeared in several different places during Sunday services. At Oceanfront MCC it is first noticeable in the parking lots behind the church's two meeting sites, where not only rainbow flags but also rainbow crosses and rainbow Christian fish decorate bumpers and rear windows.

Approaching the church's La Playa location from the street instead of the parking lot, the newcomer to OMCC would know she had arrived by the rainbow flag that hangs in the doorway. This flag, however, which belongs to Reverend Sharon's partner June, has a symbolic twist: it is a rainbow version of the U.S. flag. Rainbow stripes replace the red and white of the usual flag, and the blue field that customarily sports stars is filled instead with another symbol of LGBT identity: pink triangles.[7] Just as the cars in the church's parking lot proclaim "We are LGBT and Christian," the flag in the front announces "We are LGBT and American!"

MCCVR also has a rainbow flag. Approximately six feet by four, the flag was hanging in the front of the sanctuary the first time I visited the church, accompanied by a sign explaining that the flag is an inclusive symbol "intended to represent the whole human family." When I returned the next summer, the flag was gone, but after a few weeks it reappeared on the wall at the back of the room. The next month I spoke with Jo, who is in charge of decorations for the church, and she told me that the disappearance of the flag from the sanctuary had elicited quite a bit of concern from churchgoers.[8]

The chain of events had been innocuous: the church had acquired an overhead projector for use with song lyrics, and the screen needed to go where the flag was. The flag was removed from the front wall and then was carried in the local Pride parade, and Jo had not been able to find it immediately after the parade. However, the number of complaints she received when the flag disappeared, and the number of people who requested that it be put back up, indicate that the rainbow flag is more than a decoration in this church. As the largest and least subtle symbol of LGBT pride evident in the sanctuary, the flag is a potent reminder and a symbolic celebration of the congregation's LGBT identity. Its disappearance set that identity in the background, in effect shutting the congregation back in the closet.

Late in the summer, when decorations in MCCVR shifted from the red of Pentecost to green for the next section of the liturgical calendar, Jo put up two wall hangings that had been created by Mitchell, one of the deacons at the church. Though subtler than the rainbow flag, these hangings also conveyed a message of pride and affirmation, woven more closely with Christianity. Some of the symbolism in these hangings, in fact, is so carefully crafted that Mitchell's partner Harold had to point the images out to me.

Worked on jute, both hangings contain a caption and an image of a tree.

Stylized human figures make up the trunks of the trees, while the canopies are flames in a rainbow of colors. On the wall to the congregation's left the hanging proclaims: "The Spirit of God Has Set Us Free!" Several human figures create the impression of a tree with multiple trunks, and the flames that represent the tree's leaves take the shape of a descending dove. Both doves and flames are traditional Christian symbols of the Holy Spirit; representing them in the rainbow colors of the Pride flag adds an unusual twist to familiar imagery.

The second hanging reads: "We are standing on holy ground." It contains a single human figure as the tree trunk, with rainbow flames again representing the leaves. Harold pointed out to me that the human figure in this hanging is masculine, and there is a feminine face in the yellow tongue of flame; this was intended, he said, to represent a gender-inclusive image of God. In addition, however, the significance of the rainbow colors is again worth noticing. If this hanging offers an image of God as both female and male, it also includes LGBT identity in the deity by representing God as a tree with rainbow leaves.

While sanctuary decorations are a powerful source of affirmation, the prime place in which to join LGBT and Christian identity ought to be the altar, since it is the central location of Christian ritual. And indeed, at Oceanfront MCC, symbols of LGBT identity are ubiquitous on the altar. The communion plate and cup, for instance, are often covered with a rainbow-striped cloth napkin. On one occasion, this napkin was accompanied by a more openly political symbol: a commemorative bandana from the 1993 LGBT March on Washington. Rainbow beads are occasionally draped over the cross or the altar, and the altar candles are frequently lavender, symbolic of lesbian identity. In one of the church's two locations, Reverend Sharon also uses a lectern that has been painted lavender. Even the box for collecting private prayer requests is covered in rainbow-colored tissue paper. All of these color cues, though they might be missed by someone unfamiliar with LGBT cultures, speak loudly to MCC participants of LGBT presence at the "table of God."

At MCC Valle Rico, such symbolic elements are rarely found on the altar itself. What is present, however, is the candle of hope and healing, a common element in many MCC churches. Often a jar candle or a pillar candle, it can be many different colors; its symbolic value lies not in its appearance (except perhaps for the fact that it is long-burning) but in its use. At MCCVR, as at other MCC congregations I have visited, the candle of hope and healing is lit during the church's community prayer period. Two people from the congregation then read prayer cards while lighting the candle, and this section of the service closes with a unison prayer about God's love and healing.

Although the healing that goes on in a church can take many forms and certainly is not restricted to healing the wounds inflicted by the old world, this period in the service lends itself easily to a focus on the hope and healing of LGBT communities. It is here that the daily struggles, tragedies, and triumphs of the congregation are voiced while occasional murmurs from the audience affirm or commiserate. In this way, although the candle of hope and healing does represent hope for jobs, healing for ill family members, and so on, it also represents hope for an end to anti-LGBT rhetoric in the churches and in society and healing from the damage done by such messages.

In addition to sanctuary decoration and altar design, a third important locus of symbolism in Christian ritual is the leader: the pastor, minister, or priest. Indeed, the staunch refusal of the Catholic Church to ordain women as priests is a clear demonstration of the symbolic nature of this role. Women cannot be priests, the church claims, because a priest is the representative of Jesus and Jesus was male. By this same logic, simply having an out and proud lesbian, gay man, bisexual, or transgender person behind the altar says something profound about God's acceptance of LGBT people. Pastoral collars (worn by three of the five clergy members in these two churches) may well accentuate this effect, as they symbolically confer sacred status on a lesbian, gay, bisexual, or transgender body. Moreover, other subtle clues to such affirmation appear from time to time in the pastors' dress and jewelry. Reverend Patrick once wore a rainbow-colored stole during service, for instance, and at least one person at MCCVR wears a rainbow sash while opening the communion service. Reverend Sharon wears LGBT-themed T-shirts to church from time to time, and the astute observer can frequently spot a small cross pendant around her neck. Although at first glance the pendant looks like those worn by many Christians, closer inspection reveals a pink triangle at the center of the cross. What better symbol of integrated identities could there be?

Verbal Discourse

In addition to non-verbal symbolic discourse, for Lincoln verbal discourse also can play a significant role in deconstructing and constructing the social order. In situations where the proponents of old and new orders share the same mythology, Lincoln argues that myth can be enlisted in support of the new social order (or in this case, the new subcultural order) through three strategies.

The first strategy involves denying the validity of myths that challenge the new order; in the case of LGBT Christians, this might mean denying a literal interpretation of the Bible or even denying the Bible's status as a divinely in-

spired text. The second is to grant mythic status to a fable, legend, or historical event that supports the new order, thus granting that story transcendent
authority. Such an approach can be seen especially clearly in the reactions at
MCC Valle Rico to the murder of Matthew Shepard in the fall of 1998. Two
sermons, one given by a deacon and the other by Reverend Patrick, addressed
the murder; in the former, Shepard appeared as a kind of child saint, while
in the latter he was described in Christlike terms.[9] Another example of this
strategy is a story I heard in 1995 when I first began to do fieldwork in MCC.
A pastor who visited the church I was studying at the time told of a gay man
with AIDS who exclaimed just before he died that he could feel his angel's
wings growing. The truth or verifiability of this story is irrelevant in this
situation; the story's claim to truth is enough. Appealing to a reality beyond
the human world, the dying man in the story vividly "proves" that even gay
men with AIDS—those considered by conservative Christians to be suffering
from God's curse—do in fact go to heaven.

Finally, Lincoln suggests that the third strategy for harnessing the power
of myth involves reinterpreting existing myths in such a way that they support the new social order more clearly. In the case of MCC, this strategy involves all of the biblical interpretations used to answer those who would use
the Bible to prove that homosexuality is sinful. Also important here are the
efforts of some people, jokingly or in earnest, to "out" certain biblical figures
as lesbians or gay men. Commonly cited "same-sex couples" in the Bible include Ruth and Naomi, David and Jonathan, and Jesus and John. UFMCC
Elder Nancy Wilson has suggested that many of the eunuchs who appear in
the Bible were actually gay men.[10]

At MCC Valle Rico and Oceanfront MCC, these three strategies are utilized outside of the weekly services but generally are not evident within them.
This fact further supports my contention that MCC's central role is to affirm
integrated identities and to facilitate the continuing process of integration
rather than to begin that process. Lincoln argues that these myth-making
strategies are important in any effort to create a new world; they are important in MCC's new world as well, but as with the pink triangle and the rainbow flag, they are implicitly understood rather than being spelled out. Those
who are not familiar with these symbolic underpinnings on which MCC rests
have only to speak with a pastor or peruse a table full of pamphlets in the
back of MCCVR to find resources that explicitly map out the mythic strategies important to the construction and maintenance of MCC's world.

As several interview participants explained to me, the best resource of this
sort that is available at OMCC is Reverend Sharon herself, who has sat down
with many newcomers to hash out the theological reinterpretations necessary
to the integration of LGBT and Christian identities. Additionally, while I was

attending Oceanfront, Reverend Sharon offered a more structured approach to Lincoln's mythological strategies in a four-week class on "homosexuality and the Bible" that met one night per week. The course ended with a videotape that responded to the anti-LGBT rhetoric of the Christian right.

At MCCVR, the pastors are again an important resource. At this more affluent church, however, a newcomer could gather resources without ever speaking to anyone or even attending the service. A table at the back of the sanctuary offers a wide variety of pamphlets and flyers. Some have nothing to do with the integration of identities: Unity's monthly publication, the *Daily Word*, appears on this table, as do metaphysical pamphlets by Reverend Patrick such as "Three Ideas That Will Change Your Life" and "Pathway to Inner Peace." Also in evidence, though, are the UFMCC's "Report to the President for the White House Conference on Hate Crimes" and a letter from Reverend Patrick to the local newspaper regarding the Southern Baptists' boycott of Disney.

Then there are the more explicitly LGBT/Christian materials. "Finding the Path into the 21st Century," another of Reverend Patrick's pamphlets, addresses those LGBT people who are comfortable with their sexual or gender identity but not with religion. It explains that many lesbian and gay people have rejected organized religion and yet feel a continuing pull toward spiritual expression. As we enter the twenty-first century, the pamphlet explains, people are leaving behind "old forms and formulas" and moving "into a new space in the way we think and live." Part of this new space will be new forms of community, including "*healing communities* [italics original] where we can help each other on the path toward becoming healed and whole." MCC Valle Rico, the pamphlet says, aims to be one such community.

While this pamphlet moves beyond the integration of LGBT and Christian identities—indeed, beyond Christianity—and speaks more of integrating LGBT identity with spirituality, two other pamphlets address LGBT people from a more explicitly Christian perspective. One, entitled "So You're Going to Live," discusses the challenges faced by people with AIDS who have prepared themselves for death and then discovered that new medications can prolong their lives.[11] Opening each section with biblical quotations, the pamphlet offers suggestions from a Christian perspective for adjusting to a new lease on life.

Finally, "Free to Be Gay" is the standard MCC handout on biblical reinterpretation.[12] It takes up the problematic passages in Genesis, Leviticus, Deuteronomy, I Corinthians, I Timothy, and Romans, as well as the common perspective that homosexuality is "against nature," and briefly explains why none of these is a valid argument against same-sex relationships. For a small sum, those wishing a more in-depth presentation of the arguments can purchase from MCCVR a book written by the pamphlet's author entitled *The Bible and Homosexuality.*[13]

Services at both MCCVR and OMCC assume that those in the congregation have at least made a start at integrating their sexual or gender identities with their religious beliefs. During the course of my fieldwork, sermons rarely engaged in Lincoln's discursive strategies. Instead, they addressed the issue of identity integration in much subtler ways. While rarely making explicit links between LGBT identity and Christianity, the various people who gave these sermons nearly always managed to refer to LGBT people and their experiences. The message in these services seems to be not the activist slogan "We are everywhere," but a quieter and more assimilative "We are here like everyone else."

At MCC Valle Rico, LGBT issues were a consistent undercurrent in the sermons rather than being a central focus. On the Sunday after Independence Day, for instance, a guest speaker gave a sermon on the topic of freedom. Rather than begin with freedom in the LGBT community, however, she spoke of those who had worked for freedom from slavery in the United States and freedom from the concentration camps in Nazi Germany. When she moved on to speak of everyday struggles for freedom, the struggles of LGBT people were only one of several examples she gave. And her final point was about internal freedom: not freedom from oppressive theologies but the freedom gained by addressing internal problems and cultivating self-forgiveness.

A sermon given by Reverend Patrick later that same summer addressed LGBT experience in a similar manner. Reverend Patrick's sermons often follow monthly themes and have the feel of a lecture series; in 1998, the theme for August was M. Scott Peck's four levels of spiritual development outlined in *The Road Less Traveled.*[14] When he addressed Stage Four (the "highest" spiritual stage), Reverend Patrick began by reviewing the other three stages and explaining how they relate to the experience of LGBT people. For instance, he suggested that such people often leave Stage Two (the Formal/Institutional stage) because of rejection by their churches. This catapults them into Stage Three, the Skeptic/Individual stage. At the beginning of this stage, Reverend Patrick explained, LGBT people often feel angry and defensive because of their earlier experiences. Eventually, however, they develop a better self-understanding and begin to respect the self-understanding of others as well; this prepares them to enter the advanced Mystical/Communal stage. In this case, then, the sermon itself was about the spiritual development of the congregation; because that congregation was predominantly LGBT, relating the sermon to the lives of individual congregants meant relating it to LGBT people.

A similar process is at work in the sermons given at Oceanfront. As at

MCCVR, the LGBT content of the sermons varied from week to week. Only a few sermons explicitly addressed the integration of LGBT and Christian identities, and a few others touched briefly on issues relating to the LGBT community as a whole. Most frequent, however, were those sermons that expounded upon a spiritual lesson and then explained how that lesson related to the lives of people in the congregation—thus bringing in LGBT experience.

One sermon, for instance, was based on four passages from the Bible. Although they dealt with different topics, each of the passages emphasized a theme of reliance on God. Reverend Sharon opened her sermon by explaining the importance of remembering to ask for God's help in one's daily life. This led her to a discussion of the ways in which God could help the congregants by giving them the strength and persistence to influence the world in a positive way. Finally, she explained that this reliance on God was especially important for LGBT people because they often have difficulty believing that they have anything useful to give to the world.

In the discourse at these two MCC congregations, then, the integration of sexual or gender identity with religion is treated as something already present: it is assumed that most of the congregation are LGBT Christians, not LGBT people unsure about Christianity or Christians unsure about LGBT identity. Beyond that assumption, however, lies a wide range of symbolic and verbal discourse that helps to legitimate the world of LGBT Christians. Symbols of LGBT pride adorn the sanctuaries and altars, not to mention the pastors themselves, and speakers make frequent and casual reference during sermons to the experiences of LGBT Christians or LGBT people in general. Resources external to the service itself offer more solid support for those who are still struggling with the integration process, but the assumption seems to be that such people are in the minority. If the participants in this study are in any way representative, that assumption is correct for both churches.

It could be argued that such an assumption is actually an important strategy in the construction and maintenance of a new world at MCC. Just as Lady Macbeth was too vehement in her claims to innocence, so overemphasizing the assertion that LGBT identity and Christianity can be reconciled would draw attention to counterarguments that they cannot. Refusing to protest too much adds to the feeling at MCC that being LGBT and Christian is perfectly natural and normal.

Ritual

According to Lincoln, ritual is a second effective strategy for deconstructing old worlds and reconstructing new ones. While the rituals at MCC do incorporate material and verbal symbolism that affirms LGBT Christian identity, such symbolism is not foregrounded at all. Instead, in communion, charismatic experience, and congregational singing, it is bodily symbolism that most profoundly communicates affirmation.[15]

Jonathan Z. Smith once defined ritual as "a means of performing the way things ought to be in conscious tension to the way things are in such a way that this ritualized perfection is recollected in the ordinary, uncontrolled course of things."[16] Although his argument was made in the context of hunting rituals, it is thought-provoking in the context of MCC. However much the churches offer a new world wherein LGBT Christian identity is the accepted norm, few people can remain permanently in such a world. When they return to the old worlds, though, MCC congregants carry with them a memory of "ritualized perfection" that may sustain them in the face of challenges from heterosexual Christians, non-Christian LGBT people, and others. Here, though, "performing the way things ought to be" does not imply a recognition that such perfection is unreachable in reality. In addition to providing a world in which, for a few hours, things are the way they ought to be, MCC services support the hope that some day they will be that way universally.

While Smith's work is useful in understanding the overall effect of MCC ritual, it is Bourdieu who offers an explanation of how this effect is created. Bourdieu identifies a type of performative communication that he calls the *habitus.* This is a collection of learned behaviors, accents, and bodily postures (the "bodily hexis") and their meanings that communicate both to oneself and to others one's place in society.[17] "Symbolic power," he writes, "works partly through the control of other people's bodies and belief."[18] In a related manner, he describes ritual as a source of embodied memory, asserting that "the body believes in what it plays at. . . . What is 'learned by body' is not something that one has, like knowledge that can be brandished, but something that one is."[19] While Bourdieu is primarily concerned with class status, his ideas are applicable to LGBT people as well.

There is a *habitus,* for example, that controls the interaction between same-sex couples in public. Many people are uncomfortable holding hands unless they are certain of being in a "safe" area; more demonstrative forms of affection, such as putting arms around each other's waists or kissing in public, often are even more discomfiting. Other people intentionally hold hands or kiss when in public in a conscious effort to make same-sex couples more visible in society—but the self-awareness that is involved here suggests an intentional break from the *habitus.* Other examples of LGBT *habitus* could be cited as well, such as changes in physical demeanor that can mute or express one's LGBT identity, the use of certain words or phrases, and all of the indicators that make up what some LGBT people jokingly call "gaydar."

Communion

In the context of Christianity, it is possible to see the presence of *habitus* in the reluctance of many LGBT Christians to approach the altar. Several study participants mentioned in the surveys or in interviews that they had attended MCC for weeks before working up the courage to take communion. Trained as they had been to view the altar as a site of purity to which they were forbidden access, these people felt unworthiness, fear, or a combination of the two at the thought of approaching the altar as a self-accepting LGBT person. Yet when they do take communion, the symbolic message is clear: LGBT people can serve this sacred communal meal, and LGBT people can partake of it.

Especially important here is one of the unique aspects of communion at MCC: the opportunity for couples to take communion together. Verbal and physical violence, or the risk thereof, have trained many LGBT people to keep a low profile in public,[20] an act which often may be taken for granted but which can carry a bitter sting when compared to the casual physical affection displayed in public by many heterosexual couples. During MCC services, unlike in most other churches, same-sex couples can hold hands or put their arms around each other in the pews. More important, they can come to the "Lord's table" hand in hand, receive communion together, and have a pastor pray over them as a couple. The *habitus* that conveys second-class status to the world and to oneself is thus broken during MCC ritual. Certainly it does not disappear, but perhaps breaking this habit every Sunday allows these people to enact it more consciously during the rest of the week. In this awareness may lie the ability to resist the internalization of oppressive self-definitions.

Communing with God and with each other, MCC congregants physically express the alternative world of affirmation offered by their church. In this moment of "ritualized perfection" the *habitus* is rejected, along with the messages of inferiority and fear that it literally embodies. Clearly, there is ample reason for the popularity of the communion service at MCC. There is also an obvious importance in the fact that it is performed every week: central as this ritual is to constructing MCC's new world, Sunday services would not be the same without it.

Charisma

If taking communion as an openly LGBT person and being served communion by an openly LGBT person are powerful symbolic affirmations of LGBT Christian identity, it stands to reason that physically experiencing

God's presence during such a ritual might have an even greater impact. Although not all Christians find charismatic experiences enjoyable or meaningful, those LGBT Christians who are also charismatics have access to a strongly emotive experience through which they can communicate intimately with the divine.

Several years ago, Reverend Sharon and her partner June became involved in charismatic practices through a series of MCC conferences. As a result, some people within the church have become open to charismatic experiences and others have seen their charismatic backgrounds reaffirmed through Oceanfront MCC. During this period, the church lost a number of members who were uncomfortable with charismatic practices, but the change attracted new members as well.

Oceanfront is not a vigorously charismatic congregation. Reverend Sharon told me that charismatic expression in the church had been unusually subdued during my fieldwork, perhaps because of my presence. However, stories I heard about services prior to my attendance indicate that charismatic practices at OMCC are limited to quiet speaking or singing in tongues and the experience of being slain in the spirit.[21] Moreover, shortly after I began attending, the church held a "Service of Healing and Renewal" in celebration of its tenth anniversary. The "praise team," consisting of a music group of eight, a ninth person who ran the overhead projector, and a pastor, came from a large MCC congregation about 150 miles away to lead the service. The entire morning was distinctly charismatic, and the atmosphere was far more charged than at any other OMCC service I attended. If more boisterous charismatic expression was to be expected in the church, I doubt my presence would have impeded it during this particular service. Yet although the level and intensity of involvement were much higher, the particular forms of charismatic expression remained the same.

During interviews, several OMCC members brought up the topic of charismatic experience. Two consistent themes characterized their stories: healing and closeness to God. Beth, for instance, is a survivor of sexual abuse who had been involved in therapy for years. A few years before I met her, someone shared with Beth that being slain in the spirit "felt like Jesus was holding her in his arms and rocking her." Beth, too, wanted such an experience, so she decided to attend the annual MCC charismatic conference. At a Saturday evening healing service, she asked to be prayed for; the woman who obliged mentioned so many details about Beth's life that "it . . . was like she'd been in my therapy sessions." Beth continued the story:

> She finally said, "Now you have to forgive your father." So I'm there, I'm
> crying. I held my hands up like this [she demonstrated] and said, "I forgive

you, Dad. I forgive you, Dad." And at that point I could feel all the pain in my neck and shoulders drain out of my body. And at that point I was slain.

After this experience, Beth said, much of the trauma with which she had previously struggled was gone.[22]

Those whom I interviewed frequently described feeling an intense and emotional closeness to God when they were slain. One man told me, "It was like an old friend came back and put their arm around me."[23] June finds a unique closeness to God through both being slain and praying in tongues. Reverend Sharon described her own experiences as well as those of people she has known: "Sometimes people feel just really immensely loved. . . . Kind of feel like they're wrapped in God's arms . . . I mean, I have this thing of, just, I feel really loved, and you feel like you never want to get up."[24]

Reverend Sharon added that such an experience of intense divine love is often important for LGBT people who have been rejected by churches and families in the past. Certainly, if approaching the altar and taking communion embody a symbolic affirmation of LGBT Christians, the personal and emotional connection to God reported by charismatics is an even more unassailable affirmation.

Peter Berger has written that the mundane "massively real world of ordinary, everyday life" is broken from time to time by such experiences as dreams, hallucinations, and even "theoretical abstraction."[25] Taking his cue from the work of Alfred Schutz, Berger suggests that such experiences change one's understanding of reality. "The ordinary world, previously perceived as massive and cohesive, is now seen as being tenuously put together . . . easily collapsed into unreality. Furthermore, behind the newly revealed holes in the fabric of this world appears *another reality*. One now understands that this other reality has been there all along."[26] Praying in tongues and being slain in the spirit are experiences that break with the "ordinary" world. Demonstrating the ultimate unreality of a world wherein LGBT people are rejected by God, the charismatic experiences of LGBT Christians reveal a new reality: a world in which God does indeed love them just as much as anyone else.

Writing a decade earlier with Thomas Luckmann, Berger suggested that any version of reality requires both "routine maintenance and crisis maintenance."[27] Because of the variety of challenges their congregants face in daily life, MCC churches must offer resources for both. Communion serves primarily as routine maintenance: after spending their week in worlds where LGBT Christian identity is either unacceptable or irrelevant, at MCC, people find symbols, sermons, and rituals that affirm that identity. Some of those entering the church on Sunday may have recently been shaken by a close friend's scathing rejection of Christianity or an encounter with an anti-LGBT Christian. In these cases, it is the world of MCC that seems unreal and full of holes; communion can help to shore it up, but both churches also offer more intensive forms of "maintenance." At OMCC, charismatic experience connects believers to an affirming divine reality. At MCCVR, although charismatic experience is not evident, there is always at least one "prayer partner" available after service to offer one-on-one prayer without the public exposure or time constraints of the communion service.[28]

I have hinted above that music in MCC also can be considered to be a form of ritual. This is more clearly evident in MCCVR than in OMCC, for simple reasons of congregational size; however, music takes similar forms and has similar effects in both services. The songs themselves are often typical Christian ones: familiar hymns in the more high-church MCCVR and songs by contemporary Christian artists in the more charismatic OMCC. For many, these familiar songs provide a link back to their childhood churches, perhaps evoking a time when their status as "good Christians" was not in doubt or bridging the biographical rift that coming out sometimes leaves in its wake. Occasionally at Oceanfront, the service will include a song that makes more explicit reference to LGBT experience through its lyrics, its composer, or both.

But it is not the songs themselves that make music a ritual at MCC; rather, it is the physical involvement. The simplest form this takes is standing during the music: even such a small movement sets the music apart (as it does for the gospel readings, for which MCC congregations also stand) as a special part of the service. On more upbeat songs, hand-clapping is common in both churches, and someone may produce a tambourine to emphasize the beat further. At MCCVR, this can lead to even greater physical expression, as people sway and stomp their feet and those with charismatic leanings raise their hands over their heads.

At OMCC, hands may go up in praise during the quieter, more introspective songs. Significant physical activity during singing is rarer than at MCCVR, probably in large part because of the congregation's size. But during the July healing service, when a multivoice choir with keyboard and percussion led the music, the physical involvement approached that of MCCVR, and people clearly were touched on an emotional level by the music. Some would add emphases such as "Yes, Jesus" or "Yes, Lord" after particular lines of a song; others sat or stood quietly, swaying with their hands in the air. And tears were frequent evidence of the emotional power of this ritual for many of those present.

In a way, however, music provides a bridge between the category of ritual and that of community. While physical and emotional involvement make music a powerful ritual in MCC, it is clear that smaller groups make for a less effective ritual. At MCC, congregational singing is not simply a group of people singing praise to their deity; it is a group of LGBT people singing praise. The fervor of the singing in larger groups boldly proclaims that congregants do not just hope for God's attention and acceptance; they *expect* it. Services at MCCVR always end with everyone present joining hands before singing a final song. When the song has ended, often after several repetitions, the group remains standing, still holding hands, and recites the benediction together. With this communal affirmation of the world it has built, MCC Valle Rico sends its participants out prepared to face once again the trials of the old worlds.

Community

"My People"

When I spoke with Chris, a white gay man, in August of 1998, he was preparing to enter the seminary. Deciding in which church to seek ordination had been difficult, but he had finally chosen MCC. I asked Chris whether it was more important to him that MCC is a Christian group or that it ministers to the LGBT community. "Basically, for me," he replied, "it's about being with people who are like me, and . . . having it be an organic part of my life and my community. I really do feel that they're my people."[29] Why is this important to Chris and to others like him? Why do they choose to attend, or even minister to, congregations composed predominantly of "their people"? While community is important in many ways, one of its most central functions in MCC is to provide social support for the new world.

Barrington Moore remarks that "a very small degree of social support is sufficient to shatter the mystique of oppression and deception and permit a critical response to surface."[30] Groups that believe LGBT identity is sinful are well aware of this fact; they advise people seeking to be "healed" from homosexuality to avoid contact with LGBT people, LGBT publications, and any other influences that might tempt them back into "sin." Bill stayed in the closet for twenty years as a result of such strategies; it was a visit to MCC that convinced him that he could in fact be gay and Christian.[31]

Social Construction of a New Reality

The power of community to affirm identity is explored systematically in the work of Berger and Luckmann. "Self-production," they claim, "is always, and of necessity, a social enterprise."[32] They go on to suggest that the social site of "self-production" is the "plausibility structure," a group or social system made up of individuals who share one's version of reality and are unlikely to challenge or question it. "The plausibility structure," they argue, "is also the social base for the particular suspension of doubt without which the definition of reality in question cannot be maintained in consciousness."[33]

Plausibility structures can take a variety of forms, but as Berger notes in *The Sacred Canopy*, religion is one of the most important. Berger's work has become famous—or in some circles infamous—for his assertion that religion provides overarching social stability and his belief that a secularizing society risks losing its "sacred canopy." It is in this context that Berger speaks of the importance of plausibility structures as protective havens of belief in a world of skeptics.[34] While it is generally accepted today that religious belief is nowhere near as threatened as Berger believed it was at the time, his understanding of religious communities as plausibility structures remains useful. In the case of MCC it is generally not religious belief per se that is threatened, but a specific form of that belief that allows LGBT Christians to believe in the validity of their religion (against the challenges of non-Christian LGBT people) and in themselves as good people (against the challenges of conservative Christians).

In the immediate absence of intense personal religious experiences, Berger argues in another volume, the plausibility of past experiences

> is sustained by the same processes that keep plausible any other experience. These processes are, essentially, those of social consensus and social control: The experience is credible because everyone says it is so or acts as if it were, and because various degrees of unpleasantness are imposed on those who would deny it.[35]

MCC carries out the processes Berger describes in a variety of ways. Social consensus is expressed in multiple forms throughout the service. Wall hangings symbolically portray the inclusion of LGBT people in the divine being, and sermons often apply the day's lesson to LGBT experiences. During communion, same-sex couples come to the altar, some with children, to receive a blessing for their families. The communal song and benediction at the end of MCCVR services put congregants hand in hand with a roomful of mostly LGBT people, most of whom are Christian, presenting themselves to each other as just another community of Christians worshiping their God on a Sunday morning. In a way, it is the whole atmosphere of normalcy, so unexpected to some newcomers, that affirms the reality created in MCC. "Protesting too much" would suggest that LGBT Christian identity is in question; people come to MCC seeking a haven from such challenges, and MCC's atmosphere of normalcy helps to provide it.

Heterosexuals in MCC

Before closing the discussion of community in MCC, I want to consider a small but symbolically important component of MCC congregations: heterosexuals. As de facto representatives of a dominant group within U.S. Christianity, heterosexuals in MCC are potential symbols of both those who reject LGBT Christians and those who accept them. The presence of heterosexuals at MCC services, their understanding of their roles in the church and of LGBT responses to them, and commentary on their presence from LGBT church members are interesting because they may reflect not only interpersonal dynamics but also reactions to national and international issues.

Reverend Patrick estimates that between 5 and 10 percent of those attending any given Sunday service at MCCVR are heterosexual.[36] Among survey respondents, 5 percent were non-transgender heterosexuals. This is probably an underestimate of heterosexual involvement in MCCVR, however, because the survey focused predominantly on LGBT experience. More than one heterosexual returned blank surveys along with a note indicating that they assumed I was not interested in survey responses from heterosexuals. I did have the opportunity, however, to interview three heterosexuals who are active members of the MCCVR community: Jennifer, Anna, and Phil. What I learned from them can in no way be considered generalizable, but it is at least thought-provoking.

If there is reason to ask why an LGBT person would attend a Christian church, there is even more reason to ask why a heterosexual would choose to attend a church that is predominantly LGBT. All of those I interviewed had entered the church through the influence of others. Phil began attending because his wife enjoyed the services; Anna and Jennifer each had agreed to go church-shopping with a close friend who was gay and had found MCC in that process. Anna described the first day she and her friend came to MCC:

> When I looked at his face when we walked in the door, I thought, "Oh, my goodness, he's home. He's home!" And it was lovely. And something later on didn't work for him and he left, but I continued to go, and then I had to realize one day that I was home. I had been looking for a Christian, metaphysically-oriented church that I would be comfortable with anyhow in my mind, but I had no idea what that would look like. And so MCC just fit the bill for me.[37]

Having found MCC in the process of church-shopping with a gay man, Anna stayed because she liked the church's theology and services. It also helped that she had a strong interest in working with people with AIDS and thus felt comfortable around LGBT people.

Jennifer's story is similar in many ways to Anna's. Her friend, also a gay man, attended a funeral at MCCVR and liked the way the service was run. They attended Sunday service together, along with trying out Unity and the Church of Religious Science; MCC won out. Jennifer told me that some of her heterosexual friends are reluctant to visit the church with her because they are unsure of how the congregation will receive them. They feel unworthy, she said, or fear they will be unable to relate to the LGBT community at the church. Jennifer herself never had such concerns because she already had a number of LGBT friends when she began attending MCCVR.

I also asked Jennifer, Anna, and Phil about their roles as heterosexuals in a predominantly LGBT church. Phil, who came to the church an avowed atheist, now enjoys attending for a variety of reasons. When asked about his role in the church, though, he responded: "I consider it kind of a political statement. . . . I think that a church like this is . . . really long overdue . . . and I want to support that." Knowing that some LGBT people are averse to the inclusion of heterosexuals in LGBT organizations, I asked Phil whether he had ever felt excluded. He responded that he had not, although he was aware that social boundaries might exist. There had been some talk in the church, he said, of organizing a men's group, and he was not sure whether such a group would welcome him. Inclusion, though, was a central theme in Phil's positive response to MCCVR, because he had been very clear about his atheism when he began attending. Expecting to be ignored or shunned, he found himself instead being asked to read scripture, light the candle of hope and healing, and even speak at a men's service. During his time at the church he has given some thought to his own spiritual beliefs, and he now considers himself an agnostic rather than an atheist.[38]

When I asked Anna how she perceived her role in MCCVR, she responded: "Just a parishioner like everybody else." As someone experienced in providing support to people with AIDS, she had hoped to start an AIDS ministry within the church but was unable to attract a sufficiently large amount of interest. She says she is still available, but for now she feels that she is simply another member of MCC. Her heterosexual identity is not totally irrelevant to Anna when she is at MCC, however. She told me that she has never felt left out, but like Phil she adds: "I have real good boundaries about what's appropriate for me to be at and not." In fact, she had been concerned at first about the advisability of attending MCC at all and had asked several people at the church whether it was all right for her to come. Finally, she went up for communion one Sunday, "and the person administering communion took me in her arms and said, 'we want you here, and you don't need to ask anybody else.'"[39]

Phil and Anna protected themselves from rejection by carefully choosing the groups and activities they joined. Jennifer, however, wants to hold

MCCVR more firmly to its inclusive values. Jennifer's understanding of her position in MCC implies a division between heterosexuals and LGBT communities, with heterosexual allies of such communities serving as educators or perhaps ambassadors to heterosexuals. Many heterosexuals, Jennifer told me, have misperceptions about LGBT people, and she believes that her role in the congregation is to teach heterosexuals not to fear LGBT communities.

But Jennifer also believes (as do several of the LGBT people I interviewed) that the need for an exclusively LGBT church no longer exists. People are not different spiritually, she believes, because of their sexual or transgender identity. MCC Valle Rico, despite its efforts at inclusivity, has not yet lived up to that ideal in Jennifer's eyes. She told me of a joke about heterosexuals that had been made in a sermon and added that some of the women in the church treat her differently from the way they treat lesbian or bisexual women.[40]

The "actual" role of heterosexuals in MCC communities is impossible to define, both because there is a variety of opinions on the topic and because the views of LGBT people may differ significantly from the self-understanding of heterosexuals. What can be said, however, is that there are several possible roles for heterosexuals in such churches. The shared experiences of the heterosexuals I interviewed suggest one role: heterosexuals in MCC may be allies and friends, supporting the LGBT community wherever they can. As "ambassadors," they also might play an important role in fostering acceptance of LGBT people among their heterosexual friends.

Another possibility is suggested by Jennifer's comments: heterosexuals in MCC could be understood as part of the expression of MCC's dedication to inclusivity. As many oppressed groups have discovered, it is relatively easy to be inclusive until a representative of the oppressor group asks for admission. The UFMCC bills itself as the latest word in ecumenism, and inclusion of heterosexuals may be one of the more difficult and controversial facets of this self-definition.

Suzanne, the pastoral candidate at MCCVR, suggested a less laudable role for heterosexuals in MCC: although she valued their participation, she worried that their presence might not always be healthy for LGBT church members. "Some people," she asserted,

> need to have validation of straight people to feel real. . . . In the gay and lesbian community, often the greater honor is given to supportive straight people than it is to gay and lesbian people. . . . And I think part of that . . . is desire for acceptance by the mainstream.[41]

How much this is the case at MCCVR is impossible to say, because I did not ask respondents about the presence of heterosexuals in the church. However, when I asked LGBT interview participants to discuss heterosexual Christians' attitudes toward them, not one mentioned heterosexual MCC members. Perhaps the supportive response of such people is taken for granted. It is more likely, though, that MCCVR's heterosexual population is small enough that it is not an important force in the church. Perhaps the presence of heterosexuals is valuable for those LGBT congregants who have experienced wholesale rejection by heterosexual family and friends, but if this is the case I did not hear about it during the course of my research.

Conclusions

In summary, it appears that at least in these two congregations, MCC is a resource that people approach after having begun the process of identity reconciliation. Though all have started this process, people arrive at these churches having made varying degrees of progress, and they experience a variety of setbacks and gains during their involvement. As a result, the broad impact of OMCC and MCCVR is simple—they support and foster identity integration—but the ways in which that effect takes shape are complex.

Overall, the churches' central function in the area of identity reconciliation is to create and sustain a world in which LGBT Christian identity is normative and celebrated. For those Christians still struggling to accept their sexual or gender identity, and for those LGBT people struggling with spiritual or religious identity, MCC provides written resources and classes outside of the weekly service. Within the service, it supports and affirms LGBT Christian identity through a variety of symbolic, verbal, ritual, and social resources.

Those for whom such resources hold meaning or value are the ones who continue to attend; those for whom they are not useful—or are no longer needed—often leave. In Berger and Luckmann's terms, many of those who remain in any particular MCC are in need of a plausibility structure for LGBT Christian identity and find that particular congregation's plausibility structure effective. A committed charismatic would not be likely to find the ritual affirmations at MCC Valle Rico sufficient; however, Oceanfront MCC might touch her deeply. Likewise, someone raised in a "high-church" tradition might be uncomfortable at OMCC but strongly moved by MCCVR's services. And someone who had been comfortably out of the closet—and Christian—for decades, or who perhaps no longer considered himself Christian at all, would have other plausibility structures available and might leave the church entirely.

Part Three
Identity in Community

6 We Took the One Less Traveled

> The sociology of religion is part of the sociology of power. . . . The object of
> social science is a reality that encompasses all the individual and collective
> struggles aimed at conserving or transforming reality, in particular those that
> seek to impose the legitimate definition of reality, whose specifically symbolic
> efficacy can help to conserve or subvert the established order, that is to say,
> reality.
>
> —Pierre Bourdieu, *The Logic of Practice*

> We must not understand the exercise of power as pure violence or strict
> coercion. Power consists in complex relations: these relations involve a set of
> rational techniques, and the efficacy of those techniques is due to a subtle inte-
> gration of coercion-technologies and self-technologies.
>
> —Michel Foucault, *Religion and Culture*

As both Foucault and Bourdieu point out, the topic of power is central to the
study of society and culture. For Foucault, power acts not only through coer-
cion but also through cooptation, producing the self-policing subject so deftly
described by Judith Butler.[1] This acceptance of power and of the dominant
order is known more commonly as internalized oppression; the first section
of this chapter examines the ways in which some forms of Christianity can
create internalized oppression among LGBT people.

Diverging Roads: Hegemony and the Self-Policing Subject

The vast majority of study participants experienced at some point in
their lives a disjuncture between identifying as Christian and identifying as
lesbian, gay, bisexual, or transgender. Since nearly all identified as Christian
before identifying as LGBT, the disjuncture usually took the form of denying
or devaluing the more recent LGBT aspect of their identities rather than the
Christian aspect. Moreover, Christianity often was complicit in this denial, as
Christian teachings, leaders, or congregations communicated either implicitly or explicitly to these respondents that they could not be LGBT and still
be good Christians.

One useful theoretical approach to this devaluation of identity is Gramsci's concept of hegemony.[2] For Gramsci, hegemony was the ability of the dominant social order to present itself as natural and eternal and thus effectively to prevent the discontent and pressure for change that lead to revolt. While MCC can be understood as a counterhegemonic institution—an organization that undermines anti-LGBT hegemony—for many study participants, the Christianity of their childhood was complicit in the hegemonic order.

Consider, for instance, the rallying cry of Christian anti-LGBT activists: "God made Adam and Eve, not Adam and Steve!" At first glance, this statement is merely amusing or offensive, depending on one's point of view. At a deeper level, however, it points directly to the potential hegemonic power of traditional Christian theology. The Genesis creation story does indeed pose problems for a Christian understanding of LGBT people: if God created the first two people to be a sexual pair and God created the members of that pair male and female, what does that say about the ontological status of same-sex couples—not to mention what God might think when Eve feels s/he is really Ed?[3]

Traditional Christian theology makes much of the (apparently) stably married, procreating, heterosexual couple: such couples are the backbone of the Hebrew Bible (Adam and Eve, Abraham and Sarah) and the foundation of Jesus' biography (Mary and Joseph); their union is a sacrament in Catholicism. Except in more radical interpretations, however, same-sex couples are non-existent in the Bible. Moreover, conservative exegetes can point to several places in the Hebrew Bible and the New Testament that look suspiciously like divine condemnation of homosexuality and transgenderism.

To many people raised within traditional Christianity, then, the natural order of things seems to be heterosexuality and orthodox gender identity.[4] Christians who feel attracted to those of the same sex or who find themselves far more comfortable in the opposite gender identity from that assigned to them at birth have every reason to believe that they are breaking with that order. From this point of view, it is not surprising that people might understand their homosexual or transgender feelings to be unnatural or disapproved by God. If they continue to accept the natural order of things as the church has defined it, anti-LGBT elements in the church need do no more: the "deviants" themselves will attempt to correct their behavior and bring it in line with nature and the divine will.

This is exactly the process Foucault identifies as the "subtle integration of coercion-technologies and self-technologies"; its product is the self-policing subject discussed by Butler.[5] Coercion-technologies can include factors as subtle as gossip among members of a congregation and those as blatant as exorcism. Self-technologies, the deeper and therefore more insidious tactics, induce the LGBT Christian to monitor and attempt to eradicate same-sex or transgender feelings. It is self-technologies, in fact, that may lead the self-policing subject to voluntary participation in exorcisms or even to suicide; more commonly, they result in hours of prayer, frequent visits to the confessional, and sometimes doomed heterosexual marriages.[6]

Rifts in Reality: Cognitive Dissonance Theory

For some people, the process ends here. They make a life as "properly" gender-identified heterosexually married people, or they remain single and celibate, certain in their belief that by controlling, denying, or conquering their same-sex or transgender feelings they are doing God's bidding. For others, however, cracks begin to appear in the edifice of this reality at some point. Perhaps, they begin to think, God does not wish them to be heterosexual or male or female after all. Perhaps God loves them as they are and values same-sex relationships as well as heterosexual ones, transgender people as well as the orthodox-gendered. Perhaps the church, perhaps society, is wrong.

The events that instigate such rifts vary widely, from an encounter with an out LGBT Christian to years of unsuccessful attempts at change. A long-standing psychological theory, however, suggests that the continuing conflict between suspected LGBT identity and anti-LGBT beliefs cannot be sustained without immense psychological pressure and thus demands a resolution of some sort.

The theory of cognitive dissonance, now common in Western popular culture, was introduced by social psychologist Leon Festinger in 1957.[7] Festinger argued that an individual can experience two or more cognitions (thoughts or perceptions) as being either consonant or dissonant with each other. Dissonant cognitions produce a drive toward dissonance reduction, similar to the drive produced by hunger or thirst, and the strength of that drive is dependent upon the strength of the dissonance. The latter, in Festinger's formulation, varies according to factors such as the number and importance of the dissonant cognitions. Festinger suggested that there are several ways to eradicate or reduce dissonance, including removing dissonant cognitions, adding consonant ones, and lessening the importance of dissonant cognitions.

For the purposes of this chapter, it is most useful to consider cognitive dissonance in terms of two self-perceptions. The issue of the self, in fact, has been a central theme in more recent work on cognitive dissonance.[8] However, much of the research prompted by these ideas remains focused on the dissonance between belief and behavior; applications of dissonance theory to identity conflict have been less common.[9]

One of the exceptions to this rule is directly relevant here. In 1996, Kimberly A. Mahaffy reported the results of a study of cognitive dissonance among lesbian Christians.[10] In a survey of 163 self-identified lesbians who are or have been affiliated with Christianity, Mahaffy measured demographic variables, evangelical identity prior to coming out as lesbian, self-reported cognitive dissonance between religious and sexual identities, and strategies of dissonance resolution. Among all of these, she found that only evangelical identity prior to coming out was a reliable predictor of dissonance between sexual and religious identity.

Moreover, having defined dissonance as stemming from either an internal source (a belief that Christianity and lesbian identity could not be reconciled) or an external source (challenges from other church members or church leaders), Mahaffy found that women who experienced dissonance stemming from internal conflict most often resolved that dissonance by changing their beliefs rather than by leaving the church. Those whose sense of dissonance was rooted in an external source were more likely to leave or to live with the tension by remaining in the church.

Finally, the women in Mahaffy's study who had become Christians later in life tended to remain in the church, while those who had discovered their lesbian identity later in life were more likely to leave. Mahaffy suggests that these findings are related to identity synthesis: women who came out fairly early as lesbians may have had a longer period of time in which to integrate lesbian and Christian identity and those who came to Christianity later in life are more likely to have dealt with the conflict between religion and sexuality before ever sitting in a pew. An alternate interpretation is suggested by Berger and Luckmann's work on plausibility structures: the women in Mahaffy's study seem to remain in the community that supports the newer identity. Thus, women who came out as lesbian before becoming Christian may need more support for the Christian aspect of their identities than for the lesbian aspect, and therefore they remain in the church. For women who were Christian long before coming out as lesbian, the situation is reversed.

The concept of cognitive dissonance is especially helpful in understanding the initial rift in the reality of normative heterosexuality (also commonly called "heteronormativity") that participants in this study experienced. Given as cognitions the statements "I am a Christian" and "I am attracted to people of the same sex" or "I feel like I am in the wrong body," it is evident that traditional Christian beliefs about homosexuality and transgender identity would result in significant amount of dissonance between the two. Assuming heteronormativity and the importance of Christianity in the person's life, the obvious route to reducing such dissonance is to eradicate any suspicion of LGBT identity. However, certain experiences can shift the balance of these two cognitions and lead to a drastically different method of dissonance reduction.

A concrete example is in order here. Bill tried for twenty years to become heterosexual. Yet after praying for two decades without results, he was faced with two possible explanations: either God was ignoring him, or God meant for him to be gay and therefore was refusing to change him. Given his belief in God's love, Bill concluded that the former explanation was highly unlikely. As a result, he had a new cognition to add to the dissonant pair of Christian belief and suspected gay identity. This addition might be phrased as follows: "God makes people gay and wants them to stay that way."

In Festinger's terms, this is the addition of a consonant cognition that effectively reduces or eliminates the dissonance. Earlier in Bill's life, the combination of "I am a Christian" and "Homosexuality is sinful" made the third cognition, "I am gay," an impossibility. With the second statement changed to "God makes people gay," gay Christian identity becomes possible and the cognitive dissonance disappears. As Mahaffy points out, however, it is only internal dissonance that is resolved by such realizations. The external dissonance caused by challenges from pastors, priests, and parishioners remains to be dealt with in a variety of ways.

Individual Solutions: Vernacular and Lived Religion

For Christians from traditional theological backgrounds, the shift from denying to accepting LGBT identity requires an alteration in theology. The vast majority of participants in this study made that shift on their own; whether they left church or continued to attend, most decided that their personal beliefs encompassed a God who did not want LGBT Christians to change their sexual or gender identities. While most also were influenced by experiences of some sort, they did not make this decision at the urging of a religious leader or based upon changing teachings in their church or denomination. In fact, having decided that God might accept LGBT Christians, the participants in this study ceased to give much credence to the doctrines of anti-LGBT churches, choosing instead to identify as Christian on the basis of personal experience and belief.

Current trends toward individualism in U.S. religions have facilitated such self-definition. But it is worth noting here that another study of LGBT Christians reached a similar conclusion. In his work on Dignity, Primiano examines the conflict between Dignity members' definition of themselves as Catholic and the church's rejection of that definition.[11] Doctrinally, Dignity members are not Catholics in good standing because they deny the church's teaching that homosexual activity is sinful and LGBT identity a handicap and, more important, because they act on their beliefs. Yet the existence of Dignity chapters across the United States and Canada suggests that a significant number of people reject this definition of a "good Catholic." Tying this issue to recent theoretical discussions of popular religion, Primiano argues for a concept of vernacular religion, or "religion as it is lived."[12] Only when religion is studied at this level, Primiano explains, can a group such as Dignity be at all comprehensible as a Catholic organization. Without an appreciation of its members' self-definitions, Dignity appears to be a group that flouts Catholic teachings rather than an organization of practicing, believing Catholics. Indeed, without a concept of vernacular or lived religion, the idea of LGBT Christians would be incomprehensible in many circles.

For Primiano, the study of vernacular religion is important if we are to respect and understand the self-definitions of religious people. Yet given the data discussed in previous chapters, the concept can be applied more broadly here, for it is on the level of lived religion—the everyday beliefs of ordinary people—that self-acceptance and identity integration begin. Michel de Certeau has pointed out that a simple dichotomy between powerful active cultural producers and powerless passive cultural consumers is both misleading and inaccurate.[13] Likewise, to assume that religious leaders produce beliefs and congregations consume or follow them without contributing their own input is to oversimplify drastically the complexity of religion.

De Certeau applies Saussure's distinction between *langue* (formal language) and *parole* (informal speech) to an understanding of practice. In the context of MCC, traditional Christian teachings about sexual or gender identity might be considered as parallel to *langue:* they are the official rules that everyone is expected to follow. However, just as few people avoid split infinitives in everyday speech, few people adhere strictly and literally to every religious doctrine in their day-to-day lives. It is fortunate for LGBT Christians that this is the case, because this individual initiative on the day-to-day level of practice is what allows them to develop an understanding of their identities as morally right and even divinely ordained. Few people in this study had any significant assistance with the early stages of this process.

From Individual to Community: Tactics and Strategies

De Certeau also distinguishes between the tactics of everyday practice and the more focused long-term strategies typically employed by those in power. For him, everyday life involves an element of thinking on one's feet, of making do on the spur of the moment with the variety of resources that are immediately available—*bricolage,* as he calls it.[14] Among the participants in this study, the initial individual work of identity integration can be understood in this way. Some people have sufficient resources at hand to complete the integration and never need the support of a community. They still may join MCC or another LGBT religious organization for a variety of reasons, but not in order to complete the integration process. For others, however, individual resources are insufficient and an LGBT religious group becomes a crucial source of assistance and support. Eventually they, too, reach a point of comfort with their religious and sexual or gender identities, and spur-of-the-moment tactics become less necessary.

In this transition into MCC, and indeed in MCC congregations themselves, it is possible to see a shift from tactics to strategy. Although de Certeau uses the two terms to distinguish between the activities of the haves and the have-nots in the social arena, they are also useful in distinguishing increasing levels of social power or autonomy. The UFMCC is certainly not a dominant social institution in mainstream U.S. culture, but as an international LGBT organization it is a stable safe haven and a potential point of organization for political and social action. As such, it holds a position of considerably greater social power than does the individual LGBT Christian struggling with religious and sexual or gender identity. It is thus a logical location in which to develop long-term strategies for the acceptance of LGBT Christians within both Christianity and U.S. culture.

Individuals in Community: Revaluing Difference as Mission

From individual tactics to community strategies, there are a variety of ways in which LGBT Christians battle the internalized and external oppression they face. One notable source of self-affirmation appears both in individual belief and in community discourse: an overwhelming number of interview participants believe that LGBT people have a special mission in the world.[15] This belief is espoused by members of both MCC Valle Rico and Oceanfront MCC as well as by people who rarely attend MCC—so its ubiquity in this study is unlikely to be caused by the influence of a particular pastor or even of MCC in general.

The sense of difference among LGBT people is one legacy of a homophobic and heteronormative world. Usually that difference is a devalued one: people who are "different" in this way are considered by others, and often consider themselves, to be social and sometimes psychological deviants who are deficient rather than exceptional. One response to this differentiation is to deny it by asserting sameness, and indeed that is an important message in MCC and among its congregants. In the words of one lesbian couple I interviewed: "Lesbians [get] out of bed the same way as most people get out of bed," and "we go shopping, and we go to work, and we come home and iron our clothes and work in the yard," and "we can be participants in church services too. And . . . be Christians."[16]

Given the obvious presence of a discourse of sameness in MCC but also the existence of a message of exceptionalism, I wondered whether reclaiming and revaluing difference were as important among the group I was studying as they have been for other oppressed groups. Hoping to explore this further, I asked people during the interviews whether they believed that LGBT Christians (or, for non-Christian participants, LGBT people in general) had any sort of a special mission in the world. Although I was expecting a number of people to hold this belief, the answers to the question were in fact overwhelming: of the fifty-six people who responded, forty-seven answered in the affirmative. Five people answered with a simple negative, and four more told me that they believe each person, heterosexual or LGBT, has her or his own unique mission.

Those who did believe in a special mission often went on directly to explain what they thought it might be; when a respondent did not offer this information, I asked. Some people envisioned a single mission, while others saw multiple ones. The three most common responses concerned combating oppression, educating heterosexuals about LGBT people, and evangelizing among LGBT people who are lapsed Christians. For many, these special missions are not just an accidental result of their place in society or their experiences in the world. Rather, a number of people feel that such missions are divinely ordained. They believe, in other words, that LGBT people have been chosen by God to carry out these special tasks.

Fourteen of those I interviewed believe that LGBT people have a mission to resist oppression. On the surface, this is an unsurprising answer: those who suffer from oppression are more likely than those who do not to feel strongly about eliminating it. What is notable about these responses, however, is that in every case the oppression to be fought was not specifically that against the LGBT community but against all who are treated unjustly. As one woman put it: "What better way [to promote tolerance] than with a group that's hated?"[17] Harold explained, "I think we tend to be more tolerant of other people because people haven't been tolerant of us. And we know what that's like."[18] Rather than invoke the activist maxim that none is free until all are free, this group of respondents prefers to speak of the alliances engendered by similar experiences of oppression. Having suffered from oppression themselves, they feel that they are more acutely aware of its effects on other groups as well.

Twelve people described the special mission of LGBT people as being one of education—a mission that is no doubt related to respondents' general agreement that homophobia and anti-LGBT hate crimes stem from ignorance about the LGBT community. For some, this education takes the form of speaking to people about themselves. Many others, such as Chris, hope to educate by example:

> When I applied to [seminary], I said that really a large part of my calling was to just . . . to be there, and demonstrate by my actions that, you know, here I am, I'm a gay Christian, and . . . I'm leading a very fulfilling and challenging life. I have a lot to contribute to the world, and . . . you know, I'm not a monster; I'm not an evil person, and maybe . . . if people can see me without their usual blinders on . . . I might touch somebody that way.[19]

Ironically, for some, the special mission of LGBT people is to show that they are the same as heterosexuals. The lesbian couple quoted above expressed this understanding of their own mission, which they carry out by attending a local United Methodist church.

The third most common response to the question of mission, given by seven of the people I interviewed, was evangelization. Most of these respondents stressed that theirs is a very circumscribed definition of the term: it applies only to LGBT people who have been rejected by their churches and have rejected Christianity in turn. There is a sense among these respondents, often based on personal experience, that many former Christians in the LGBT community are unaware, despite their self-acceptance as LGBT people, that God accepts them as well. These respondents feel that the most important function they can perform as LGBT Christians is to bring the "good news" of God's love and acceptance to those who have not yet heard it.

Other responses included a sense that LGBT people are more spiritual or more artistically creative than heterosexuals and that sharing these special gifts is a mission. A few respondents went so far as to argue that difference is a necessary force that keeps mainstream society from becoming complacent; Jeffrey described LGBT people as being "part of the perfect plan of chaos."[20]

Many people turned to biblical sources to explain the unique location of LGBT people and other oppressed groups within Christianity. Noting that Jesus paid special attention to social outcasts and had little respect, on a spiritual level, for those in power, respondents claimed a place for LGBT people among the chosen outcasts. This strategy highlights especially well the explicit reclaiming of difference among some LGBT Christians. Told repeatedly by religious groups and by society at large that they are deviant, that their sexuality is not honored by God and was not created by God, that their relationships are farces of or insults to heterosexual marriage, some LGBT people respond not by denying difference but by revaluing it. Like those who reclaim the epithet "queer," these people transform deviance into exceptionalism and claim a place not just at the table but at its head.

MCC as an Institution

MCC's most central role in this study is to serve as a source of community. It is also a sizeable and politically active institution—a fact that affects its influence in the lives of both members and nonmembers.

The UFMCC in the Political Arena

The UFMCC has been a politically active organization since its inception. In addition to making a strong political statement simply by existing, the denomination has been represented at innumerable rallies and marches for LGBT rights. It claims a commitment as well to the struggles of other minority groups and recently joined forces with Jesse Jackson and other religious leaders to agitate for more effective hate crimes legislation.[21] Within Christianity, the UFMCC is visible on both the national and international levels. As an observer at the World Council of Churches, it has played a part in attempts to raise awareness of LGBT civil rights issues worldwide. The denomination has applied for both membership and observer status in the National Council of Churches, but both requests have been denied.[22] And MCC Minister of Justice Mel White, a former ghostwriter for Jerry Falwell, was instrumental in organizing a 1999 détente between LGBT and conservative Christians.[23]

Is MCC effective politically because of its status as a church? Several current theories support this contention; here I examine the intersection of Pierre Bourdieu's concept of symbolic capital with Christian Smith's analysis of social activism in religious organizations.[24]

Bourdieu defines symbolic capital in the context of the ultimate illusory nature of social power. Applying an economic concept to cultural analysis, Bourdieu suggests that just as economic capital represents one's buying power, so symbolic (or social) capital represents one's social power. In a way, this idea is linked to Gramsci's concept of hegemony: both authors argue that social control remains in place largely through symbolic means rather than though overt ones such as threatened or actual violence. For Bourdieu, though, symbolic capital does more than determine who is in power and who is not; its effects are more nuanced than that. The level of symbolic capital possessed by a group or institution determines the amount of respect and power society assigns it.

Applying this idea to MCC, we might suggest that although its identity as an LGBT organization puts its register of symbolic capital in the red, its status as a church might go a long way toward correcting that balance. To put the argument more concretely, given the common accusation that LGBT people are somehow less morally upright than the average heterosexual, and given the frequent assumption that churches and their members represent the best in moral rectitude, it is possible that an LGBT church might go farther in some circles toward gaining respect and equal rights for LGBT people than would a secular organization. At least in some areas of U.S. society, a church has a higher level of social capital than does a secular political group.[25]

Christian Smith agrees with this analysis, which he summarizes in his concept of privileged legitimacy. Examining a broad spectrum of religio-political coalitions, Smith suggests six religious assets for activism, three of which are particularly helpful in understanding MCC's role in the struggle for LGBT civil rights.[26] First on Smith's list is what he calls transcendent motivation. Religious beliefs, he argues, provide a variety of motivations for political involvement. These include moral imperatives, ritual, and ideologies, myths, or symbols that encourage social protest. In addition, the transcendent aspect of these motivations is important. They are strengthened, Smith argues, by the fact that they stem from a source beyond the human realm. In the context of LGBT Christians, I have already discussed the critical importance of believing in God's acceptance of LGBT identity. That belief alone, however, is motivation enough for self-acceptance but not necessarily for political protest.

On a more practical level, Smith cites organizational resources as a second asset that religious groups offer to activists. In addition to motivation, any social or political movement needs resources in order to spread its message, including everything from meeting space to office supplies and communications equipment. In the movement for LGBT rights as a whole, groups with such resources already existed when Perry founded MCC, and a powerful grassroots organization was soon to arise that would generally reject organized religion—so here MCC is not as helpful. However, in the movement for LGBT acceptance within Christianity, MCC has been a major resource. Indeed, this is due in part to the rejection just mentioned. Because the Marxist-influenced gay liberation movement was deeply suspicious of organized religion and especially of Christianity, it was of little help in the struggle for LGBT rights within the churches. MCC, on the other hand, was an explicitly Christian organization and was the first LGBT religious organization to develop beyond the local level; it thus was and is a potential source of organizational resources for LGBT rights movements within Christianity.

The third part of Smith's analysis that is applicable to MCC is the concept of privileged legitimacy. Smith applies this idea in the context of repressive political regimes, arguing that in such societies, the official voices of the dominant religion often can be heard even when explicitly political groups have been repressed. This concept works slightly differently in the case of

MCC: although the denomination is part of the dominant religion in the United States, its identity as an LGBT organization would make it vulnerable under a repressively anti-LGBT regime. In such a case, only the mainline denominations could be influential in supporting LGBT rights. In most areas of the United States, however, the fiercest repression of LGBT people comes from grassroots sources rather than governmental ones. Thus, a different application of the idea of privileged legitimacy suggests that the symbolic capital provided by MCC's status as a Christian denomination may make it a more effective source of political action, in at least some areas of the country, than secular LGBT organizations.[27]

MCC and LGBT Christians

Important as MCC's role may be in political and social activism, these considerations are less directly relevant for the two congregations in this study, neither of which is strongly activist. Certainly both have taken part in protests and in coalition-building, but such activities are far from being central areas of focus. MCC congregations are obviously sources of social and symbolic support. But what can be said about MCC's role as an institution among LGBT Christians?

The key point here is that MCC serves not the general population, but a subset of it. It is a subcultural institution rather than a cultural one, and as such it acts as a bridge, intermediary, or buffer between individual congregants and the community at large. Warner provides an important clue to understanding MCC's role as a subcultural institution when he notes that "Perry and his early followers had the audacity to claim for homosexuals the social space given over to subcultural groups through American churches."[28] What other subcultural groups claim social space through American churches? One need only investigate Warner's other recent works to see what he might have had in mind: the religious organizations of minority ethnic communities.

In 1998, Warner and Judith G. Wittner co-edited a volume representing the culmination of the New Ethnic and Immigrant Congregations Project.[29] Ten studies appear in the book, covering everything from Rastafarians in New York to Iranian Jews in Los Angeles. The most important overarching theme in the book is, in fact, the divergence between these communities, as each serves differing needs in a variety of ways. However, beyond these differences stands the fact that religious organizations serve as gathering places, sources of identity affirmation, and havens of familiarity for recent immigrants. They also can provide crucial social networks that help new immigrants to find jobs and to navigate the customs and bureaucracies of their new home.

It is not only among recent immigrants, however, that religious organizations serve as subcultural enclaves. A mass of literature on African American religions has made the same point, especially about the black churches. Similar cases could in fact be cited for most of the ethnic subcultures in the country. But can the LGBT community truly be compared to an ethnic minority?

This is in fact an extremely difficult question. As the literature on essentialism in LGBT identity makes clear, many LGBT people see a parallel between minority sexual or gender identity and minority ethnicity.[30] Some non-LGBT members of ethnic minority groups also see such similarities, yet in practice the comparison has become problematic. The most obvious distinction between the experiences of LGBT people and ethnic minorities is that the former have a far greater possibility of passing as straight or orthodox-gendered than the latter have of passing as white, since any visible physical characteristics that indicate LGBT identity are more cultural than biological. LGBT children do not suffer from the same prejudices regarding their intelligence and work ethic as do the children of some ethnic minorities, although those who come out in junior high and high school may suffer immensely in other ways at the hands of both classmates and teachers.

Furthermore, because of their questionable status as a "people" before the twentieth century, LGBT people *as a community* do not have the same history of brutal oppression and genocide that some ethnic groups have in the United States—in part because without a community LGBT people were a less easily identifiable target.[31] Nor do lesbians, gay men, and bisexuals—again, taken as a group—suffer from the severe economic disadvantages that still plague some minority groups.[32]

Finally, there is the complicating factor that one can be LGBT and still be of any ethnic background—thus, these communities are multicultural in composition, even though they have their own subcultures as well. Minority ethnicity adds further complications to LGBT experiences and identities. Ideals regarding gender and the family among some ethnic minority groups can buttress conservative Christian values, making it all the more difficult for LGBT Christians in these communities to find self-acceptance or acceptance from others. Moreover, racism is alive and well in many LGBT communities, which only increases the difficulty, for LGBT people of color, of finding a safe and supportive community.

So LGBT communities are not the same as ethnic minority communities, and the oppression suffered as a result of homophobia or transphobia differs in substantial ways from that resulting from racism. That much must be said. But the question remains whether it might be fruitful to examine the *functional* parallels between LGBT communities and various ethnic communities.

Like members of other subcultures, LGBT people live in a world where they do not fit the invisible unspoken norm. Just as white is the default ethnic category in mainstream culture, heterosexuality and orthodox gender identity are also default categories. How often does someone say, for instance, "I went to a straight wedding this weekend," or "I met an orthodox-gendered woman yesterday"? LGBT organizations, like organizations based on minority ethnicity, provide a space wherein non-normative identity becomes normative—where one might indeed need to specify that the wedding one attended last weekend was that of a heterosexual couple.

LGBT groups such as MCC also provide a source of community networking. Through the church, someone with few contacts in the LGBT community could find a lawyer specializing in discrimination law if he believed he had been fired from his job on the basis of his sexual orientation, someone else might track down a lead on a job in an LGBT-friendly company, and others might be warned to avoid a certain restaurant where a same-sex couple had received stares and substandard service.

Finally, MCC is parallel to many ethnic churches in its symbolic integration of subcultural identity into religious services. Among ethnic minority communities, such identity is expressed in language choice, music, decoration of the worship space, culturally specific sacred stories or sacred images, and even the identity of the religious leader. With the exception of language, these same factors play a part in MCC's symbolic affirmation of LGBT Christian identity. Far from being a remarkable religious development, then, MCC is simply an interesting new variation on the historic theme of the subcultural religious institution.[33]

Conservative or Radical?

In the United States, many of the groups promoting civil rights over the past few decades have held ambivalent attitudes toward religion. Christianity has been a central target of suspicion because of its complicity in misogyny and in European conquest and colonization. Thus, some black radicals have found a new spiritual home in Islam, some Native American and Latino activists have reclaimed or revived traditional rituals, and some radical feminists have turned to feminist spirituality or Goddess religion. Likewise, the gay liberation movement and its descendants have turned a cold shoulder to Christianity, returning the favor done them by many congregations and pastors.

From the point of view of such activists, anyone in the LGBT community who continues to identify as Christian is either reactionary, hopelessly optimistic, or a victim of false consciousness. Displaying the somewhat unnerving convergence of views that seems to be typical between radicals and reactionaries, some LGBT people join conservative Christians in claiming that it is literally impossible to be a self-respecting LGBT person and also a Christian. To them, the idea of an LGBT Christian organization is at worst repugnant and at best a sad example of people being severely misled. Although these views represent a more radical contingent, many LGBT people who are suspicious of traditional religion consider MCC to be a fundamentally conservative organization.

In many ways, they are right. In terms of the literal definition of the word, MCC has a clear conservative side. Within LGBT communities, the denomination conserves traditional religious values and practices. Although the topic of ethics is a delicate one in MCC because of the moralizing many LGBT Christians have endured from unsympathetic heterosexual pastors, MCC does also offer a certain amount of ethical guidance to its members—and for the most part it follows traditional Christian ethics.[34] And what better way is there to argue for the conservative nature of the denomination as a whole than to consider Troy Perry's original goal of putting himself out of business by successfully promoting the integration of LGBT Christians into mainstream Christian churches?

Yet classifying MCC as a conservative institution is far too simplistic. Certainly the National Council of Churches, which has refused membership to the denomination for so many years, does not consider it conservative. To those Christians more commonly called conservative, in fact, it probably seems to be on par with Goddess worship. And this side, too, has a strong case. It could begin, in fact, where the last one left off: Perry's goal was to integrate LGBT Christians fully into mainstream Christian churches. From the point of view of a conservative Christian, this is a truly radical and perhaps even blasphemous move made by people who are misguided at best and downright evil at worst.

Is MCC a radical organization or a conservative one, then? One possible answer is that MCC is actually a centrist organization, attacked as too conservative by those on the left and as too radical by those on the right. And perhaps if the discussion were about economic reforms proposed by a presidential candidate, this would be an accurate analysis. But the situation of MCC is far more complex. I would suggest, rather, that MCC is *both* radical and conservative, holding the two perspectives in tension just as in its early years it balanced between identifying its members as "lesbian and gay Christians" or "Christian gays and lesbians."

Although Protestant Christianity has produced its share of social radicals, and although UFMCC leaders are often on the forefront of social activism, the denomination in general is not radical in this way. Some of its congregations may be theologically radical, but they are so even relative to the denomination itself. And while there are plenty of participants in this study who wish to affirm LGBT difference rather than pressing for assimilation into heterosexual society, the difference they affirm is not a radical one in the strict definition of the word. No one spoke to me about destabilizing the mating-pair model of love relationships or about developing new social and domestic arrangements—both of which are important themes in the more radical areas of LGBT/queer activism. Instead, they spoke of difference in terms of creativity or spiritual gifts, a different perspective on the world, or simply the obvious difference in sexual or gender identity. These are differences that do not threaten radical social change.

On one front, however, MCC does in fact threaten radical change, especially within Christianity: it represents the demands of LGBT people for full inclusion and equal rights in society at large and in every subculture. Lest it be thought that change in a single area is not earth-shaking enough to offset the general conservative aspects of the church, it is important to notice what portion of society MCC is implicitly and explicitly altering: marriage and family organization. As the recent spate of legislation against same-sex marriages proves, this is a fiercely defended social arena. It is also not one given to large-scale alterations; a brief glance at the long and cross-cultural history of heterosexual marriage makes this abundantly clear.

The UFMCC as an institution, then, serves as a political resource for both secular and religious struggles. It is a source of cultural capital and subcultural support and a wellspring of both conservative and radical impulses. Ultimately, MCC congregations play a complex variety of roles in U.S. society as a whole as well as in the lives of their members.

Epilogue

Roads Less Traveled

The convergence of LGBT identity and Christian belief is becoming familiar to an increasing number of people, but it remains a road less traveled. On April 29, 2000, Troy Perry officiated at a non-sectarian demonstration and same-gender wedding in Washington, D.C. A precursor to the next day's massive LGBT Millennium March on Washington, the event called "The Wedding: Now More Than Ever" brought an estimated 3,000 couples from forty-eight states and seven countries to the Lincoln Memorial to exchange or renew their vows.

On the West Coast, news coverage was brief and was indicative of the tenacity of misunderstanding. One prominent news radio station in San Francisco reported that the event had been a "mock wedding," while a Sacramento television station illustrated its story with footage of a small group of people protesting the wedding. In a stunning clash of voice and image, the camera zoomed in on placards reading: "Got AIDS yet?" as the reporter informed audiences that lesbian and gay couples had gathered for a demonstration.

But despite misunderstanding and the perseverance of anti-LGBT sentiment, LGBT Christians find ways to affirm their own identities. At times this self-affirmation comes at great cost, at times it never comes, and at times, conversely, it seems effortless—but many reach the point of integration. One of the most important findings of this study concerns the role of individualized religious beliefs in this process. Although the vast majority of study participants had contact at some point with anti-LGBT Christian teachings, fewer than half of them ever took those messages to heart. Turning to their personal beliefs, to spirituality, and to an essentialist understanding of LGBT identity, many of those in this study reached their own conclusions regarding the appropriateness of being both LGBT and Christian. Rather than following the guidance of pastor and church (though some did this at first), they studied their Bibles and prayed to their God and then chose a church that affirmed the conclusions they had reached on their own. For the respondents in this study, that church was MCC; for others it might be a chapter of Evangelicals Concerned, a Unitarian church, a Dignity chapter, or a Welcoming and Affirming Baptist congregation. But MCC offers something that some of these other groups cannot: a new world.

The old world of divergent identities persists, although it has been changing rapidly in recent years. In some religious quarters its presence is clear: LGBT Christians are not welcome unless they are committed to seeking a future as heterosexual or orthodox-gendered Christians. In other areas, the remnants of the old world are more subtle. Though a congregation as a whole may welcome LGBT Christians, for instance, individual members may be less accepting. Or, subtlest of all but still quite tangible to those in this study, accepting congregations may be wholly welcoming and inclusive yet may lack one crucial element: community.

As Jane pointed out, for LGBT Christians it is a rare and potentially moving experience to walk into a sanctuary that is decorated with rainbow flags. Like her, many study participants came to MCC not to integrate their sexual or transgender identities with their Christian beliefs but to gain support for an already integrated identity. Though accepting churches in non-LGBT denominations offer such support upon request, it is rarely a regular part of the weekly service. But at MCC one might almost say that affirmation is in the air, present as it is in symbolic and verbal discourse, in ritual, and in the congregational community itself. For LGBT people, as for other minorities in the United States, Sunday remains the most segregated day of the week, but this is by intent as well as by necessity. As Chris put it, being with "my people" remains an important factor in some respondents' choice of congregation.

LGBT communities are an unusual case for the study of individualism in religion. Most work on this topic examines the religious and spiritual choices that people make during the course of their lives. While the same approach applies to LGBT communities, the religious life stories of many LGBT people begin with a forced or constrained choice between LGBT identity and religious affiliation. This factor puts a new twist on the study of religious individualism: Does this phenomenon look different when it is forced upon people through religious rejection rather than being chosen freely? According to those in this study, in the former case the initial adjustment process may be turbulent, but the eventual result is often similar to the religious individualism found in other U.S. communities. Whether they take what they need from the Bible and ignore the rest or spend long hours working to align their biblical interpretations with their personal beliefs, these people have benefited from the trend toward individualism in U.S. religiosity because it has allowed them to create a subcultural space wherein they can exist comfortably both as LGBT people and as Christians.

The study of LGBT people in religion also raises interesting issues for the analysis of identity and the self—issues, in fact, that are becoming increasingly important in a world of mixed identities and *bricolage*. Travelers on these new but increasingly popular paths of identity refuse to choose when offered traditional options for religious affiliation, ethnicity, and the like: they claim instead combined or multiple identities. These are the people who cause survey researchers endless headaches by selecting three or four options on questions about religion or ethnicity, but they are also the ones who force us to acknowledge the shifting nature of identity in postmodern societies.

The religious identities and the coming-out processes of LGBT people offer an opportunity to explore what happens when the dominant culture defines two aspects of one's identity as irreconcilable. Dissonance theory offers one fruitful approach to this puzzle, but other analytical angles can be found in theories on the self that come from outside the field of psychology. Indeed, the interdisciplinary analysis necessary in work such as this forces researchers to examine our own identities as well: it seems that increasing levels of *bricolage* are in our future, too. This book reflects that possible future, refusing theoretical boundaries and exploring instead the application of ideas from sociology, religious studies, psychology, and other fields to the research at hand.

Finally, studying the dynamics involved in LGBT religious organizations can further our understanding of the role of religion and religious communities among socially disadvantaged groups in general. Religion is not, Marx suggested, simply a tool of those in power—though it certainly can be at times. Neither is it always an open door to liberation—though, again, it can be at times. Instead, the role of religion is multifaceted and complex. It is affected by group and individual dynamics, by the nature of a religious organization and the beliefs of its leaders, by locale, by the group's function (or lack thereof) as a source of community, and by many other factors.

The stories of participants in this study are cases in point: within their own lives, these people often have seen religion acting as oppressor, liberator, and neutral party. Many chose to name these roles differently, reflecting a contemporary understanding of religion as doctrinally bound and restrictive and of spirituality as open-ended and freeing. But whatever words they chose, it was the latter option that led many respondents into MCC (and sometimes out again), and it was this aspect of religiosity that allowed them to alter the cultural geography. Where two roads once diverged in the yellow wood of identity, these people created converging paths. They built a road less traveled by, and that truly has made all the difference.

Appendix A

Index of Participants

Stories or comments from study participants appear on the pages listed after each name.

Appendix B

UFMCC Mission Statement, Vision Statement, and Doctrine

Reprinted by permission of the Universal Fellowship of Metropolitan Community Churches

UFMCC Mission Statement (adopted July 1997)

The Universal Fellowship of Metropolitan Community Churches is a Christian Church founded in and reaching beyond the Gay and Lesbian communities. We embody and proclaim Christian salvation and liberation, Christian inclusivity and community, and Christian social action and justice. We serve among those seeking and celebrating the integration of their spirituality and sexuality.

UFMCC Vision Statement (adopted July 1997)

The vision of the UFMCC is to embody the presence of the Divine in the world, as revealed through Jesus Christ; to challenge the conscience of the universal Christian Church; and to celebrate the inherent worth and dignity of each person. As we move toward this vision, by 2003, the UFMCC will be comprised of at least 70,000 members and adherents who are all called and equipped to minister with excellence. This diverse global body will be widely recognized as a prophetic light and driving force for an inclusive Christian spirituality which celebrates the integration of spirituality and human sexuality. Through our strengthened local churches, we will meet the justice and faith needs of people in increasing numbers of countries and cultures.

UFMCC Doctrine (By-laws, July 1997)

Christianity is the revelation of God in Jesus Christ and is the religion set forth in the Scriptures. Jesus Christ is foretold in the Old Testament, presented in the New Testament, and proclaimed by the Christian Church in every age and in every land.

Founded in the interest of offering a church home to all who confess and believe, the Universal Fellowship of Metropolitan Community Churches moves in the mainstream of Christianity.

Our faith is based upon the principles outlined in the historic creeds: Apostles and Nicene.

We believe:

1. In one triune God, omnipotent, omnipresent and omniscient, of one substance and of three persons: God—our Parent-Creator; Jesus Christ, the only begotten son of God, God in flesh, human; and the Holy Spirit—God as our Sustainer.

2. That the Bible is the divinely inspired Word of God, showing forth God to every person through the law and the prophets, and finally, completely and ultimately on earth in the being of Jesus Christ.

3. That Jesus . . . the Christ . . . historically recorded as living some 2,000 years before this writing, is God incarnate, of human birth, fully God and fully human, and that by being one with God, Jesus has demonstrated once and forever that all people are likewise Children of God, being spiritually made in God's image.

4. That the Holy Spirit is God making known God's love and interest to all people. The Holy Spirit is God, available to and working through all who are willing to place their welfare in God's keeping.

5. Every person is justified by grace to God through faith in Jesus Christ.

6. We are saved from loneliness, despair and degradation through God's gift of grace, as was declared by our Savior. Such grace is not earned, but is a pure gift from a God of pure love. We further commend the community of the faithful to a life of prayer; to seek genuine forgiveness for unkind, thoughtless and unloving acts; and to a committed life of Christian service.

7. The Church serves to bring all people to God through Christ. To this end, it shall arrange for regular services of worship, prayer, interpretation of the Scriptures, and edification through the teaching and preaching of the Word.

Appendix C
Survey Demographics

Percentages are given for the relevant mailing list: MCCVR, OMCC, or all participants.

Gender of Survey Participants

| | Female | | Male | |
	N	%	N	%
MCCVR	37	41.1	53	58.9
OMCC	15	55.6	12	44.4
Total	52	44.4	65	55.6

Number and Percent of
Transgender/Transsexual Respondents

	N	% Survey Population
MCCVR	5	5.6
OMCC	—	—
Total	5	4.3

Sexual Orientation of Survey Participants

| | Lesbian | | Gay Male | | Bisexual | | Heterosexual | | Questioning | |
	N	%	N	%	N	%	N	%	N	%
MCCVR	24	26.7	47	52.3	8	8.9	7	7.8	4	4.4
OMCC	15	55.6	9	33.3	1	3.7	1	3.7	1	3.7
Total	39	33.3	56	47.8	9	7.7	8	6.8	5	4.3

Age of Survey Participants in 1998

	Under 30		30–39		40–49		50–59		60–69		70 +	
	N	%	N	%	N	%	N	%	N	%	N	%
MCCVR	1	1.1	20	22.7	29	33.0	26	29.6	9	10.2	3	3.4
OMCC	1	3.8	5	19.2	10	38.5	4	15.4	4	15.4	2	7.7
Total	2	1.8	25	21.9	39	34.2	30	26.3	13	11.4	5	4.4

Ethnicity of Survey Participants

	Asian/ Pacific Islander		European/ Caucasian		Chicano/ Latino		Native American		Biracial: White + Native American		Biracial: White + Asian/ Pacific Islander		Multiracial	
	N	%	N	%	N	%	N	%	N	%	N	%	N	%
MCCVR	4	4.4	77	85.6	3	3.3	1	1.1	2	2.2	2	2.2	1	1.1
OMCC	—	—	18	69.2	2	7.7	—	—	3	11.5	1	3.8	2	7.7
Total	4	3.4	95	81.9	5	4.3	1	0.9	5	4.3	3	2.6	3	2.6

Primary Childhood Residence of Survey Participants

	South U.S.		New England/ East U.S.		Mid- west U.S.		South- west U.S.		West Coast U.S.		Non-U.S. (Inter- national)		Multiple	
	N	%	N	%	N	%	N	%	N	%	N	%	N	%
MCCVR	6	6.7	10	11.2	17	19.1	5	5.6	45	50.6	5	5.6	1	1.1
OMCC	—	—	6	22.2	6	22.2	—	—	13	48.1	1	3.7	1	3.7
Total	6	5.2	16	13.8	23	19.8	5	4.3	58	50.0	6	5.2	2	1.7

Highest Educational Level Attained by Survey Participants

	High School		Some College		Associate's Degree or Equivalent		Bachelor's Degree or Equivalent		Some Graduate School		Graduate Degree	
	N	%	N	%	N	%	N	%	N	%	N	%
MCCVR	5	5.5	20	22.2	10	11.1	22	24.4	9	10.0	24	26.7
OMCC	1	3.7	7	25.9	5	18.5	2	7.4	3	11.1	9	33.3
Total	5	4.3	27	23.1	15	12.8	24	20.5	12	10.3	33	28.2

Approximate Annual Income of Survey Participants

	Below $15,000		$15,000 to $25,000		$25,000 to $40,000		$40,000 to $65,000		$65,000 to $90,000		Over $90,000	
	N	%	N	%	N	%	N	%	N	%	N	%
MCCVR	8	9.2	15	17.2	29	33.3	22	25.3	9	10.3	4	4.6
OMCC	6	22.2	4	14.8	9	33.3	5	18.5	3	11.1	—	—
Total	14	12.3	19	16.7	38	33.3	27	23.7	12	10.5	4	3.5

Primary Religious Upbringing of Survey Participants

	Catholic		Con- servative Protestant		Mainline Protestant		Liberal Protestant		Pagan		Other*		None	
	N	%	N	%	N	%	N	%	N	%	N	%	N	%
MCCVR	29	32.2	12	13.3	31	34.4	4	4.4	—	—	8	8.9	6	6.7
OMCC	6	22.2	2	7.4	8	29.6	3	11.1	2	7.4	3	11.1	3	11.1
Total	35	29.9	14	12.0	39	33.3	7	6.0	2	1.7	11	9.4	9	7.7

* Includes Protestant (unspecified denomination), Jewish, Russian Orthodox, Christian Scientist, atheist, agnostic, and multiple

MCC Attended Most Frequently by Survey Participants

	MCCVR		OMCC		Other Local MCC		Other West Coast MCC	
	N	%	N	%	N	%	N	%
MCCVR	52	75.4	1	1.5	11	15.9	5	7.2
OMCC	2	8.7	20	87.0	1	4.3	—	—
Total	54	58.7	21	22.8	12	13.0	5	5.4

Frequency of Attendance of Survey Participants at MCCVR and OMCC in 1998

	Once a week or more		2–3 times per month		Once a month		Several times per year		Once or twice a year		Less than once a year		Never	
	N	%	N	%	N	%	N	%	N	%	N	%	N	%
MCCVR	19	21.8	2	2.3	15	17.2	13	14.9	6	6.9	24	27.6	8	9.2
OMCC	5	20.0	5	20.0	2	8.0	2	8.0	3	12.0	5	20.0	3	12.0
Total	24	21.4	7	6.3	17	15.2	15	13.4	9	8.0	29	25.9	11	9.8

Length of Attendance at MCCVR and OMCC by Survey Participants*

	Less than 6 months		6 months to 1 year		1 to 3 years		3 to 5 years		5 to 7 years		8 to 10 years		Over 10 years	
	N	%	N	%	N	%	N	%	N	%	N	%	N	%
MCCVR	11	13.8	4	5.0	9	11.3	19	23.8	7	8.8	7	8.8	23	28.8
OMCC	4	17.4	1	4.3	4	17.4	2	8.7	6	26.1	1	4.3	5	21.7
Total	15	14.6	5	4.9	13	12.6	21	20.4	13	12.6	8	7.8	28	27.2

*Includes current and past attenders

Coding of Denominational Affiliation

Participants who listed "Protestant Christian" as their former or current religious affiliation were asked to give the name of their denomination. The denominations were then classed as conservative, mainline, or liberal Protestant based on several guidelines. Roof and McKinney's classifications in *American Mainline Religion* (New Brunswick, N.J.: Rutgers University Press, 1987) proved helpful, as did Tom W. Smith's article, "Classifying Protestant Denominations," *Review of Religious Research* 31 (March 1990): 225–45. Coding also took into account the official and unofficial attitudes of a given denomination toward LGBT people (as reflected in formal statements and in denominational practices across the United States) and respondents' comments on the congregation in question. In some cases, churches that normally would be classed as mainline Protestant were coded instead as conservative Protestant because respondents indicated that theirs was a particularly conservative congregation. In the absence of such evidence, Protestant denominations were coded as follows.

Conservative Protestant: Southern Baptist, Lutheran-Missouri Synod, Pentecostal, fundamentalist, Evangelical Free Church, Pentecostal/Holiness, evangelical, Shiloh youth revivals, non-denominational charismatic, Assemblies of God, Southern Church of Christ, Southern Methodist, charismatic Episcopalian, Jehovah's Witness, Missionary Baptist, Conservative Baptist, Salvation Army, Seventh-day Adventist, Mormon, Mennonite, Foursquare Gospel, Vineyard Fellowship

Mainline Protestant: United Methodist, American Baptist, unspecified Baptist, Presbyterian, Lutheran, Congregational, non-denominational Protestant

Liberal Protestant: Episcopalian, Disciples of Christ, United Church of Christ, Unitarian, Quaker, Moravian

Notes

Prologue

1. While MCCVR interprets the rainbow flag as a representation of human diversity, it is widely recognized and most often used as a symbol of pride in lesbian, gay, bisexual, and transgender identity.

2. Unity is one of the many metaphysical movements that developed out of the New Thought movement in the nineteenth-century United States.

3. The UFMCC is the denominational organization, headquartered in Los Angeles, to which each individual Metropolitan Community Church (MCC) belongs.

4. Lengthy notes on terminology are de rigueur in any study of LGBT people. The early term "homosexual" leaves invisible the bisexuals and transgender people who also make up an important part of many communities. "Gay" is problematic because it often refers specifically to men, thus rendering lesbians invisible. "Gay and lesbian" has the same problems as "homosexual," and although "queer" has come to be the all-inclusive term of choice in many areas of LGBT studies, I avoid it in fieldwork-based research out of respect for those respondents who remain uncomfortable with the idea of reclaiming such a pejorative word. I thus use "LGBT" throughout this work. At times, I discuss a study or group that explicitly excludes one or more subgroups of this population; I make this clear by altering my terminology to speak, for instance, of "lesbians and gay men." In other cases, an author's use of more limited terminology is indicative of the standard usage at the time of writing, and the work itself does not specify either the presence or the absence of the excluded groups. In these situations, I continue to use the term "LGBT," assuming that if the population in question was large enough, it probably included the unnamed groups as well.

A second clarification is necessary regarding my use of the term "transgender." Transgender women and men are usually those whose sense of gender identity does not match their genetic sex: they are genetic females who identify as men and genetic males who identify as women (though of late these definitions have become increasingly fluid, and some now use the term to refer to identification with both genders or with neither gender). Among those who acknowledge and accept their internal sense of gender, some address the tension between identity and social expectations simply by living their internal identities (an older vocabulary called these people "transvestites" or "cross-dressers"), while others change their bodies through hormone therapy and/or surgery (these individuals are often designated as "transsexuals"). Although some drag performers are transgender, many are not, and the categories of drag performance and transgender identity should not be conflated.

I follow current usage among many in the transgender community by utilizing "transgender" as a blanket term to refer to anyone whose gender identity does not match her or his genetically determined sex. When referring to the gender of a transgender person, I respect her or his self-identification. Thus, someone who would technically be referred to as "male-to-female transgender" is simply described herein as a transgender woman.

Transsexual or transgender identity also has little to do with sexual orientation. Some transgender women, for example, are heterosexual (in other words, they are attracted to men) while others are bisexual or lesbian. But because transgender identity and homosexual orientation were confused for so many decades in Western scientific and popular literature, transgender communities are often allied with lesbian, gay, and bisexual communities (although not without tension and misunderstandings). Thus, it is logical in a study such as this one to refer to "LGBT people" or "the LGBT community." This tactic also carries certain risks, but I believe it to be the best choice.

5. Gary David Comstock's denominational study, *Unrepentant, Self-Affirming, Practicing: Lesbian/Gay/Bisexual People within Organized Religion* (New York: Continuum, 1996), has an exhaustive literature review. More recently, Edward Gray and Scott Thumma have put together an anthology of current research on LGBT religiosity in their forthcoming book, *Gay Religion: Innovation and Tradition in Spiritual Practice* (Walnut Creek, Calif.: Alta Mira).

6. Gray and Thumma's introduction to *Gay Religion* may in fact prove to be the first such effort.

7. Ronald M. Enroth, "The Homosexual Church: An Ecclesiastical Extension of a Subculture," *Social Compass* 21, no. 3 (1974): 355–360; Ronald M. Enroth and Gerald E. Jamison, *The Gay Church* (Grand Rapids, Mich.: Eerdmans, 1974).

8. Paul F. Bauer, "The Homosexual Subculture at Worship: A Participant Observation Study," *Pastoral Psychology* 25, no. 2 (1976): 115–127.

9. E. Michael Gorman, "A New Light on Zion: A Study of Three Homosexual Religious Congregations in Urban America" (Ph.D. diss., University of Chicago, 1980).

10. This sort of comparative work, incidentally, has not been repeated since, and to my knowledge the dissertation was never published.

11. It is possible, of course, that the congregations studied by Enroth, Jamison, and Bauer were in fact shallow and focused largely on sex. Certainly this complaint is not unknown among those dissatisfied with some LGBT congregations today. Moreover, both congregations were quite new—as was the denomination—and may have been developing their culture as they grew. It is also possible that LGBT congregations, and LGBT subcultures in general, underwent a critical phase of development between the completion of Bauer's work in the early 1970s and the beginning of Gorman's in the late 1970s. But it is also relevant that heterosexual researchers (which Bauer insistently declares himself to be; Enroth and Jamison are more subtle but do not give any indication of being homosexual) tend to be extremely sensitive to, critical of, and at times overtly threatened by sexual overtones in LGBT communities, accustomed as they are to having their own gender and sexual orientation be the unmarked "default" category.

12. Scott Thumma, "Negotiating a Religious Identity: The Case of the Gay Evangelical," *Sociological Analysis* 52, no. 4 (1991): 333–347.

13. Leonard Norman Primiano, "Intrinsically Catholic: Vernacular Religion and Philadelphia's 'Dignity'" (Ph.D. diss., University of Pennsylvania, 1993); Moshe Shokeid, *A Gay Synagogue in New York* (New York: Columbia University Press, 1995). See also Primiano, "'I Would Rather Be Fixated on the Lord': Women's Religion, Men's Power, and the 'Dignity' Problem," *New York Folklore* 19, no. 1–2 (1993): 89–99.

14. Glenn Wagner, et al., "Integration of One's Religion and Homosexuality: A Weapon against Internalized Homophobia?" *Journal of Homosexuality* 26, no. 4 (1994): 91–110.

15. Shokeid, *A Gay Synagogue in New York,* 239.

16. R. Stephen Warner, "The Metropolitan Community Churches and the Gay Agenda: The Power of Pentecostalism and Essentialism," in *Sex, Lies, and Sanctity: Religion and Deviance in Contemporary North America,* ed. Mary Jo Neitz and Marion S. Goldman (Greenwich, Conn.: JAI, 1995), 81–108.

17. Edward R. Gray and Scott L. Thumma, "The Gospel Hour: Liminality, Identity, and Religion in a Gay Bar," in *Contemporary American Religion: An Ethnographic Reader,* ed. Penny Edgell Becker and Nancy L. Eiesland (Walnut Creek, Calif.: Alta Mira Press, 1997), 79–98.

18. Comstock, *Unrepentant, Self-Affirming, Practicing.* Because Comstock does not address transgender people in his study (indeed, he was one of the first to consider bisexuals), I use "LGB" when discussing his work.

19. Kimberly A. Mahaffy, "Cognitive Dissonance and Its Resolution: A Study of Lesbian Christians," *Journal for the Scientific Study of Religion* 35, no. 4 (1996): 392–402.

20. Andrew K. T. Yip, "Gay Christian Couples and Blessing Ceremonies," *Theology and Sexuality* 4 (1996): 100–117; and "Gay Christians and Their Participation in the Gay Subculture," *Deviant Behavior* 17 (1996): 297–318. Among Yip's 1997 works are "Attacking the Attacker: Gay Christians Talk Back," *British Journal of Sociology* 48, no. 1 (1997): 113–127; and *Gay Male Christian Couples: Life Stories* (Westport, Conn.: Praeger, 1997). See also Sean Gill, ed., *The Lesbian and Gay Christian Movement: Campaigning for Justice, Truth, and Love* (London: Cassell, 1998).

21. Yip, "The Persistence of Faith Among Nonheterosexual Christians: Evidence for the Neosecularization Thesis of Religious Transformation," *Journal for the Scientific Study of Religion* 41, no. 2 (2002): 199–212.

22. Eric M. Rodriguez and Suzanne C. Ouellette, "The Metropolitan Community Church of New York: A Gay and Lesbian Community," *The Community Psychologist* 32, no. 3 (1999): 24–29, and "Gay and Lesbian Christians: Homosexual and Religious Identity Integration in the Members and Participants of a Gay-Positive Church," *Journal for the Scientific Study of Religion* 39, no. 3 (2000): 333–347. See also Eric M. Rodriguez and Suzanne C. Ouellette, "Religion and Masculinity in Latino Gay Lives," in *Gay Masculinities,* ed. Peter Nardi (Thousand Oaks, Calif.: Sage, 2000), 101–129.

23. Also worthy of mention is Michele Dillon's *Catholic Identity: Balancing Reason, Faith, and Power* (New York: Cambridge University Press, 1999), which came to my attention too late to be included here in any depth. In a chapter entitled "Gay and Lesbian Catholics: 'Owning the Identity Differently,' " Dillon reports on fieldwork conducted at Dignity/Boston in 1995. Although her discussion is succinct, her findings correlate well with those of other researchers discussed in this section, as well as with my own.

24. A second recent study of MCC is W. Bernard Lukenbill, "Observations on the Corporate Culture of a Gay and Lesbian Congregation," *Journal for the Scientific Study of Religion* 37, no. 3 (1998): 440–452. Lukenbill, however, as his title suggests, is more interested in the organizational aspects of MCC than in questions of identity among individual members. His study is thus somewhat tangential to the work presented here.

25. The most notable of these gaps is the in-depth study of bisexuals, transgender people, and LGBT people of color; all three groups were underrepresented in this study, due in part to MCC's own demography and in part to the complex social dynamics of LGBT communities. Also all but missing in the literature to date (it has been discussed only by Yip so far), and addressed only in passing here, is any examination of unchurched LGBT people—those who have left organized religion behind in favor of a more individu-

alized form of spirituality. I am currently working on a project designed to address some of these missing elements. Other helpful work can be found in Gray and Thumma's forthcoming anthology, *Gay Religion: Innovation and Tradition in Spiritual Practice*.

26. The coming-out process and its attendant narratives have been studied extensively by psychologists, sociologists, and literary theorists (see, for instance, Richard Troiden, "The Formation of Homosexual Identities," *Journal of Homosexuality* 17, no. 1–2 [1989]: 43–73). The entire process, which may take decades in some cases, generally involves several phases, including acknowledging and eventually accepting one's LGBT identity (coming out to oneself); telling others about that identity (coming out to others); and making that identity more generally public through symbolic jewelry, bumper stickers, public displays of affection with a member of the same sex, and the like (being out).

27. R. Stephen Warner, "Immigration and Religious Communities in the United States," in *Gatherings in Diaspora: Religious Communities and the New Immigration,* ed. R. Stephen Warner and Judith G. Wittner (Philadelphia: Temple University Press, 1998), 9.

28. Comstock, *Unrepentant, Self-Affirming, Practicing,* xiv.

29. Universal Fellowship of Metropolitan Community Churches, "Mission Statement" (http://www.ufmcc.com/missionstatement.htm [Accessed January 14, 2003]). This version was adopted in 1997. The UFMCC's Mission Statement, Vision Statement, and Doctrine are reproduced in Appendix B.

30. Frank Zerilli, personal communication.

31. Universal Fellowship of Metropolitan Community Churches By-Laws, 1997, Article 3a. In author's possession.

32. Ibid., Article 8a.

33. Although many of those involved in this study would have preferred that I use their real names and those of their churches, out of concern for those who are still vulnerable to exposure I have chosen to use pseudonyms for the two congregations, the cities in which they are located, and all people affiliated with them. Facts given about the churches and cities are real, as are the names of public figures in the UFMCC, such as Troy Perry, and the names of MCC churches other than the two involved in this study.

34. Census data from the 2000 U.S. census (http://factfinder.census.gov [Accessed January 13, 2003]).

35. A good source for further information on the charismatic movement in the United States is Mary Jo Neitz's *Charisma and Community: A Study of Religious Commitment within the Charismatic Renewal* (New Brunswick, N.J.: Transaction Books, 1987).

36. However, Andrew K. T. Yip is currently conducting a study of bisexual Christians in Britain, and a groundbreaking book on transgender issues was released as the present work was going to press (Justin E. Tanis, *Trans-Gendered: Theology, Ministry, and Communities of Faith* [Cleveland, Ohio: Pilgrim Press, 2003]). Deborah R. Kolodny's *Blessed Bi Spirit: Bisexual People of Faith* (New York: Continuum, 2000) is one of the few exceptions to the lack of primary literature; essays by bisexual and transgender people are also scattered thinly through the various anthologies on religion and spirituality. See, for instance, David Shallenberger's *Reclaiming the Spirit: Gay Men and Lesbians Come to Terms with Religion* (New Brunswick, N.J.: Rutgers, 1998); and David Shneer and Caryn Aviv, eds., *Queer Jews* (New York: Routledge, 2002).

37. This is in part due to the influence of the congregational studies model on the sociology of LGBT religion; influenced more strongly than men by feminism, women may be more likely to leave organized religion even before they come out. My own forthcoming

work attempts to address some of these problems by focusing on a religiously and ethnically diverse group of lesbian, bisexual, and transgender women in Los Angeles.

38. Guy A. M. Widdershoven, "The Story of Life: Hermeneutic Perspectives on the Relationship Between Narrative and Life History," in *The Narrative Study of Lives*, vol. 1, ed. Ruthellen Josselson and Amia Lieblich (Newbury Park, CA: Sage, 1993), 1–20.

39. Kenneth L. Cuthbertson, "Coming Out/Conversion: An Exploration of Gay Religious Experience," *Journal of Men's Studies* 4, no. 3 (1996): 193–207. This is also suggested by Plummer's argument that stories of coming out, recovery from rape, and self-help share a common progression from suffering to epiphany to transformation—although he does not mention the conversion narrative. See Ken Plummer, *Telling Sexual Stories: Power, Change, and Social Worlds* (London: Routledge, 1995).

40. For other considerations of this issue, see Norman K. Denzin, *Interpretive Ethnography: Ethnographic Practices for the 21st Century* (Thousand Oaks, Calif.: Sage, 1997); Carolyn Ellis and Michael G. Flaherty, eds., *Investigating Subjectivity: Research on Lived Experience* (Newbury Park, Calif.: Sage, 1992); Donald E. Polkinghorne, *Narrative Knowing and the Human Sciences* (Albany: State University of New York, 1988); and Catherine Kohler Riessman, *Narrative Analysis* (Newbury Park, Calif.: Sage, 1993).

41. José I. Cabezón, "Tibetan Intelligent Agency," public lecture, University of California at Santa Barbara, November 9, 2001.

42. Wade Clark Roof, *Spiritual Marketplace: Baby Boomers and the Remaking of American Religion* (Princeton, N.J.: Princeton University Press, 1999), 152.

1. Converging and Diverging Roads

1. Interview 1206; August 27, 1998.

2. Survey 1241.

3. Interview 1133; September 3, 1998.

4. See John Boswell, *Christianity, Social Tolerance, and Homosexuality: Gay People in Western Europe from the Beginning of the Christian Era to the Fourteenth Century* (Chicago: University of Chicago Press, 1980); Wayne R. Dynes and Stephen Donaldson, eds., *Ethnographic Studies of Homosexuality* (New York: Garland, 1992); and Evelyn Blackwood and Saskia E. Wieringa, eds., *Female Desires: Same-Sex Relations and Transgender Practices across Cultures* (New York: Columbia University Press, 1999).

5. Michel Foucault, *The History of Sexuality*, Vol. 1, *An Introduction*, trans. Robert Hurley (New York: Vintage Books, 1978). This brief overview of Western developments does not do justice to the growing depth and complexity of the field; narratives of LGBT history and challenges to those narratives have multiplied rapidly in recent years. For a fairly traditional version of nineteenth- and twentieth-century Western developments, see Barry D. Adam, *The Rise of a Gay and Lesbian Movement*, rev. ed. (New York: Twayne, 1995). Leila J. Rupp's *A Desired Past: A Short History of Same-Sex Love in America* (Chicago: University of Chicago Press, 1999) takes up the issues of terminology that have plagued the field of LGBT history. Two other works offer additional complexity: Jeffrey Escoffier's *American Homo: Community and Perversity* (Berkeley: University of California Press, 1998) adds economic considerations to the mix, while Scott Bravmann provides much-needed coverage of the complicating effects of race and gender on LGBT history in *Queer Fictions of the Past: History, Culture, and Difference* (New York: Cambridge University Press, 1997).

6. Cf. Vernon A. Rosario, ed., *Science and Homosexualities* (New York: Routledge, 1997).

7. See John D'Emilio, *Sexual Politics, Sexual Communities: The Making of a Homosexual Minority in the United States, 1940–1970* (Chicago: University of Chicago Press, 1983).

8. Cf. Thomas Furman Hewitt, "The American Church's Reaction to the Homophile Movement, 1948–1978" (Ph.D. diss., Duke University, 1983).

9. See Adam, *The Rise of a Gay and Lesbian Movement*; D'Emilio, *Sexual Politics*; Toby Marotta, *The Politics of Homosexuality* (Boston: Houghton Mifflin, 1981); Jonathan Ned Katz, *Gay American History: Lesbians and Gay Men in the U.S.A.*, rev. ed. (New York: Meridian, 1992).

10. For an in-depth discussion of the Stonewall Riots and the gay liberation movement, see Chapter 3.

11. Homosexuality did not disappear from the manual, however; it remained as a condition that could be treated if the client so wished. Cf. Adam, *The Rise of a Gay and Lesbian Movement*, 88.

12. As many have pointed out, these "traditional" values and family structures were not traditional at all but rather represented the stereotypical upper-middle-class white U.S. family of the 1950s.

13. That these questions were generated and debated by heterosexuals without the input of LGBT people is evident from the glaring heterosexism that underlies them. Asking whether homosexuals deserve full human rights implies that they might not be fully human; questioning whether homosexuality is a curable "perversion" or whether it can perhaps be tolerated suggests that the answers to such questions should be reached analytically by "objective" observers rather than through consultation with the persons themselves. These dynamics are reminiscent of the all-male debates within early Christianity over whether women had souls or the all-white Christian colonial musings on the feasibility of and effective methods for "saving" Native Americans and Africans.

14. See Gordon Melton, *The Churches Speak on Homosexuality* (Detroit: Gale Research, 1991); and Comstock, *Unrepentant, Self-Affirming, Practicing*.

15. National Conference of Catholic Bishops, "Principles to Guide Confessors in Questions of Homosexuality," in Melton, *The Churches Speak*, 5–6. In addition to resonating with the Vatican's response to the sexual abuse scandals in 2002, the latter claim is especially ironic in light of the sizeable body of literature that connects lack of social support to depression and low self-esteem among both gay men and lesbians. Cf. Karen M. Jordan and Robert H. Deluty, "Coming Out for Lesbian Women: Its Relation to Anxiety, Positive Affectivity, Self-Esteem, and Social Support," *Journal of Homosexuality* 35, no. 2 (1998): 41–63; John Vincke and Ralph Bolton, "Social Support, Depression, and Self-Acceptance Among Gay Men," *Human Relations* 47, no. 9 (1994): 1049–1062.

16. Assemblies of God, "Statement on Homosexuality," in Melton, *The Churches Speak*, 49–50.

17. United Church of Christ, "Resolution on Human Sexuality and the Needs of Gay and Bisexual Persons," ibid., 207.

18. For a study of several North Carolina churches in the throes of these debates, see Keith Hartman, *Congregations in Conflict: The Battle over Homosexuality* (New Brunswick, N.J.: Rutgers University Press, 1996).

19. The translations of "*to'evah*" and "*qadesh*" are currently the focus of considerable controversy; see below for a discussion of pro-LGBT interpretations of these texts.

20. A classic example is the virulently homophobic rhetoric of anti-gay activist Fred Phelps, whose views on homosexuality can be accessed on his Web site: http://www.godhatesfags.com (Accessed January 13, 2003). The Jewish Publication Society's 1985 translation of this verse reads: "If a man lies with a male as one lies with a woman, the two of them have done an abhorrent thing; they shall be put to death—their bloodguilt is upon them." The New Revised Standard Version (1989) reads: "If a man lies with a male as with a woman, both of them have committed an abomination; they shall be put to death; their blood is upon them." It is worth noting that the same chapter of Leviticus also prescribes capital punishment for adultery, incest, bestiality, and insulting one's parents.

21. A sampling of official statements expressing such views can be found in Melton, *The Churches Speak*.

22. The UFMCC publishes a small book that outlines each of the biblical texts in question and refutes anti-gay interpretations of them, using many of the strategies described here. See Michael E. England, *The Bible and Homosexuality*, 5th ed. (Gaithersburg, Md.: Chi Rho Press, 1998).

23. Troy D. Perry with Thomas L. P. Swicegood, *Don't Be Afraid Anymore: The Story of Reverend Troy Perry and the Metropolitan Community Churches* (New York: St. Martin's Press, 1990), 31–35.

24. Nancy Wilson, *Our Tribe: Queer Folks, God, Jesus, and the Bible* (San Francisco: Harper, 1995), 26; italics in original.

25. Interview PI 2A; September 14, 1998.

26. J. Michael Clark, Joanne Carlson Brown, and Lorna M. Hochstein, "Institutional Religion and Gay/Lesbian Oppression," *Marriage and Family Review* 14, no. 3–4 (1989): 268.

27. Tables of these results can be found in Appendix C.

28. $p < 0.001$.

29. The survey defined coming out as "that period of time when you began to acknowledge your sexual orientation and to tell others about it." While coming out is indeed a single period of time for many, for some people this question conflates two separate processes. Those respondents who found it impossible to define a single time period for their coming out usually elaborated on the problem in writing. Most commonly, the discrepancy arose because a respondent had acknowledged her sexual or gender identity to herself and a few others but had waited for a period of time before telling more than one or two people. Due to the frequency with which religious leaders were involved in the first part of the process, two-stage coming-out processes were coded using the earlier age.

30. Interview 1004; August 28, 1998.

31. Interview 1103; August 13, 1998.

32. Interview 1197; August 20, 1998.

33. Interview 2085; September 2, 1998.

2. Christians Coming Out

Portions of this chapter appeared in *Sociology of Religion* 63, no. 4 (2002): 497–513.

1. Survey 1293.

2. Interview 1211; August 19, 1998.

3. Interview 1128; August 26, 1998.

4. Robert N. Bellah, Richard Madsen, William M. Sullivan, Ann Swidler, and Steven

M. Tipton, *Habits of the Heart: Individualism and Commitment in American Life* (Berkeley: University of California Press, 1985).

5. For a discussion of this, see R. Stephen Warner, "Work in Progress Toward a New Paradigm for the Sociological Study of Religion in the United States," *American Journal of Sociology* 98 (March 1993): 1044–1093. Such negative evaluations of increasing religious disaffiliation in the United States have their roots in Max Weber's assertion that the secularization of society would lead to a "disenchantment of the world" and a dull, mechanistic future. See Weber, *The Protestant Ethic and the Spirit of Capitalism* (New York: Routledge, 1992).

6. See C. Daniel Batson, Patricia Schoenrade, and W. Larry Ventis, *Religion and the Individual: A Social-Psychological Perspective* (New York: Oxford University Press, 1993). Although Freud's relationship to his Jewish heritage was complex, he is one of the most famous psychologists to have held negative views of religion.

7. Martin E. Marty, "Revising the Map of American Religion," *Annals of the American Academy of Political and Social Science* 558 (July 1998): 13–27.

8. Robert Wuthnow, *After Heaven: Spirituality in America Since the 1950s* (Berkeley: University of California Press, 1998). See especially Chapter 1.

9. Ibid., 9–10.

10. Ibid., 147.

11. Interview PI 2A; September 14, 1998.

12. See Wade Clark Roof, *Spiritual Marketplace*, 41. As Roof notes, the term "lived religion" has its origins in a book edited by David D. Hall: *Lived Religion in America: Toward a History of Practice* (Princeton, N.J.: Princeton University Press, 1997).

13. Roof, *Spiritual Marketplace*, 43.

14. Ibid., 169, 166.

15. Interview 1154 (Ben); August 27, 1998.

16. Lynn Resnick Dufour, "Sifting Through Tradition: The Creation of Jewish Feminist Identities," *Journal for the Scientific Study of Religion* 39, no. 1 (2000): 104.

17. Judith Butler, *Gender Trouble: Feminism and the Subversion of Identity* (New York: Routledge, 1990); and *The Psychic Life of Power: Theories in Subjection* (Stanford, Calif.: Stanford University Press, 1997).

18. Adrienne Rich, "Compulsory Heterosexuality and Lesbian Existence," *Signs* 5, no. 4 (1980): 647.

19. Diana Fuss, *Essentially Speaking: Feminism, Nature and Difference* (New York: Routledge, 1989). Fuss's central line of argument appears in two chapters that read the anti-essentialist work of Monique Wittig against the essentialist writings of Luce Irigaray.

20. Warner, "The Metropolitan Community Churches," 81–108.

21. See, for instance, Troiden, "The Formation of Homosexual Identities"; Michele J. Eliason, "Identity Formation for Lesbian, Bisexual, and Gay Persons: Beyond a 'Minoritizing' View," *Journal of Homosexuality* 30, no. 3 (1996): 31–58; and Vera Whisman, *Queer by Choice: Lesbians, Gay Men, and the Politics of Identity* (New York: Routledge, 1996).

22. The only group with a higher average was liberal Protestants, but with only six respondents in that category I am reluctant to assign the statistic too much importance.

23. On the phenomenon of switching in general, see Wade Clark Roof and William McKinney, *American Mainline Religion: Its Changing Shape and Future* (New Brunswick, N.J.: Rutgers University Press, 1987).

24. Cf. Roof, *Spiritual Marketplace*, 33–35.

25. Roof defines baby boomers as having been born between 1946 and 1962; see ibid., 315. Among survey respondents in this study, 59.7 percent fit this category.

26. Survey 1103.

27. Interview 1133; September 3, 1998.

28. Interview 1108; September 8, 1998.

29. Carrie is not the only one in this study to report alcohol and/or drug abuse. Like some ethnic minority groups in this country, LGBT communities have been hard hit by these problems as their members seek ways to cope with both external and internalized oppression. In recognition of this fact, many MCC churches (MCCVR and OMCC included) offer only grape juice at communion.

30. Interview 1217; August 11, 1998.

31. The song that Terry mentions was written by singer-songwriter Marsha Stevens, who subsequently came out as a lesbian herself.

32. Interview 1288; August 21, 1998. The biblical quotation is from Isaiah 45:9.

33. Interviews 1051 and 1052; August 28, 1998.

34. Interview 2012; August 9, 1998.

35. It is difficult to argue, of course, that such memories are reliable proof of the early existence of LGBT identity. While it is quite possible that transgender and minority sexual identity begin to manifest at an early age, it is also likely that coming out functions much like religious conversion: the radical shift in identity encompassed in the transition necessitates a rereading of the past in a way that supports the development of the new identity. On religious conversion, see Lorne Dawson, *Comprehending Cults: The Sociology of New Religious Movements* (Toronto: Oxford University Press Canada, 1998); on its parallel to coming-out narratives, see Kenneth L. Cuthbertson, "Coming Out/Conversion: An Exploration of Gay Religious Experience."

36. In *Queer by Choice,* Whisman reports that a greater number of women than men in her study claimed their homosexual or bisexual identities to be chosen. While this is strictly true for the present study as well, here the differences are weak. Moreover, it was the less strongly Christian and the non-Christian women in my study who were more likely to claim choice in their sexual identity. This adds the nuance of religious context to Whisman's analysis: while feminism and gendered differences in social power make a constructivist view of identity more accessible and plausible to women than to men, she argues that other influences can lead women to claim an essentialist understanding. In this case, essentialism is a much stronger argument than constructivism against claims that lesbian and bisexual Christian women are "living in sin."

37. Interview 1031; August 4, 1998.

38. Interview 1032; August 4, 1998.

39. Interview 1103; August 13, 1998.

40. Interview 1282; August 7, 1998.

41. Interview 1277; August 30, 1998.

42. Interview 1155; August 26, 1998.

43. Interview 1197; August 20, 1998.

44. Interview 1108; September 8, 1998.

45. Interview 1182; August 7, 1998. This interchange raises provocative questions about the role of the researcher, which I have addressed in depth elsewhere. See Melissa M. Wilcox, "Dancing on the Fence: Researching Lesbian, Gay, Bisexual, and Transgender Christians," in *Personal Knowledge and Beyond: Reshaping the Ethnography of Religion,* ed.

James V. Spickard, J. Shawn Landres, and Meredith B. McGuire (New York: New York University Press, 2001), 47–60.

46. Howard Eilberg-Schwartz, *God's Phallus and Other Problems for Men and Monotheism* (Boston: Beacon Press, 1994).

47. See Caroline Walker Bynum, *Holy Feast, Holy Fast: The Religious Significance of Food to Medieval Women* (Berkeley: University of California Press, 1987); and *Fragmentation and Redemption: Essays on Gender and the Human Body in Medieval Religion* (New York: Zone Books, 1991); Amanda Porterfield, *Female Piety in Puritan New England* (New York: Oxford University Press, 1992). Though it is possible to argue for homoeroticism in the visions that male mystics had of Jesus during the medieval period, that homoeroticism was sublimated under the understanding of Jesus as a mother. On this issue, see Bynum, *Jesus as Mother: Studies in the Spirituality of the High Middle Ages* (Berkeley: University of California Press, 1982).

48. Comstock, *Unrepentant, Self-Affirming, Practicing.*

49. Interview 2050; September 1, 1998.

50. Interview 1217; August 11, 1998.

51. See especially Warner, "The Metropolitan Community Churches," 97–99.

52. Ibid., 99.

53. Wuthnow, *After Heaven,* 10.

54. Roof, *Spiritual Marketplace,* 41.

55. Ibid., 43.

3. Creating a Space

An earlier version of this chapter appeared in *Religion and American Culture* 11, no. 1 (Winter 2001): 83–108.

1. Interview 1189; August 6, 1998.

2. Rev. Troy D. Perry, as told to Charles L. Lucas, *The Lord Is My Shepherd and He Knows I'm Gay* (Los Angeles: Nash Press, 1972), 192.

3. Frances FitzGerald, *Cities on a Hill: A Journey through Contemporary American Cultures* (New York: Simon and Schuster, 1986).

4. The Second Great Awakening, which historians usually locate in the early decades of the nineteenth century, not only involved Protestant revivalism but also led to the foundation of a number of new religious movements, such as Spiritualism, the utopian Oneida community, and the Church of Jesus Christ of Latter-Day Saints. Comparing nineteenth- and twentieth-century periods of social change, FitzGerald comments: "There were very few periods in American history in which the dominant sector—the white middle class—transformed itself as thoroughly as it did in the [nineteen-] sixties and seventies. . . . In fact since the Revolution there was probably only one other such period . . . the Age of Jackson and the Second Great Awakening" (*Cities on a Hill,* 390).

5. See ibid., 20, 386. The human potential movement, developed during the 1960s from an unlikely mixture of neurology, psychology, Buddhism, and twentieth-century forms of New Thought, focused on maximizing the supposedly untapped possibilities of the human mind.

6. Data for this estimate come from worship directories and new mission reports printed in the UFMCC newsletter, *In Unity.*

7. The UFMCC Web site can be found at http://www.ufmcc.com (Accessed January 15, 2003).

8. Bauer, "The Homosexual Subculture," 115–127; Warner, "The Metropolitan Community Churches," 81–108.

9. See, for instance, Perry and Lucas, *The Lord Is My Shepherd,* 121–25 and 222–223; the sermon by Rev. Brad Wilson that appears in *In Unity* 2, no. 7 (1971): 6–20; and Perry and Swicegood, *Don't Be Afraid Anymore,* 41–42, 345. The denomination's documentary video *God, Gays, and the Gospel: This Is Our Story* (Los Angeles: Universal Fellowship of Metropolitan Community Churches, 1984) also places strong emphasis on this factor.

10. Bauer, "The Homosexual Subculture," 118. "Homophile," as Bauer uses it here, is an older synonym for "homosexual." It was coined in the 1950s with the goal of shifting emphasis from sexual attraction to the importance of same-sex love in homosexual identity.

11. This assertion is somewhat problematic because the gay liberation movement was already in full swing by the mid-1970s. This movement's message of pride and visibility would have provided, for many, a strong challenge to earlier conditioning.

12. Warner, "The Metropolitan Community Churches," 84–85.

13. Ibid., 85. It is worth noting that a lesbian subculture also had been growing since the Second World War, and some of its members, too, although fewer initially than the men, were attracted to the UFMCC.

14. Ibid., 82.

15. See, for example, "Hymn for Gay Freedom" (which is intended to be sung to the melody of the "Battle Hymn of the Republic"), *In Unity* 2, no. 7 (1971): 13; the sermon by Rev. Brad Wilson, 6–20; and Rev. Howard Wells's sermon, 29–32.

16. Troy Perry, "From the Pulpit," *In Unity* 1, no. 2 (1970): 3.

17. Troy Perry, "Freedom and Justice for All?" *In Unity* 2, no. 6 (1971): 2.

18. Charles David, "A Response to Editor, *The Prodigal,* MCC-San Diego," *In Unity* 2, no. 9 (1971): 18–19.

19. Joanie Kettles, "Fulfillment of My Impossible Dream," *In Unity* 2, no. 6 (1971): 5–17.

20. "Gays and the Gospel: An Interview with Troy Perry," *Christian Century* 113, no. 27 (September 25, 1996): 896–901. It is important to keep in mind, though, that the UFMCC is not a denomination in which the founder's theology determines that of member churches—as is evident from the existence of MCC Valle Rico and other distinctly non-evangelical MCC churches.

21. UFMCC, *God, Gays, and the Gospel.*

22. David, "A Response to Editor," 18.

23. "Gays and the Gospel," 897–898.

24. See Perry and Swicegood, *Don't Be Afraid Anymore,* 175–205 (a chapter tellingly entitled "The Freedom Train"). The vast majority of UFMCC activism is centered around LGBT civil rights issues.

25. Perry and Lucas, *The Lord Is My Shepherd,* 126.

26. Kettles, "Fulfillment of My Impossible Dream," 17.

27. UFMCC, *God, Gays, and the Gospel.*

28. See Roof and McKinney, *American Mainline Religion.* In *Righteous Empire: The Protestant Experience in America* (New York: Dial, 1970), Martin E. Marty notes a division between "private Protestants" and "public Protestants" that stretches much farther back in U.S. history (177–187).

29. Roof and McKinney, *American Mainline Religion,* 23.

30. Ibid., 23; see also 19.

31. This innovation is mentioned in UFMCC, *God, Gays, and the Gospel.* According to an interview I conducted with an MCC minister in 1995, it was still a central topic of discussion at UFMCC General Conferences.

32. A good overview of these early events can be found in Hewitt, "The American Church's Reaction to the Homophile Movement, 1948–1978."

33. Harry Emerson Fosdick, *On Being a Real Person* (New York: Harper and Brothers, 1943), cited in Comstock, *Unrepentant, Self-Affirming, Practicing,* 4. For a full discussion of the historical development of Christian responses to homosexuality, see also Melton, *The Churches Speak.*

34. Derrick Sherwin Bailey, *Homosexuality and the Western Christian Tradition* (London: Longmans, Green, 1955); see Comstock, *Unrepentant, Self-Affirming, Practicing,* 4.

35. Useful sources on the pre-Stonewall and immediately post-Stonewall history of the LGBT community include Marotta, *The Politics of Homosexuality;* John D'Emilio, *Sexual Politics* and *Making Trouble: Essays on Gay History, Politics, and the University* (New York: Routledge, 1992); Katz, *Gay American History;* Adam, *The Rise of a Gay and Lesbian Movement;* and Charles Kaiser, *The Gay Metropolis, 1940–1996* (Boston: Houghton Mifflin, 1997).

36. See Marotta, *The Politics of Homosexuality,* 17.

37. Ibid., 67.

38. Katz, *Gay American History,* 417. An open Communist, Hay was deposed from the Mattachine's leadership during the reorganization and retrenchment of 1953.

39. Marotta, *The Politics of Homosexuality,* 162–195.

40. Ibid., 236n. LGBT people of color encountered similar problems within both the gay liberation movement and the feminist movement, resulting in a double or even triple bind: their sexuality was not accepted within their own cultures and their ethnicity was not affirmed within the LGBT community. Lesbians of color, furthermore, encountered sexism in addition to racism and homophobia in their multiple communities.

41. Max Weber, "The Sociology of Religion," in *Economy and Society,* ed. Guenther Roth and Claus Wittich (Berkeley: University of California Press, 1978), 399–640.

42. I do not wish to argue that Perry is a prophet in the popular sense of the term, only that through his charisma, leadership, dedication, and sense of call he bears a strong resemblance to the Weberian figure of the charismatic prophet.

43. Perry and Swicegood, *Don't Be Afraid Anymore,* 48.

44. See, for example, ibid., 34–35.

45. UFMCC Committee on Evangelism, General Conference Report. Reproduced in *In Unity* 3, no. 1 (1972): 15.

46. Perry and Lucas, *The Lord Is My Shepherd,* 130. This is an interesting organizational adaptation of Dufour's sifting. See Lynn Resnick Dufour, "Sifting through Tradition."

47. Perry and Lucas, *The Lord Is My Shepherd,* 202.

48. See Melton, *The Churches Speak,* xviii–xix; Comstock, *Unrepentant, Self-Affirming, Practicing,* 9; and Melissa M. Wilcox, "Innovation in Exile: Religion and Spirituality in Lesbian, Gay, Bisexual, and Transgender Communities," in *Sexuality and the World's Religions,* ed. David W. Machacek and Melissa M. Wilcox (Goleta, Calif.: ABC-CLIO, 2003).

49. Ronald Enroth and Gerald Jamison noted this tension about identity in *The Gay Church.*

50. C. Shawn Farrell, "Viewpoint," *In Unity* 2, no. 9 (October 1971): 4.

51. "Ten Golden Rules for a Happy Gay Marriage," *In Unity* 2, no. 11 (1971–72): 12.

52. This conclusion is supported by similar findings in Gorman, "A New Light on Zion."

53. It would be interesting to discover whether this experience holds true for MCC members in regions with a higher Christian population, such as the southern United States. The California locale of this pastor's church is also home to many alternative religions that have attracted LGBT people, such as the neopagan Radical Faeries and Dianic witchcraft, various New Age groups, and Eastern religions. This alternative religious climate may contribute, in part, to anti-Christian sentiment. The vocal presence of the religious right in California politics also may play a role.

54. The interview appears in UFMCC, *God, Gays, and the Gospel*; see also Perry and Swicegood, *Don't Be Afraid Anymore*, 102–119.

55. Perry and Swicegood, *Don't Be Afraid Anymore*, 117.

56. The most comprehensive coverage I have found of the UFMCC's international efforts appears in Perry and Swicegood, *Don't Be Afraid Anymore*, 206–229.

57. The church in Nigeria is the only MCC that is not primarily LGBT. According to Perry and Swicegood, the Biafran congregation was attracted to the UFMCC's ecumenicity.

58. FitzGerald, *Cities on a Hill*, 409.

4. Creating New Worlds

1. Interview PI 1A; September 3, 1998.

2. Survey 1032 and Interview 1032; August 4, 1998.

3. Survey 1075.

4. Survey 2037.

5. See Comstock, *Unrepentant, Self-Affirming, Practicing*, 56–69.

6. Comstock's description of the difficulties encountered by LGBT clergy in the United Church of Christ during the ordination process suggests that the greatest resistance came from relatively anonymous groups. While 10 to 20 percent reported problems with support from the local pastor or congregation, 30 to 40 percent encountered difficulties at the district level, and over 60 percent had trouble finding employment. See Comstock, *Unrepentant, Self-Affirming, Practicing*, 142–144.

7. See Hartman, *Congregations in Conflict*, 25–65. The boycott was undertaken in protest of Disney's policy of offering benefits to the domestic partners of its employees.

8. On attitudes toward LGBT people in the black churches, see Saul M. Olyan and Martha C. Nussbaum, eds., *Sexual Orientation and Human Rights in American Religious Discourse* (New York: Oxford University Press, 1998), 171–211. Broader mention of the experiences of LGBT people of color is made in Comstock, *Unrepentant, Self-Affirming, Practicing*, 189–193. In addition to risking rejection from their communities and families, people of color frequently feel excluded from the LGBT community. Even when overt racism is not a factor, the whiteness of mainstream LGBT culture itself can be oppressive. It is likely, in fact, that this is a central reason for the underrepresentation of people of color in the UFMCC—and for the success of the Unity Fellowship Church Movement, a national movement whose churches minister primarily to LGBT African Americans.

9. On the Progressive National Baptist Convention, see Comstock, *Unrepentant, Self-Affirming, Practicing*, xiv. On Jackson, see "Jesse Jackson, Troy Perry Hold L.A. Hate Crimes Rally," UFMCC Press Release, October 23 1998.

10. "The Evangelical Closet," *Christianity Today* 34 (November 5, 1990): 56–57.

11. Didi Herman, *The Antigay Agenda: Orthodox Vision and the Christian Right* (Chicago: University of Chicago Press, 1997), 54–59.

12. See Edward R. Gray and Scott L. Thumma, "The Gospel Hour," 79–98; and Scott Thumma, "Negotiating a Religious Identity," 333–347.

13. Some Catholic parishes and even some archdioceses have developed fairly supportive programs for gay and lesbian Catholics (but not yet for bisexual and transgender Catholics). Some of these are more radical than others, but several rely on the growing importance of conscience and individual discernment among Catholics in the United States.

14. There are several excellent summaries of the positions of Christian groups on issues affecting the LGBT community. Because of the volatile nature of this topic, summaries become outdated rapidly; however, combining existing sources with a perusal of recent issues of *Christianity and Crisis* or *Christianity Today* yields a fairly accurate picture of the current situation. For an overview of Christian denominations, the best sources are Melton, *The Churches Speak;* Hartman, *Congregations in Conflict,* 175–181; and Comstock, *Unrepentant, Self-Affirming, Practicing,* 13–20. More recent sources include Ken Garfield, "Presbyterians in Stalemate over Homosexual Ordination," *Christianity Today* 42, no. 9 (1998): 22; "Gay-friendly Church Leaves Denomination," *Christian Century* 113, no. 32 (1996): 1068–1069; Timothy C. Morgan, "Anglicans Deem Homosexuality 'Incompatible with Scripture,'" *Christianity Today* 42, n. 10 (1998): 32–33; "UMC Bishops Split on Ordaining Gays," *Christian Century* 113, no. 6 (1996): 504; "UMC Bishops' Stance Draws Praise, Criticism," *Christian Century* 115, no. 16 (1998): 521–522; and James K. Wellman, Jr., ed., "Religious Organizational Identity and Homosexual Orientation: A Case Study of the Presbyterian Church, U.S.A.," *Review of Religious Research* 41, no. 2 (1999).

15. In addition to the sources listed above, an excellent discussion of these debates is contained in John J. Carey, ed., *The Sexuality Debate in North American Churches, 1988–1995: Controversies, Unresolved Issues, Future Prospects* (Lewiston, N.Y.: Edwin Mellen, 1995).

16. A similar movement exists within the Jewish communities of greater Los Angeles, where synagogues that welcome LGBT people sometimes include on their signs and literature the phrase: "A place to belong." Thanks to Michelle Jacobs for bringing this to my attention.

17. The accepting status of a church can strongly influence how open a congregant is about her or his sexual identity. Comstock found that among the LGBT members of Welcoming congregations of the United Methodist Church and the United Church of Christ, 84 percent and 75 percent, respectively, reported being out. In congregations without the Welcoming designation, only 29 percent of Methodists and 28 percent in the UCC reported being out. See Comstock, *Unrepentant, Self-Affirming, Practicing,* 78.

18. Ralph G. McFadden, "If We Would Just Turn Purple," *Brethren Life and Thought* 36 (Winter 1991): 35–41.

19. Comstock, *Unrepentant, Self-Affirming, Practicing,* 219–228.

20. Survey 2063.

21. Interview 1040; August 31, 1998.

22. Interview 1032; August 4, 1998.

23. See Melton, *The Churches Speak,* xix; Comstock, *Unrepentant, Self-Affirming, Practicing,* 18–20. Other sources include Sam Francis, "A Mormon Paradox: Fellowship in the Shadow of Intolerance," *Advocate* 758 (April 28, 1996): 16; and David Davidson, "Dignity,

Inc.: An Alternative Experience of Church," in *Homosexuality and Religion and Philosophy,* ed. Wayne R. Dynes and Stephen Donaldson (New York: Garland, 1992), 152–161.

24. http://www.dignityusa.org (Accessed January 15, 2003).

25. Primiano, "Intrinsically Catholic," 221. Gorman's "A New Light on Zion" also discusses Dignity.

26. See James S. Tinney, "Why a Gay Black Church?" in *In the Life: A Black Gay Anthology,* ed. Joseph Beam (Boston: Alyson Publications, 1986); and Comstock, *Unrepentant, Self-Affirming, Practicing,* 191. In 1985, Bean and several associates founded the mother church of the Unity Fellowship Church Movement in Los Angeles; in August 2002, the movement had a roster of fourteen churches nationwide.

27. See Scott Thumma, "Negotiating a Religious Identity."

28. Comstock, *Unrepentant, Self-Affirming, Practicing,* 184–189.

29. Primiano, "'I Would Rather Be Fixated on the Lord,'" 88–99. Dignity/USA now lists women's ordination as one of its main concerns; see http://www.dignityusa.org.

30. Interview 1091; September 8, 1998.

31. One woman, in fact, had the impression that Dignity requires its members to be celibate (interview 2087; September 1, 1998).

32. Interview 1093; August 31, 1998. Whether any of the members of these "heterosexual couples" was bisexual or transgender is unclear.

33. Interview 2064; September 14, 1998.

34. Interview 1277; August 30, 1998.

35. Interview 1288; August 21, 1998.

36. Beth E. Schneider reported similar findings in her 1980 study of lesbians in the workplace: women's tendency to come out at work was positively influenced by the development of close friendships in the workplace. See "Coming Out at Work: Bridging the Private/Public Gap," *Work and Occupations* 13, no. 4 (1986): 463–487.

37. Interview 1108; September 8, 1998.

38. Interview 2085; September 2, 1998.

39. Interview 1165; September 3, 1998.

40. Interview 1211; August 19, 1998.

41. Interview 1217; August 11, 1998.

42. Interview 1271; August 11, 1998.

43. On the topic of seekers, see Wade Clark Roof, *A Generation of Seekers: The Spiritual Journeys of the Baby Boom Generation* (San Francisco: Harper, 1993). More recent discussions of seeking and the quest mentality in contemporary U.S. religion can be found in Roof, *Spiritual Marketplace;* and Wuthnow, *After Heaven.*

44. Other less well-represented paths to MCC include the following: childhood religious affiliation to LGBT religious group other than MCC, 5.3 percent; childhood religious affiliation to mainline Protestant to MCC, 4.4 percent; childhood religious affiliation to no religious affiliation, 3.5 percent; childhood religious affiliation to Catholic to MCC, 2.7 percent; no religious affiliation to MCC, 2.7 percent.

45. Cf. Wade Clark Roof and William McKinney, *American Mainline Religion.*

46. See Roof and McKinney, *American Mainline Religion,* especially Chapter 5.

47. Because I have coded the pathways to ignore shifts within a religious group, the liberal Protestants represented here are those who moved to metaphysical or New Age groups before coming to MCC.

48. Additionally, shifts from metaphysical and New Age groups to MCC are likely to be overrepresented in this sample relative to the UFMCC as a whole. MCCVR has marked

metaphysical leanings and would therefore be a far more congenial setting than most MCCs for those accustomed to metaphysical and New Age groups. Indeed, some of those I interviewed who attend MCCVR indicated that they would not be comfortable in other MCC churches.

49. Survey 1042.

50. Interview 1091; September 8, 1998. Soteriology is not emphasized at MCCVR, nor is human sinfulness. In the UFMCC as a whole, however, as well as among some individual members of MCCVR, these are still important issues.

51. See Primiano, "Intrinsically Catholic," 158–159; Shokeid, *A Gay Synagogue in New York,* 2. Both are excellent and sorely needed studies, but even scholars, who like to believe we are trained to think objectively, are vulnerable to cultural prejudices. Both of these research projects were carried out in the 1980s, before there were many positive images of LGBT people in mainstream culture. Both Primiano and Shokeid had close friends who came out as gay or lesbian before the fieldwork projects began; like other heterosexuals mentioned in this study, their perception of LGBT people may have been positively influenced by personal interaction. Furthermore, it is to the credit of both scholars that they reevaluated their initial misunderstandings as soon as experience proved them incorrect and that they went on to produce two important book-length studies of LGBT congregations.

52. Interview 1128; August 26, 1998.

53. Interview 1103; August 13, 1998.

54. Interview PI 2A; September 14, 1998.

55. Interview 1206; August 27, 1998.

56. Interview 1004 (Peter); August 28, 1998.

57. Interview 1081 (Eileen); September 3, 1998 and Interview 1154 (Ben); August 27, 1998.

58. Survey 1123.

59. Interview 2090; August 27, 1998.

60. Survey 1031.

61. Survey 1032.

62. Interview 2085; September 2, 1998.

63. Interview 2038 (Niki); August 7, 1998.

64. Survey 2071.

65. See Roof and McKinney, *American Mainline Religion.*

66. Interview 1282; August 7, 1998.

67. Survey 1128 and Interview 1128; August 26, 1998.

68. Survey 2063.

69. Survey 1053.

70. Interview 1053; August 11, 1998.

71. Respondents who currently do not attend MCC were excluded from these figures.

72. Twelve-step programs are probably underrepresented in these figures, as the question asked specifically about attendance at religious organizations and many do not consider twelve-step groups to be religious. However, a number of people mentioned either in interviews or survey responses that groups such as Alcoholics Anonymous, Al-Anon, and Narcotics Anonymous had been and continued to be important resources for their spiritual growth.

73. In some cases, this is because of overlapping reporting: when both partners filled out surveys, each reported his own attendance but was also reported as an attending part-

ner by the other. Yet 12.5 percent of partners were reported to attend twelve-step groups, as opposed to the 5.3 percent who reported their own attendance at such groups. Perhaps respondents' partners do in fact attend twelve-step groups more often than the respondents themselves. It is also likely, however, that some respondents were reluctant to report such attendance on their own behalf. The 12.5 percent, then, may be a more accurate estimate of twelve-step attendance among study participants.

74. See Wuthnow, *After Heaven*, 1–18.

75. It is quite probable, of course, that these figures do not generalize to all those affiliated with OMCC and MCCVR. People who are or were more highly involved in MCC would be more likely to see this study as being relevant to their lives and therefore would be more likely to participate.

76. Also interesting is the fact that changes in attitude toward spirituality and homosexuality, measured between the year after coming out and the time at which the respondent completed the survey, were negligible. Nearly half of all respondents reported no change in their attitude toward either issue, and although the mean change for both was positive, it was less than 1 on the five-point scale.

77. The first two questions exclude transgender respondents; this was an error on the original survey. However, the number of such respondents was small enough that had all of the heterosexual transgender people in the study taken the question literally, their responses would have had little effect on the results.

78. Survey 1155.

79. Survey 1217.

80. Interview 1053; August 11, 1998.

81. Survey 1052.

82. Survey 1108.

5. Re-Creating the World

1. Interview 1100; August 24, 1998.

2. Interview PI 1B; September 15, 1998.

3. Fieldnotes, September 6, 1998.

4. Bruce Lincoln, *Discourse and the Construction of Society* (New York: Oxford University Press, 1989).

5. Clifford Geertz, *The Interpretation of Cultures* (New York: Basic Books, 1973), 24–30.

6. Pierre Bourdieu, *The Logic of Practice*, trans. Richard Nice (Stanford, Calif.: Stanford University Press, 1990), 141.

7. The pink triangle has its roots in the Nazi era, when it was used to identify gay men in the concentration camps. In the first part of the century, Germany led Europe in the development of a gay and lesbian subculture, and those involved were targeted when Hitler came into power. Because of this history, the pink triangle has been challenged by some as being a poor symbol for LGBT pride. It continues to be widely used, however, along with the newer rainbow colors. For this history, see Richard Plant, *The Pink Triangle: The Nazi War against Homosexuals* (New York: Henry Holt, 1986).

8. Interview 1179; August 31, 1998.

9. A full analysis of reactions to Shepard's murder appears in Melissa M. Wilcox, "Murderers and Martyrs: Violence, Discourse, and the (Re)construction of Meaning," *Culture and Religion* 2, no. 2 (Autumn 2001): 155–178.

10. Wilson, *Our Tribe,* 121–134.

11. Steve Pieters, "So You're Going to Live: Facing Life after Facing Death" (West Hollywood, Calif.: Universal Fellowship of Metropolitan Community Churches, 1997).

12. Michael England, "Free to Be Gay: A Brief Look at the Bible and Homosexuality" (n.p., n.d.).

13. See England, *The Bible and Homosexuality.*

14. M. Scott Peck, *The Road Less Traveled: A New Psychology of Love, Traditional Values, and Spiritual Growth* (New York: Simon and Schuster, 1978).

15. Chiara Manodori has found that more verbal rituals such as commitment ceremonies and baby-naming ceremonies help to "solidify lesbian identity through the confrontation of internalized and external homophobia." See "This Powerful Opening of the Heart: How Ritual Affirms Lesbian Identity," *Journal of Homosexuality* 36, no. 2 (1998): 41–58.

16. Jonathan Z. Smith, *Imagining Religion: From Babylon to Jonestown* (Chicago: University of Chicago Press, 1982), 63.

17. Bourdieu, *The Logic of Practice* and *Language and Symbolic Power,* ed. John B. Thompson, trans. Gino Raymond and Matthew Adamson (Cambridge, Mass.: Harvard University Press, 1991).

18. Bourdieu, *The Logic of Practice,* 69.

19. Ibid., 73.

20. On this issue, see Wilcox, "Murderers and Martyrs."

21. Charismatic Christians describe "being slain" as an overwhelmingly intimate contact with God; it tends to occur while they are being prayed over and manifests physically in a collapse akin to fainting (thus the term "slain").

22. Interview 2012; August 9, 1998.

23. Interview 2051; August 10, 1998.

24. Interview PI 2A; September 14, 1998.

25. Peter L. Berger, *The Heretical Imperative: Contemporary Possibilities of Religious Affirmation* (Garden City, N.Y.: Anchor/Doubleday, 1979), 38–39.

26. Ibid., 40; italics in original.

27. Peter L. Berger and Thomas Luckmann, *The Social Construction of Reality: A Treatise in the Sociology of Knowledge* (Garden City, N.Y.: Doubleday, 1966), 137.

28. This is not to suggest, of course, that communion, charismatic experience, and personal prayer are only tools for affirming LGBT Christian identity. As in any church, they are resources for emotional support in many different situations.

29. Interview 2090; August 27, 1998. The nature of "my people" is complicated in many cases by issues of race, class, and gender; community can be found in very different places. For some, the local MCC congregation may *not* be "my people," while for others, such as Chris, it is.

30. Barrington Moore, Jr., *Injustice: The Social Bases of Obedience and Revolt* (White Plains, N.Y.: M. E. Sharpe, 1978), 116.

31. Interview 1211; August 19, 1998.

32. Berger and Luckmann, *The Social Construction of Reality,* 48.

33. Ibid., 142.

34. Peter L. Berger, *The Sacred Canopy: Elements of a Sociological Theory of Religion* (Garden City, N.Y.: Doubleday, 1967). See especially 45–52.

35. Berger, *The Heretical Imperative,* 47–48.

36. Interview PI 1A; September 3, 1998. Because OMCC has no regularly attending heterosexual members, this discussion focuses solely on MCCVR.

37. Interview 1255; September 11, 1998.

38. Interview 1073; August 23, 1998.

39. Interview 1255; September 11, 1998.

40. Interview 1074; August 23, 1998. That a heterosexual woman interacting socially with lesbians would experience a certain lack of acceptance is not surprising considering the battles for inclusion that have taken place in the lesbian community. Defensive of their social space against both heterosexuals and men, some lesbians have objected to the participation in lesbian organizations not only of heterosexual women but also of bisexuals, transgender women, and even transgender lesbians. One occasionally sees a women's group advertised as being open only to "biological [i.e., genetic] women," and in recent years such questions of inclusion have been the subject of heated debate and protest at the famed Michigan Womyn's Music Festival, which does not allow participation by transgender women. These issues are covered insightfully, though briefly, in Joshua Gamson, "Must Identity Movements Self-Destruct? A Queer Dilemma," *Social Problems* 42, no. 3 (1995): 390–407.

41. Interview 1206; August 27, 1998.

6. We Took the One Less Traveled

1. Judith Butler, *The Psychic Life of Power: Theories in Subjection* (Stanford, Calif.: Stanford University Press, 1997).

2. Antonio Gramsci, *Selections from the Prison Notebooks of Antonio Gramsci,* ed. Quintin Hoare and Geoffrey Nowell Smith (New York: International, 1971); and *Further Selections from the Prison Notebooks,* trans. and ed. Derek Boothman (London: Lawrence and Wishart, 1995).

3. This discussion of Christian hegemony relates specifically to traditional Christian beliefs about gender and sexuality; I would consider not only MCC but all of the various rewritings of that tradition—feminist, womanist, liberationist, queer, and so on—to be efforts to counter or undermine such hegemonic discourse.

4. This same "natural order," of course, reigns supreme outside the confines of Christianity as well. Here I am interested in the role that Christianity specifically plays in buttressing this worldview.

5. Michel Foucault, *Religion and Culture,* ed. Jeremy R. Carrette (New York: Routledge, 1999), 162–163; Butler, *The Psychic Life of Power.*

6. Several other authors have taken slightly different routes to similar conclusions about the ability of social institutions to create and define reality. See, for instance, Moore, *Injustice;* Peter L. Berger, *The Sacred Canopy,* 81–101; Peter L. Berger and Thomas Luckmann, *The Social Construction of Reality,* 50–103; and Pierre Bourdieu, *The Logic of Practice,* 135–146.

7. Leon Festinger, *A Theory of Cognitive Dissonance* (Evanston, Ill.: Row, Peterson, 1957). Within religious studies, Festinger is best known for his application of dissonance theory to the study of a new religious movement in *When Prophecy Fails* (co-authored with Henry W. Riecken and Stanley Schachter; Minneapolis: University of Minnesota Press, 1956). An excellent summary of Festinger's original theory and subsequent developments, to which this section is greatly indebted, can be found in Eddie Harmon-Jones

and Judson Mills, eds., *Cognitive Dissonance: Progress on a Pivotal Theory in Social Psychology* (Washington, D.C.: American Psychological Association, 1999), 3–21. The theory is certainly not without its detractors and has been challenged on many fronts; Harmon-Jones and Mills's book contains both critiques and reformulations of dissonance theory. My purpose here is not to wade into this debate—a move I am not qualified to make in any case—but to suggest the ways in which recent work on dissonance theory is thought-provoking in the context of LGBT Christian identity. In fact, three authors have already found this to be a useful angle; see Bauer, "The Homosexual Subculture," 115–127; Thumma, "Negotiating a Religious Identity," 333–347; and Mahaffy, "Cognitive Dissonance and Its Resolution," 392–402.

8. See Harmon-Jones and Mills, *Cognitive Dissonance,* 103–232.

9. A superb work that does take self-concept into account is Ruth Thibodeau, "The Threatened Self: Toward a Comprehensive Theory of Dissonance Processes" (Ph.D. diss., University of California, Santa Cruz, 1995). Combining dissonance theory with recent research on the self, Thibodeau suggests that dissonance always arises from conflicts between three factors: information on the self, self-expectancies that are based on prior self-knowledge, and desired self-conceptions that reflect the ideal self.

10. See Mahaffy, "Cognitive Dissonance and Its Resolution."

11. See Primiano, "Intrinsically Catholic."

12. Primiano argues, as others have as well, that the dichotomy between "official religion" and "popular religion" is both demeaning and oversimplified. It implies that "official religion" is the true or more sophisticated form of religion, while "popular religion" (literally, the religion of the people) is a simplified and superstitious version. Primiano points out that this dichotomy also manages to suggest that religious officials adhere to no beliefs beyond official doctrine and no practices beyond official rites—an assumption that is clearly erroneous. See Primiano, "Intrinsically Catholic," 1–151, 429–481; and "Vernacular Religion and the Search for Method in Religious Folklife," *Western Folklore* 54 (1995): 37–56. See also Hall, *Lived Religion in America.*

13. Michel de Certeau, *The Practice of Everyday Life,* trans. Steven Rendall (Berkeley: University of California Press, 1984).

14. The term was used earlier by Lévi-Strauss in his discussions of myth; see *The Savage Mind* (Chicago: University of Chicago Press, 1966), 16–22.

15. I rely on interviews in this section for the sake of simplicity. Although themes of uniqueness run through sermons as well as casual remarks made by congregants during the Sunday services at both churches, during the interviews, I asked outright whether participants believed that LGBT people had a special mission.

16. Interviews 2063 and 2087; September 1, 1998.

17. Interview 2047; September 1, 1998.

18. Interview 1039; August 31, 1998.

19. Interview 2090; August 27, 1998.

20. Interview 1155; August 26, 1998.

21. See "Jesse Jackson, Troy Perry Hold L.A. Hate Crimes Rally."

22. "NCC Rejects Ties with Gay Church," *Christian Century* 109 (December 2, 1992): 1097–1098; Bruce W. Robbins, "UFMCC and NCC: Unity over Justice?" *Christianity and Crisis* 52 (4 January 1993): 424–425.

23. "Falwell Tames His Rhetoric," *Christianity Today* 43, no. 14 (1999): 29. The meeting was an attempt to open a dialogue between LGBT Christians and anti-LGBT Christians. Although its main outcome was an agreement to disagree over the ontological and

soteriological status of LGBT Christians, Falwell did issue a statement after the meeting that emphasized the importance of showing love and support for LGBT friends and family members.

24. Pierre Bourdieu, *The Logic of Practice* and *Language and Symbolic Power;* Christian Smith, ed., *Disruptive Religion: The Force of Faith in Social-Movement Activism* (New York: Routledge, 1996).

25. On this point, it would be interesting to explore the differences in symbolic power among majority and minority religions or the extent to which minority status and perhaps cultural prejudices counteract the symbolic capital of religious organizations. For instance, are there areas of the country in which a synagogue or an association of rabbis holds more sway than a secular organization? Could an LGBT synagogue be more convincing than, say, the National Gay and Lesbian Task Force on some issues, even among the general population? What about a non-LGBT group like the Union of American Hebrew Congregations? Would a Muslim or Buddhist association hold any sway over the general public in the United States? It would not be surprising to find that as cultural misconceptions of a group increase and the group's population decreases, its symbolic capital decreases as well.

26. Smith, *Disruptive Religion,* 9–23.

27. There is also a potential counterargument here that cannot be proved or disproved in this study because of lack of evidence. Although MCC's status as a Christian group could lend it greater credibility in areas of the country that are strongly Christian, the egregious contradiction that conservative Christians would see in the idea of an LGBT church might produce the opposite result instead: MCC might be *less* effective in such areas rather than more so. In that case, it might be that MCC's symbolic capital as a religious organization is more effective in liberal areas, where religious groups and religious leaders are accorded respect but religious diversity is also valued. Although this question cannot be answered here, it is an interesting topic for future study.

28. Warner, "The Metropolitan Community Churches," 89.

29. R. Stephen Warner and Judith G. Wittner, eds., *Gatherings in Diaspora: Religious Communities and the New Immigration* (Philadelphia: Temple University Press, 1998).

30. See, for instance, Steven Epstein, "Gay Politics, Ethnic Identity: The Limits of Social Constructionism," *Socialist Review* 17, no. 3–4 (1987): 9–54.

31. This portion of the debate about parallels between LGBT and ethnic identities is particularly volatile, because the claims of minority groups to a consistent and immutable historical identity also have been challenged. Moreover, although the concept of an LGBT community has shallow historical roots, LGBT popular culture has assiduously reclaimed as symbolic ancestors people throughout history and across cultures who are suspected of homosexual or cross-gender activities.

32. This does not hold for transgender and transsexual people, however, who continue to face severe employment discrimination and who are rarely protected by the same anti-discrimination laws that cover homosexuals in some states. And LGB people are far from being immune to economic discrimination; the point is that such discrimination is not as severe overall among these communities as it is among some ethnic minority communities.

33. And since, despite the denomination's ecumenicity, MCC services tend to reflect mostly the subcultures of white LGBT Christians, the variations have multiplied further. Carl Bean's Unity Fellowship Church Movement appeals to those LGBT African Americans who feel that their culture is not visibly affirmed in LGBT churches such as MCC and that their sexual or gender identities are not affirmed in the historic black churches.

34. Especially noticeable because of their importance in anti-LGBT rhetoric are the topics of marriage, monogamy, and fidelity, on which the UFMCC in general tends to hold fairly traditional views. These are hardly unusual ethical concerns for a church, but they are important as central issues in the struggle of LGBT people for respectability in the mainstream culture.

Selected Bibliography

Adam, Barry D. *The Rise of a Gay and Lesbian Movement.* Rev. ed. New York: Twayne, 1995.

Allen, David J., and Terry Oleson. "Shame and Internalized Homophobia in Gay Men." *Journal of Homosexuality* 37, no. 3 (1999): 33–43.

Altman, Dennis. "Rupture or Continuity? The Internalization of Gay Identities." *Social Text* 48, vol. 14, no. 3 (1996): 77–94.

Ammerman, Nancy Tatom. *Congregation and Community.* New Brunswick, N.J.: Rutgers University Press, 1997.

Aronson, Elliot. "A Theory of Cognitive Dissonance." *American Journal of Psychology* 110, no. 1 (1997): 127–136.

Batson, C. Daniel, Patricia Schoenrade, and Larry W. Ventis. *Religion and the Individual: A Social-Psychological Perspective.* New York: Oxford University Press, 1993.

Bauer, Paul F. "The Homosexual Subculture at Worship: A Participant Observation Study." *Pastoral Psychology* 25, no. 2 (1976): 115–127.

Beemyn, Brett, and Mickey Elianon. *Queer Studies: A Lesbian, Gay, Bisexual, and Transgender Anthology.* New York: New York University Press, 1996.

Bell, Catherine. *Ritual Theory, Ritual Practice.* New York: Oxford University Press, 1992.

Bellah, Robert N., Richard Madsen, William M. Sullivan, Ann Swidler, and Steven M. Tipton. *Habits of the Heart: Individualism and Commitment in American Life.* Berkeley: University of California Press, 1985.

Berger, Peter. *The Sacred Canopy: Elements of a Sociological Theory of Religion.* Garden City, N.Y.: Doubleday, 1967.

———. *The Heretical Imperative: Contemporary Possibilities of Religious Affirmation.* Garden City, N.Y.: Anchor/Doubleday, 1979.

Berger, Peter, and Thomas Luckmann. *The Social Construction of Reality: A Treatise in the Sociology of Knowledge.* Garden City, N.Y.: Doubleday, 1966.

Berkstresser, Charles Frank. "Christian Gay Men's Understanding of the Relationship between Their Gayness and Their Spirituality." M.A. thesis, Pacific School of Religion, 1991.

Billings, Dwight. "Religion as Opposition: A Gramscian Analysis." *American Journal of Sociology* 96, no. 1 (1990): 1–31.

Billings, Dwight, and Shaunna L. Scott. "Religion and Political Legitimation." *Annual Review of Sociology* 20 (1994): 173–201.

Birchard, Roy. "Metropolitan Community Church: Its Development and Significance." *Foundations: A Baptist Journal of History and Theology* 20 (April–June 1977): 127–132.

Blackwood, Evelyn, and Saskia E. Wieringa, eds. *Female Desires: Same-Sex Relations and Transgender Practices across Cultures.* New York: Columbia University Press, 1999.

Boswell, John. *Christianity, Social Tolerance, and Homosexuality: Gay People in Western*

Europe from the Beginning of the Christian Era to the Fourteenth Century. Chicago: University of Chicago Press, 1980.

Bourdieu, Pierre. *The Logic of Practice.* Translated by Richard Nice. Stanford, Calif.: Stanford University Press, 1990.

———. *Language and Symbolic Power.* Edited by John B. Thompson. Translated by Gino Raymond and Matthew Adamson. Cambridge, Mass.: Harvard University Press, 1991.

Bradley, Don E. "Religious Involvement and Social Resources: Evidence from the Data Set *Americans' Changing Lives.*" *Journal for the Scientific Study of Religion* 34, no. 2 (1995): 259–267.

Brasher, Brenda. *Godly Women: Fundamentalism and Female Power.* New Brunswick, N.J.: Rutgers University Press, 1998.

Bravmann, Scott. *Queer Fictions of the Past: History, Culture, and Difference.* New York: Cambridge University Press, 1997.

Burr, Chandler. *A Separate Creation: The Search for the Biological Origins of Sexual Orientation.* New York: Hyperion, 1996.

Butler, Judith. *Gender Trouble: Feminism and the Subversion of Identity.* New York: Routledge, 1990.

———. *The Psychic Life of Power: Theories in Subjection.* Stanford, Calif.: Stanford University Press, 1997.

Bynum, Caroline Walker. *Jesus as Mother: Studies in the Spirituality of the High Middle Ages.* Berkeley: University of California Press, 1982.

———. *Holy Feast, Holy Fast: The Religious Significance of Food to Medieval Women.* Berkeley: University of California Press, 1987.

———. *Fragmentation and Redemption: Essays on Gender and the Human Body in Medieval Religion.* New York: Zone Books, 1991.

Carbaugh, Donal. *Situating Selves: The Communication of Social Identities in American Scenes.* Albany, N.Y.: SUNY Press, 1996.

Carey, John Jesse, ed. *The Sexuality Debate in North American Churches, 1988–1995: Controversies, Unresolved Issues, Future Prospects.* Lewiston, N.Y.: Edwin Mellen, 1995.

Cherry, Kittredge, and James Mitulski. "We Are the Church Alive, the Church with AIDS." *Christian Century* 105, no. 3 (1988): 85–88.

Clark, J. Michael, Joanne Carlson Brown, and Lorna M. Hochstein. "Institutional Religion and Gay/Lesbian Oppression." *Marriage and Family Review* 14, no. 3–4 (1989): 265–284.

Clark, J. Michael, and Robert E. Goss, eds. *A Rainbow of Religious Studies.* Las Colinas, Tex: Monument, 1996.

Clifford, James. *The Predicament of Culture: Twentieth Century Ethnography, Literature, and Art.* Cambridge, Mass.: Harvard University Press, 1988.

———. *Routes: Travel and Translation in the Late Twentieth Century.* Cambridge, Mass.: Harvard University Press, 1997.

Comstock, Gary David. *Unrepentant, Self-Affirming, Practicing: Lesbian/Gay/Bisexual People within Organized Religion.* New York: Continuum, 1996.

Comstock, Gary David, and Susan E. Henking. *Que(e)rying Religion: A Critical Anthology.* New York: Continuum, 1997.

Cooper, Aaron. "No Longer Invisible: Gay and Lesbian Jews Build a Movement." *Journal of Homosexuality* 18, no. 3–4 (1989): 83–94.

Cuthbertson, Kenneth L. "Coming Out/Conversion: An Exploration of Gay Religious Experience." *Journal of Men's Studies* 4, no. 3 (1996): 193–207.

D'Emilio, John. *Sexual Politics, Sexual Communities: The Making of a Homosexual Minority in the United States, 1940–1970.* Chicago: University of Chicago Press, 1983.

———. *Making Trouble: Essays on Gay History, Politics, and the University.* New York: Routledge, 1992.

Dart, John. "Gay-Oriented Church Joins Ecumenical Group." *Los Angeles Times,* February 21, 1997.

Dashefsky, Arnold. "And the Search Goes On: The Meaning of Religio-Ethnic Identity and Identification." *Sociological Analysis* 33, no. 4 (1972): 239–245.

Davidson, David. "Dignity, Inc.: An Alternative Experience of Church." In *Homosexuality and Religion and Philosophy,* edited by Wayne R. Dynes and Stephen Donaldson, 152–161. New York: Garland, 1992.

Dawson, Lorne. *Comprehending Cults: The Sociology of New Religious Movements.* Toronto: Oxford University Press Canada, 1998.

de Certeau, Michel. *The Practice of Everyday Life.* Translated by Steven Rendall. Berkeley: University of California Press, 1984.

Demerath, N.J., III, and Rhys H. Williams. *A Bridging of Faiths: Religion and Politics in a New England City.* Princeton, N.J.: Princeton University Press, 1992.

Denzin, Norman K. *Interpretive Ethnography: Ethnographic Practices for the Twenty-First Century.* Thousand Oaks, Calif.: Sage, 1997.

Dillon, Michele. *Catholic Identity: Balancing Reason, Faith, and Power.* New York: Cambridge University Press, 1999.

Douglas, Mary. *Purity and Danger: An Analysis of Concepts of Pollution and Taboo.* New York: Praeger, 1966.

Dudley, Carl S., Jackson W. Carroll, and James P. Wind, eds. *Carriers of Faith: Lessons from Congregational Studies.* Louisville, Ky.: Westminster/John Knox, 1991.

Dufour, Lynn Resnick. "Sifting through Tradition: The Creation of Jewish Feminist Identities." *Journal for the Scientific Study of Religion* 39, no. 1 (2000): 90–106.

Dynes, Wayne R., and Stephen Donaldson, eds. *Ethnographic Studies of Homosexuality.* New York: Garland, 1992.

———. *Homosexuality and Religion and Philosophy.* New York: Garland, 1992.

Eilberg-Schwartz, Howard. *God's Phallus and Other Problems for Men and Monotheism.* Boston: Beacon, 1994.

Eliason, Michele J. "Identity Formation for Lesbian, Bisexual, and Gay Persons: Beyond a 'Minoritizing' View." *Journal of Homosexuality* 30, no. 3 (1996): 31–58.

Ellis, Carolyn, and Michael G. Flaherty, eds. *Investigating Subjectivity: Research on Lived Experience.* Newbury Park, Calif.: Sage, 1992.

England, Michael E. *The Bible and Homosexuality.* 5th ed. Gaithersburg, Md.: Chi Rho, 1998.

Enroth, Ronald M. "The Homosexual Church: An Ecclesiastical Extension of a Subculture." *Social Compass* 21, no. 3 (1974): 355–360.

Enroth, Ronald M., and Gerald E. Jamison. *The Gay Church.* Grand Rapids, Mich.: Eerdmans, 1974.

Epstein, Steven. "Gay Politics, Ethnic Identity: The Limits of Social Constructionism." *Socialist Review* 17, no. 3–4 (1987): 9–54.

Erikson, Erik. *Identity, Youth, and Crisis.* New York: W. W. Norton, 1968.

Escoffier, Jeffrey. *American Homo: Community and Perversity.* Berkeley: University of California Press, 1998.

Fischer, Clare B. "A Bonding of Choice: Values and Identity among Lesbian and Gay Religious Leaders." *Journal of Homosexuality* 18, no. 3-4 (1989): 145-174.

FitzGerald, Frances. *Cities on a Hill: A Journey through Contemporary American Cultures.* New York: Simon and Schuster, 1986.

Foucault, Michel. *The History of Sexuality.* Vol. 1, *An Introduction.* Translated by Robert Hurley. New York: Vintage, 1978.

———. *Power/Knowledge: Selected Interviews and Other Writings, 1972-1977.* Edited and translated by Colin Gordon. New York: Pantheon, 1980.

———. *Religion and Culture.* Edited by Jeremy R. Carrette. New York: Routledge, 1999.

Frame, Randy. "The Evangelical Closet." *Christianity Today* 34 (1990): 56-57.

Francis, Sam. "A Mormon Paradox: Fellowship in the Shadow of Intolerance." *Advocate* 758 (April 28, 1996): 16.

Fuss, Diana. *Essentially Speaking: Feminism, Nature, and Difference.* New York: Routledge, 1989.

———, ed. *Inside/Out: Lesbian Theories, Gay Theories.* New York: Routledge, 1991.

Garfield, Ken. "Presbyterians in Stalemate over Homosexual Ordination." *Christianity Today* 42, no. 9 (August 10, 1998): 22.

"Gay-Friendly Church Leaves Denomination." *Christian Century* 113, no. 32 (November 6, 1996): 1068-1069.

Geertz, Clifford. *The Interpretation of Cultures.* New York: Basic Books, 1973.

Giddens, Anthony. *Modernity and Self-Identity: Self and Society in the Late Modern Age.* Stanford, Calif.: Stanford University Press, 1991.

Gill, Sean, ed. *The Lesbian and Gay Christian Movement: Campaigning for Justice, Truth, and Love.* London: Cassell, 1998.

Goffman, Erving. *Stigma: Notes on the Management of Spoiled Identity.* Englewood Cliffs, N.J.: Prentice-Hall, 1963.

Gorman, E. Michael. "A New Light on Zion: A Study of Three Homosexual Religious Congregations in Urban America." Ph.D. diss., University of Chicago, 1980.

Gramsci, Antonio. *Selections from the Prison Notebooks of Antonio Gramsci.* Edited by Quintin Hoare and Geoffrey Nowell Smith. New York: International, 1971.

———. *Further Selections from the Prison Notebooks.* Translated and edited by Derek Boothman. London: Lawrence and Wishart, 1995.

Gray, Edward R., and Scott L. Thumma. "The Gospel Hour: Liminality, Identity, and Religion in a Gay Bar." In *Contemporary American Religion: An Ethnographic Reader,* edited by Penny Edgell Becker and Nancy L. Eiesland, 79-98. Walnut Creek, Calif.: Alta Mira, 1997.

———. *Gay Religion: Innovation and Tradition in Spiritual Practice.* Walnut Creek: Alta Mira, forthcoming.

Hall, David D., ed. *Lived Religion: Toward a History of Practice.* Princeton, N.J.: Princeton, 1997.

Hammond, Phillip E. "Religion and the Persistence of Identity." *Journal for the Scientific Study of Religion* 27, no. 1 (1988): 1-11.

Hannigan, John A. "New Social Movement Theory and the Sociology of Religion: Synergies and Syntheses." In *A Future for Religion? New Paradigms for Social Analysis,* edited by William H. Swatos, Jr., 1-18. Newbury Park, Calif.: Sage, 1993.

Harmon-Jones, Eddie, and Judson Mills, eds. *Cognitive Dissonance: Progress on a Pivotal*

Theory in Social Psychology. Washington, D.C.: American Psychological Association, 1999.

Hartman, Keith. *Congregations in Conflict: The Battle over Homosexuality.* New Brunswick, N.J.: Rutgers University Press, 1996.

Hasbany, Richard, ed. *Homosexuality and Religion.* New York: Haworth, 1989.

Herman, Didi. *The Antigay Agenda: Orthodox Vision and the Christian Right.* Chicago: University of Chicago Press, 1997.

Hewitt, Thomas Furman. "The American Church's Reaction to the Homophile Movement, 1948–1978." Ph.D. diss., Duke University, 1983.

Humphreys, Laud, and Brian Miller. "Identities in the Emerging Gay Culture." In *Homosexual Behavior: A Modern Reappraisal,* edited by Judd Marmon, 142–156. New York: Basic Books, 1980.

In Unity. Universal Fellowship of Metropolitan Community Churches. April 1970 to October/November 1978.

Jordan, Karen M., and Robert H. Deluty. "Coming Out for Lesbian Women: Its Relation to Anxiety, Positive Affectivity, Self-Esteem, and Social Support." *Journal of Homosexuality* 35, no. 2 (1998): 41–63.

Josselson, Ruth, and Amia Lieblich, eds. *The Narrative Study of Lives.* Vol. 1. Newbury Park, Calif.: Sage, 1993.

———. *The Narrative Study of Lives.* Vol. 5. Thousand Oaks, Calif.: Sage, 1997.

Kaiser, Charles. *The Gay Metropolis, 1940–1996.* Boston: Houghton Mifflin, 1997.

Katz, Jonathan Ned. *Gay American History: Lesbians and Gay Men in the U.S.A.* Rev. ed. New York: Meridian, 1992.

Kertzer, David I. *Ritual, Politics, and Power.* New Haven, Conn.: Yale University Press, 1988.

Kolodny, Deborah R., ed. *Blessed Bi Spirit: Bisexual People of Faith.* New York: Continuum, 2000.

Lincoln, Bruce. *Discourse and the Construction of Society.* New York: Oxford University Press, 1989.

———, ed. *Religion, Rebellion, Revolution: An Interdisciplinary and Cross-Cultural Collection of Essays.* New York: St. Martin's, 1985.

Lukenbill, W. Bernard. "Observations on the Corporate Culture of a Gay and Lesbian Congregation." *Journal for the Scientific Study of Religion* 37, no. 3 (1998): 440–452.

McEwen, Mary Anne. *God, Gays, and the Gospel: This Is Our Story.* Videocassette. Directed by Mary Anne McEwen. Produced by Troy D. Perry. 60 min. Los Angeles: Universal Fellowship of Metropolitan Community Churches, 1984.

McGuire, Meredith B. "Religion and the Body: Rematerializing the Human Body in the Social Sciences of Religion." *Journal for the Scientific Study of Religion* 29, no. 3 (1990): 283–294.

Maduro, Otto. *Religion and Social Conflicts.* Maryknoll, N.Y.: Orbis Books, 1982.

Mahaffy, Kimberly A. "Cognitive Dissonance and Its Resolution: A Study of Lesbian Christians." *Journal for the Scientific Study of Religion* 35, no. 4 (1996): 392–402.

Malcolm, Teresa. "Vatican Approves Changes to Message for Parents of Gays." *National Catholic Reporter* 34, no. 34 (July 17, 1998): 12.

Manodori, Chiara. "This Powerful Opening of the Heart: How Ritual Affirms Lesbian Identity." *Journal of Homosexuality* 36, no. 2 (1998): 41–58.

Marotta, Toby. *The Politics of Homosexuality.* Boston: Houghton Mifflin, 1981.

Marty, Martin E. *Righteous Empire: The Protestant Experience in America.* New York: Dial, 1970.

———. "Revising the Map of American Religion." *Annals of the American Academy of Political and Social Science* 558 (July 1998): 13–27.

Melton, Gordon. *The Churches Speak on Homosexuality.* Detroit: Gale Research, 1991.

Miller, Neil. *In Search of Gay America: Women and Men in a Time of Change.* New York: Atlantic Monthly, 1989.

Mishler, Elliott G. *Research Interviewing: Context and Narrative.* Cambridge, Mass.: Harvard University Press, 1986.

Monroe, Irene. "The Aché Sisters: Discovering the Power of the Erotic in Ritual." In *Women at Worship: Interpretations of North American Diversity,* edited by Marjorie Procter-Smith and Janet R. Walton, 127–135. Louisville, Ky.: Westminster/John Knox, 1993.

Moore, Barrington, Jr. *Injustice: The Social Bases of Obedience and Revolt.* White Plains, N.Y.: M. E. Sharpe, 1978.

Morgan, Timothy C. "Anglicans Deem Homosexuality 'Incompatible with Scripture.' " *Christianity Today* 42, no. 10 (1998): 32–33.

Neitz, Mary Jo. *Charisma and Community: A Study of Religious Commitment within the Charismatic Renewal.* New Brunswick, N.J.: Transaction, 1987.

Nesti, Arnaldo. "Gramsci et la Religion Populaire." *Social Compass* 22, no. 3–4 (1975): 343–354.

Nicholson, Linda, and Steven Seidman, eds. *Social Postmodernism: Beyond Identity Politics.* New York: Cambridge University Press, 1995.

Nungesser, Lon G. *Homosexual Acts, Actors, and Identities.* New York: Praeger, 1983.

Olyan, Saul M., and Martha C. Nussbaum, eds. *Sexual Orientation and Human Rights in American Religious Discourse.* New York: Oxford University Press, 1998.

Oppenheimer, Mark. "Inherent Worth and Dignity: Gay Unitarians and the Birth of Sexual Tolerance in Liberal Religion." *Journal of the History of Sexuality* 7, no. 1 (1996): 73–101.

Perry, Troy D. "Gays and the Gospel: An Interview with Troy Perry." *Christian Century* 113, no. 27 (1996): 896–901.

Perry, Troy D., with Thomas L. P. Swicegood. *Don't Be Afraid Anymore: The Story of Reverend Troy Perry and the Metropolitan Community Churches.* New York: St. Martin's, 1990.

Perry, Troy D., as told to Charles L. Lucas. *The Lord Is My Shepherd and He Knows I'm Gay.* Los Angeles: Nash, 1972.

Pierce, Janet E. "Outside the Gate: The Challenge of the Universal Fellowship." In *Women and Church: The Challenge of Ecumenical Solidarity in an Age of Alienation,* edited by Melanie A. May, 49–54. Grand Rapids, Mich.: Eerdmans, 1991.

Plant, Richard. *The Pink Triangle: The Nazi War against Homosexuals.* New York: Henry Holt, 1986.

Plummer, Ken. *Telling Sexual Stories: Power, Change, and Social Worlds.* London: Routledge, 1995.

Polkinghorne, Donald E. *Narrative Knowing and the Human Sciences.* Albany, N.Y.: SUNY, 1988.

Primiano, Leonard Norman. "Intrinsically Catholic: Vernacular Religion and Philadelphia's 'Dignity.' " Ph.D. diss., University of Pennsylvania, 1993.

——. "'I Would Rather Be Fixated on the Lord': Women's Religion, Men's Power, and the 'Dignity' Problem." *New York Folklore* 19, no. 1–2 (1993): 89–99.

——. "Vernacular Religion and the Search for Method in Religious Folklife." *Western Folklore* 54 (1995): 37–56.

Rich, Adrienne. "Compulsory Heterosexuality and Lesbian Existence." *Signs* 5, no. 4 (1980): 631–660.

Riessman, Catherine Kohler. *Narrative Analysis.* Newbury Park, Calif.: Sage, 1993.

Robbins, Bruce W. "UFMCC and NCC: Unity over Justice?" *Christianity and Crisis* 52 (January 4, 1993): 424–425.

Robbins, Thomas, and Dick Anthony, eds. *In Gods We Trust: New Patterns of Religious Pluralism in America.* 2nd ed. New Brunswick, N.J.: Transaction, 1990.

Roof, Wade Clark. *A Generation of Seekers: The Spiritual Journeys of the Baby Boom Generation.* San Francisco: Harper, 1993.

——. "Modernity, the Religious, and the Spiritual." *Annals of the American Academy of Political and Social Science* 558 (1998): 211–224.

——. *Spiritual Marketplace: Baby Boomers and the Remaking of American Religion.* Princeton, N.J.: Princeton University Press, 1999.

Roof, Wade Clark, and William McKinney. *American Mainline Religion: Its Changing Shape and Future.* New Brunswick, N.J.: Rutgers University Press, 1987.

Rosario, Vernon A., ed. *Science and Homosexualities.* New York: Routledge, 1997.

Ross, Michael W., and B. R. Simon Rosser. "Measurement and Correlates of Internalized Homophobia: A Factor Analytic Study." *Journal of Clinical Psychology* 52, no. 1 (1996): 15–21.

Rupp, Leila J. *A Desired Past: A Short History of Same-Sex Love in America.* Chicago: University of Chicago Press, 1999.

Schneider, Beth E. "Coming Out at Work: Bridging the Private/Public Gap." *Work and Occupations* 13, no. 4 (1986): 463–487.

Sedgwick, Eve Kosofsky. *Epistemology of the Closet.* Berkeley: University of California Press, 1990.

Seidman, Steven. *Difference Troubles: Queering Social Theory and Sexual Politics.* Cambridge: Cambridge University Press, 1997.

Shallenberger, David. *Reclaiming the Spirit: Gay Men and Lesbians Come to Terms with Religion.* New Brunswick, N.J.: Rutgers University Press, 1998.

Shneer, David, and Caryn Aviv, eds. *Queer Jews.* New York: Routledge, 2002.

Shokeid, Moshe. *A Gay Synagogue in New York.* New York: Columbia University Press, 1995.

Silverstein, Charles. *Man to Man: Gay Couples in America.* New York: William Morrow, 1981.

Smith, Christian, ed. *Disruptive Religion: The Force of Faith in Social-Movement Activism.* New York: Routledge, 1996.

Smith, Jonathan Z. *Imagining Religion: From Babylon to Jonestown.* Chicago: University of Chicago Press, 1982.

——. *To Take Place: Toward Theory in Ritual.* Chicago: University of Chicago Press, 1987.

Solheim, James. "National Council of Churches Denies Observer Status to UFMCC." *Ecumenical Trends* 22, no. 13 (1993): 13.

Stacey, Judith. *Brave New Families: Stories of Domestic Upheaval in Late Twentieth Century America.* New York: Basic Books, 1990.

Tanis, Justin Edward. *Trans-Gendered: Theology, Ministry, and Communities of Faith.* Cleveland, Ohio: Pilgrim Press, 2003.

Thibodeau, Ruth. "The Threatened Self: Toward a Comprehensive Theory of Dissonance Processes." Ph.D. diss., University of California Santa Cruz, 1995.

Thumma, Scott. "Negotiating a Religious Identity: The Case of the Gay Evangelical." *Sociological Analysis* 52, no. 4 (1991): 333–347.

Tinney, James S. "Why a Black Gay Church?" In *In the Life: A Black Gay Anthology,* edited by Joseph Beam, 70–86. Boston: Alyson, 1986.

Troiden, Richard. "Self, Self-Concept, Identity, and Homosexual Identity: Constructs in Need of Definition and Differentiation." *Journal of Homosexuality* 10, no. 3–4 (1984): 97–109.

———. "The Formation of Homosexual Identities." *Journal of Homosexuality* 17, no. 1–2 (1989): 43–73.

Turner, Victor. *The Ritual Process: Structure and Anti-Structure.* New York: Aldine de Gruyter, 1969.

"UMC Bishops Split on Ordaining Gays." *Christian Century* 113, no. 16 (May 8, 1996): 504.

"UMC Bishops' Stance Draws Praise, Criticism." *Christian Century* 115, no. 16 (May 20, 1998): 521–522.

Vincke, John, and Ralph Bolton. "Social Support, Depression, and Self-Acceptance among Gay Men." *Human Relations* 47, no. 9 (1994): 1049–1062.

Wagner, Glenn, James Serafini, Judith Rabkin, Robert Remien, and Janet Williams. "Integration of One's Religion and Homosexuality: A Weapon against Internalized Homophobia?" *Journal of Homosexuality* 26, no. 4 (1994): 91–110.

Warner, R. Stephen. *New Wine in Old Wineskins: Evangelicals and Liberals in a Small-Town Church.* Berkeley: University of California Press, 1988.

———. "Work in Progress toward a New Paradigm for the Sociological Study of Religion in the United States." *American Journal of Sociology* 98 (March 1993): 1044–1093.

———. "The Metropolitan Community Churches and the Gay Agenda: The Power of Pentecostalism and Essentialism." In *Sex, Lies, and Sanctity: Religion and Deviance in Contemporary North America,* edited by Mary Jo Neitz and Marion S. Goldman, 81–108. Greenwich, Conn.: JAI, 1995.

Warner, R. Stephen, and Judith G. Wittner, eds. *Gatherings in Diaspora: Religious Communities and the New Immigration.* Philadelphia: Temple University Press, 1998.

Warren, Carol A. B. *Identity and Community in the Gay World.* New York: John Wiley and Sons, 1974.

Weber, Max. "The Sociology of Religion." In *Economy and Society,* edited by Guenther Roth and Claus Wittich, 399–634. Berkeley: University of California, 1978.

———. *The Protestant Ethic and the Spirit of Capitalism.* New York: Routledge, 1992.

Wellman, James K., Jr., ed. *Religious Organizational Identity and Homosexual Ordination: A Case Study of the Presbyterian Church, U.S.A.* Special issue of *Review of Religious Research* 41, no. 2 (1999).

Whisman, Vera. *Queer by Choice: Lesbians, Gay Men, and the Politics of Identity.* New York: Routledge, 1996.

Wilcox, Melissa M. "Dancing on the Fence: Researching Lesbian, Gay, Bisexual, and Transgender Christians." In *Personal Knowledge and Beyond: Reshaping the*

Ethnography of Religion, edited by James V. Spickard, J. Shawn Landres, and Meredith B. McGuire, 47–60. New York: New York University Press, 2001.

———. "Murderers and Martyrs: Violence, Discourse, and the (Re)construction of Meaning." *Culture and Religion* 2, no. 2 (2001).

———. "Innovation in Exile: Religion in Lesbian, Gay, Bisexual, and Transgender Communities." In *Sexuality and the World's Religions,* edited by David W. Machacek and Melissa M. Wilcox. Goleta, Calif.: ABC-CLIO, 2003.

Williams, Peter W. *Popular Religion in America: Symbolic Change and the Modernization Process in Historical Perspective.* Englewood Cliffs, N.J.: Prentice Hall, 1980.

Williams, Rhys H. "Religion as Political Resource: Culture or Ideology?" *Journal for the Scientific Study of Religion* 35, no. 4 (1996): 368–378.

Wilson, Nancy. *Our Tribe: Queer Folks, God, Jesus, and the Bible.* San Francisco: Harper, 1995.

Wind, James P., and James W. Lewis, eds. *American Congregations.* Vol. 1, *Portraits of Twelve Religious Communities.* Chicago: University of Chicago Press, 1994.

———. *American Congregations.* Vol. 2, *New Perspectives in the Study of Congregations.* Chicago: University of Chicago Press, 1994.

Wood, Richard. "Faith in Action: Religious Resources for Political Success in Three Congregations." *Sociology of Religion* 55, no. 4 (1994): 397–417.

Wuthnow, Robert. *Rediscovering the Sacred: Perspectives on Religion in Contemporary Society.* Grand Rapids, Mich.: Eerdmans, 1992.

———. *Producing the Sacred: An Essay on Public Religion.* Urbana: University of Illinois Press, 1994.

———. *After Heaven: Spirituality in America Since the 1950s.* Berkeley: University of California Press, 1998.

Yinger, J. Milton. *Religion in the Struggle for Power: A Study in the Sociology of Religion.* New York: Russell and Russell, 1961.

Yip, Andrew K. T. "Gay Christians and Their Participation in the Gay Sub-culture." *Deviant Behavior* 17 (1996): 297–318.

———. "Gay Christian Couples and Blessing Ceremonies." *Theology and Sexuality* 4 (1996): 100–117.

———. "Attacking the Attacker: Gay Christians Talk Back." *British Journal of Sociology* 48, no. 1 (1997): 113–127.

———. *Gay Male Christian Couples: Life Stories.* Westport, Conn.: Praeger, 1997.

———. "The Persistence of Faith among Nonheterosexual Christians: Evidence for the Neosecularization Thesis of Religious Transformation." *Journal for the Scientific Study of Religion* 41, no. 2 (2002): 199–212.

Index

Study participants are indexed only in Appendix A, at the wishes of the author. *Illustrations and charts are indicated by italicized page numbers.*

accepting movements: beginning of, 106; process, 106; Protestant, 106; reasons for leaving MCC, 106
activism: for equal access, 40; and Stonewall Riots, 40, 90–91. *See also* gay liberation movement
Advocate, 94
Affirmation, 95, 108
al-Fatiha, 108
American Baptist Conference: expulsion of churches from, 43. *See also* Baptist
American Psychological Association: demedicalization of homosexuality, 40–41
Anderson, C. Alan, 2
Assemblies of God, 42
AXIOS, 108

Bailey, Derrick Sherwin, 89
Baptist: American Baptists Concerned, 108; Welcoming and Affirming, 106. *See also* American Baptist Conference; Progressive National Baptist Convention; Southern Baptist churches
Bauer, Paul F., 12, 83–84, 95
Bean, Carl. *See* black lesbian and gay churches
Bellah, Robert, et al.: on expressive individualism, 53–54; Sheila Larson (participant in study), 53, 54, 77
Berger, Peter: on experience and reality, 142; on religion as stabilizer, 145. *See also* Schutz, Alfred
Berger, Peter, and Thomas Luckmann: on plausibility structures, 16, 144, 156
Beth Chayim Chadashim, 95
biblical sources for anti-LGBT views, 43–44. *See also* LGBT approaches to the Bible
bisexuality: invisibility of, 43; in study, 29–30
black lesbian and gay churches, 95, 108
Black Power movement, 91

Bourdieu, Pierre: on *habitus,* 139; on power, 153; on symbolic capital, 162; on symbolism, 131
bricolage, 170–171
British ethnographic studies. *See* Yip, Andrew K. T.
Brown, Joanne Carlson. *See* Clark, J. Michael
Butler, Judith: on self-policing subject, 153, 154; on socially-determined gender, 56

Cabezón, José, 32
Candle of Hope and Healing, 4, 133–134
Cathedral of Hope, 18
Catholic church: on celibacy, 105; and homosexual essentialism, 70. *See also* Dignity
Certeau, Michel de, 158
charismatic: experience, 7, 141–142; at MCC Long Beach, 22; at MCCVR, 4; at OMCC, 9, 22. *See also glossolalia,* slain in the spirit
choice and LGBT identity, 69
Christian New Testament, 43–44. *See also* LGBT approaches to the Bible
Church of God in Prophecy, 18. *See also* Perry, Troy
Civil Rights Movement, 85
Clark, J. Michael, Joanne Carlson Brown, and Lorna M. Hochstein: on effects of anti-homosexual teachings, 46
cognitive dissonance theory, 14–15, 155–156. *See also* Festinger, Leon; Mahaffy, Kimberly A.
coming out as LGBT: and Christianity, 97; and religion, 17, 47–48, 58–59, 60–61, 62; and religious individualism, 55; and spirituality of seeking, 54–55
commitment ceremony. *See* same-sex marriage
Comstock, Gary David: on conservative churches, 106; on inclusion of LGBT people in accepting churches, 108; on LGB experiences of religiosity, 14, 17–18; on LGBT iden-

gion, 17; as God-given, 44, 70–71, 75 (*See also* essentialism)

Independent Fundamentalist Churches of America, 52

Integrity, 95, 109, 111

Interweave, 108

In Unity (UFMCC newsletter), 85, 87, 89, 93, 96

Islam. *See* al-Fatiha

Jackson, Jesse, 162

Jamison, Gerald E. *See* Enroth, Ronald M.

Jesus: as a gay man, 135; historical sexuality of, 73–74; on loving unconditionally, 44; Paul's teaching about, 43

Job, 129

King, Martin Luther, Jr., 85

Kinsey Report, 42

Knight Initiative, ix

lesbian feminism, 91–92

Leviticus: and death penalty, 43; and homosexuality, 43, 74–75 (See also *to'evah*); and hypocrisy, 74

LGBT (Lesbian, Gay, Bisexual, and Transgender)

—LGBT approaches to the Bible: as a condemnation, 71; refusing church teachings, 67; same-sex couples in, 135; taking what is needed, 53, 56, 74–75

—LGBT Christian groups within churches, 106–107. *See also* Baptist; Integrity; Interweave; Lutheran; Presbyterian; United Church Coalition for Lesbian and Gay Concerns

—LGBT community responses to LGBT Christians, 48–49

—LGBT people and ethnic minorities, 165–166

liberation theology: and ecumenism in MCC, 86–87; and Marxism, 95. *See also* Gutierrez, Gustavo

Lincoln, Bruce: on discourse, 130; on ritual, 138; on strategies of myth, 134–135

Luckmann, Thomas, 16, 34, 142, 144. *See also* Berger, Peter

Lutheran: Lutherans Concerned, 111; Reconciled in Christ movement, 106

Maduro, Otto, 17

Mahaffy, Kimberly A.: on cognitive dissonance, 14–15, 155–157. *See also* Festinger, Leon

Marotta, Toby: on Gay Liberation Front, 91; on homophile movement, 90

Marty, Martin, 54

Marxism and Christianity, 17, 163

Mattachine Society, 89–90, 91; and *One*, 90. *See also* Hay, Harry; homophile; movement; ONE, Incorporated

MCC (Metropolitan Community Churches): activism, 87 (*See also* hate crimes); attempts to join National Council of Churches, 162; and Civil Rights Movement, 85; demographics, 18–19; evangelism, 93–94; founding of, 18; and gender equality, 18, 97; growth rate of, 83; inaugural conference, 18; international outreach by, 97; and mainstream Christianity, 19; membership, 18; mission, 18; non-Christian converts, 95–96; as observer at World Council of Churches, 162; and people of color, 18–19; as radical and conservative, 167; and Rainbow Coalition, 104, 162; as subcultural enclave, 164–165; and theology, 14, 19, 86 (*See also* liberation theology, ecumenism); and traditional Christian ethics, 167. *See also* Perry, Troy

MCCVR (MCC "Valle Rico"): description of, 2, 20; founding of, 20; healing services, 3, 23 (*See also* Reiki); metaphysics, 2, 3, 20–21; religious belief, 4, 21

McFadden, Ralph, 106

McKinney, William. *See* Roof, Wade Clark

medicalization of homosexuality, 38–40

Millennium March, 34, 169. *See also* Perry, Troy

mission of LGBT Christians, 159–161

Moore, Barrington, 144

morality, 41

More Light movement, 43, 106. *See also* Presbyterian

Mormon. *See* Affirmation

National Coming Out Day, 130

National Council of Churches: rejection of MCC by, 162, 167

National Gay Pentecostal Alliance, 108

New Left, 91

New Testament. *See* Christian New Testament

Old Testament. *See* Hebrew Bible

OMCC ("Oceanfront" MCC): founding of, 21; in "La Playa" 5–6; membership crisis, 22–23; in "Seaview" 6; slain in the spirit (*See also* charismatic)

ONE, Incorporated, 90. See also Mattachine Society

Open and Affirming movement, 43, 106. *See also* Disciples of Christ; United Church of Christ

ordination of LGBT Christians: in Southern
Baptist Church, 103, 105; in United Church
of Christ, 42, 43. *See also* MCC
Orthodox Christians. *See* AXIOS
Ouellette, Suzanne C. *See* Rodriguez, Eric M.

Paul: on homosexuality, 44; on Jesus, 43;
reinterpretations of, 44
Peck, M. Scott, 3, 137
Perry, Troy: activism of, 34, 87; charisma of,
93; and Church of God in Prophecy, 18; ecumenical belief of, 87; on essentialism, 57; as
evangelist, 84, 86, 93; founding of MCC by,
18, 45, 81–82; as Pentecostal, 19; as religious
entrepreneur, 84. *See also* hate crimes; MCC;
Millennium March
PFLAG (Parents, Families, and Friends of Lesbians and Gays), 111
plausibility structures, 144–145. *See also* Berger,
Peter, and Thomas Luckmann
Ploen, Rev. Richard, 87–94
pluralism, 67, 82
population of areas studied, 20–21
praying in tongues. *See* glossolalia
Presbyterian: Presbyterians for Lesbian and
Gay Concerns, 108. *See also* More Light movement
Primiano, Leonard Norman: on gender and
Dignity, 108–109; on individualistic religiosity, 13; on vernacular religion, 157–158
Progressive National Baptist Convention: and
anti-LGBT discrimination, 104
pseudonyms: use of, 27

qadesh: biblical source and translations, 43–44.
See also LGBT approaches to the Bible

Radicalesbians, 94
Rainbow Coalition, 104
rainbow flag, 128, 131–132, 133
Reform and Reconstructionist Judaism, 105
Reiki, 3; described, 23
religious individualism, described, 13; and
MCC, 33; necessity of, 16, 77. *See also* Roof,
Wade Clark
religious right, 45. *See also* Wilson, Rev. Elder
Nancy
Rich, Adrienne, 56–57
Rodriguez, Eric M. and Suzanne C. Ouellette,
15, 16
Roof, Wade Clark: lived religion, 55, 76–77; re-
ligious individualism, 33; spirituality versus
religion, 61

Roof, Wade Clark and McKinney: religious
groups' growth rates, 88; leaving Protestantism, 115
Routes to MCC, *115*

same-sex marriage: in a Methodist church,
107; in a Southern Baptist church, 103; and
United Church of Christ, 43; and wedding,
34, 89, 169
Schutz, Alfred, 142
sexual revolution, 41
Shepard, Matthew, 135
Shokeid, Moshe, 13–14
sifting, 56
slain in the spirit: 9, 141–142. *See also* charismatic
Smith, Christian, 162, 163
Smith, Freda, 97
Smith, Jonathan Z., 139
Smith, Willie, 87
Sodom and Gomorrah. *See* Hebrew Bible;
LGBT approaches to the Bible
sodomy statutes, 94
Southern Baptist churches: and commitment
ceremony, 103; licensing of a gay minister by,
103; boycott of Disneyland by, 103, 136. *See
also* Baptist
switchers, 61

temple prostitute. *See* qadesh
Thumma, Scott. *See* Gray, Edward
to'evah: biblical source and translations, 43–44.
See also LGBT approaches to the Bible
transgender people: acceptance of, in mainstream culture and religious groups, 106–107;
invisibility of, 43; at MCCVR, 20; at OMCC,
21–22

UFMCC (Universal Fellowship of Metropoli-
tan Community Churches). *See also* MCC
Unitarian. *See* Interweave
Unitarian Universalist Association, 105
United Church Coalition for Lesbian and Gay
Concerns, 107–108
United Church of Christ (UCC): 105; Open
and Affirming movement, 106; Tenth General
Synod, 42. *See also* ordination of LGBT Chris-
tians, same-sex marriage
United Methodist Church, 14; and Reconciling
movement, 106

Vatican, 105

MELISSA M. WILCOX is the Visiting Johnston Professor of Religion at Whitman College. The author of several articles on various aspects of LGBT religiosity and on religious responses to violence, she is also co-editor of *Sexuality and the World's Religions* and is a member of the advisory committee for the Lesbian, Gay, Bisexual, and Transgender Religious Archives Network.